MW00464418

The Pillars of Reaganomics

The Pillars of Reaganomics

A Generation of Wisdom from Arthur Laffer and
the Supply-Side Revolutionaries

Edited by
Brian Domitrovic

THE
LAFFER
CENTER
at the Pacific Research Institute

ISBN   978-1-934276-19-8

Published in the United States by:

The Laffer Center at the Pacific Research Institute
One Embarcadero Center, Suite 350
San Francisco, CA 94111
Tel: 415-989-0833
Fax: 415-989-2411
Email: info@pacificresearch.org
www.pacificresearch.org

In Memoriam Jack French Kemp

CONTENTS

*It is time to reawaken this industrial giant,
to get government back within its means,
and to lighten our punitive tax burden. And
these will be our first priorities, and on these
principles, there will be no compromise.*
　—Ronald Reagan
　First Inaugural Address, 1981

Introduction
Brian Domitrovic

The aftermath of the Great Recession is looking ever more uninspiring with the passage of time. Since the deep trough of the 2008-09 downturn, the recovery has been as weak as any on record. By the middle of 2013, economic growth since that trough amounted to all of 2.2 percent per year. Employment still lags the pre-recession mark by more than a million. The dollar remains near historic lows against major currencies. And stocks are little better in real terms than they were at the turn of the millennium.

This nation endured a fair number of recessions over the seventy years following the granddaddy of them all, the Great Depression of the 1930s—eleven of them, in fact, from 1945 to 2007. But in no case of *recovery* from these previous recessions can you find the comprehensive mediocrity that characterizes the period of 2009–13.

In no case of recovery from the previous recessions can you find the comprehensive mediocrity that characterizes the period of 2009–13.

Here is what typically happened in the post-World War II era when we were hit with a bad recession. From 1945 to 1947, there was a steep recession as wartime government spending plummeted. But the private sector was on a tear the whole while. Total employment surged past the World War II peak for good within a year of the war's end, in 1946.

In 1957–58, there was a downturn nearly as bad as in 2008–09, with a two-quarter drop in Gross Domestic Product (GDP) actually worse than we saw to close 2008. Yet the next four quarters in 1958–59 delivered as much growth as came in three-and-a-half years of recovery from the Great Recession.

From 1973–75, five negative-growth quarters stalked the economy, just as in 2008–09. But the next three years saw 5 percent growth per annum, even if consumer price inflation remained high.

Ours today is the worst recovery since the Great Depression. And it must be remembered that the New Deal-supervised recovery from the Great Contraction of the early 1930s was a feeble one. Hence we speak of the 1930s as a lost decade. Six years into Franklin D. Roosevelt's presidency in 1939, living standards, employment totals, and real-sector output remained below the 1929 marks.

Now in the second decade of the twenty-first century, we have another example of an extended period after a serious recession, call it a depression, in which the old norms are not met for a very long time. Barack Obama and Franklin D. Roosevelt have a similar record as of their second terms in office. They are the two presidents who could not promptly overcome the economic crises they inherited.

The lameness of the current recovery can serve a productive purpose. By realizing how insufficient this recovery is, compared to all others in the post-World War II period, we might helpfully remind ourselves—we might discover—what qualified as the *best* recovery from recession in our recent history.

Without question, and everything from statistics to anecdote bears this out, the recovery that emerged in 1983, following the three straight recessionary years of 1980–82, was the most powerful recovery from a significant recession that we have seen in modern times. The only competition is the Roaring Twenties that followed the big downturn of 1919–21.

From 1980 until late 1982, the United States spent twenty-two months in recession. GDP went down six times in a ten-quarter stretch. Two million jobs bit the dust, inflation was cruising at 10 percent per year, and stocks were off 70 percent in real terms compared to highs set fifteen years prior. It remains debatable whether we should ever have called our own Great Recession the worst since the Great Depression, given the horror story of 1980–82. The important point is that 1980–82 was very bad—and the era that followed outstanding.

Beginning in late 1982, and lasting consistently through 1989, a span of seven years, the economy of the United States plowed ahead at a 4.3 percent annual rate of growth. This growth was itself about a third higher than the historical norm, even that of the "postwar prosperity" era after World War II. Yet growth was only the half of it. Inflation, which had bedeviled the 1970s and the early 1980s at high, often double-digit rates, fell in 1983 to 3 percent and stayed there. Stocks tripled in value. And jobs—they rained on the economy. Total employment in this country swelled by twenty million from 1982 to 1989.

Then the great run lasted into two further decades. There was a short and shallow recession in 1990–91, but it gave way to another stupendous period of non-inflationary growth which lasted through the turn of the millennium. In 2001, there was a recession of small magnitude, but it too yielded to a substantial recovery, if one less marvelous than the previous two. The whole blooming span of 1982–2007 came to be known in economics circles as the "Great Moderation." It was a quarter century of very good growth, rare and mild recessions, minor inflation and unemployment, and a cascade of jobs and opportunity.

THE SUPPLY-SIDE ERA

The Great Moderation got underway in the early 1980s just as a series of policy reforms inspired by supply-side economics were put in place. These reforms largely remained in place for twenty-five years, only to be vacated during the run-up to the Great Recession and then the Obama presidency.

Supply-side economics was a new perspective on the fiscal-monetary policy mix. The central notion was that given conditions of low output and stubborn inflation—the "stagflation" conditions of the 1970s and early 1980s—the proper response is to relax fiscal policy and to strengthen monetary policy. Specifically, there should be tax cuts at marginal rates so as to spur investment, output, and jobs; and an establishment of a good monetary standard beyond fiat management of the dollar, so as to kill off inflation.

In the early 1980s, the major arms of federal economic policy—the president, the Congress, and the Federal Reserve—effectively cooperated to implement the supply-side revolution. Tax cuts at the margin became law, and monetary policy was coordinated with a stable gold price. Once these two elements of the supply-side policy mix came on line together in late 1982, the great recovery began. For two some decades, the consensus on low taxes and stable money held. Prosperity was the order of the day.

The years in which supply-side economics held sway formed one of the grandest periods of American economic history, while the years prior and after are second only to the Great Depression as the worst things that have ever happened to the modern American economy.

The turning away from the supply-side policy mix began with the loose-money, weak-dollar combination of the early and mid-2000s, the prerequisite of the housing bubble. The *coup de grace* came with the Obama presidency and the raising of marginal tax rates, along with calls for more of the same in the context of trillion-dollar budget deficits.

Thus the era of supply-side economics is wholly defined. The years in which supply-side economics held sway formed one of the grandest periods of American economic history (the Great Moderation), while the years prior (stagflation) and after (Great Recession) are second only to the Great Depression as the worst things that have ever happened to the modern American economy.

READING SUPPLY-SIDE HISTORY

Those who first developed supply-side economics laid out their ideas over the course of some fifteen years before the initial stages of policy implementation in 1981. Thereafter, the original supply-siders did not at all fade away, but absorbed the practical experiences of the immense recovery of the 1980s and beyond to test, bolster, and substantiate the views that they had elaborated in the decade and a half prior. One thing we need to be aware of with respect to supply-side economics is this: its advocates wrote down a great deal over a period now amounting to nearly half a century.

The two men who established supply-side economics—*avant la lettre*: the name did not come about until 1977—were fellow faculty members at the University of Chicago in the late 1960s, one on the economics and the other on the business faculty. The former was Robert A. Mundell (the recipient of the 1999 Nobel Prize in economic sciences) and the latter Arthur B. Laffer, father of what is probably the most famous economics graph of the twentieth century, the "Laffer Curve."

Mundell and Laffer were at once the *sine qua non* of the supply-side revolution and its efficient cause. There would have been no supply-side revolution without these two; and it was they who encouraged and challenged others to join in the cause. It was specifically Mundell and Laffer who reeled in virtually all the major advocates of supply-side economics in the 1970s, from Robert L. Bartley, Paul Craig Roberts, and Jude Wanniski at the *Wall Street Journal* to Jack Kemp in Congress and Ronald Reagan on the presidential ticket. To be sure, there was ferment in the economics profession and within policy circles at large in the direction of reform along supply-side lines in the 1970s, but it remains a fact that during these years, Mundell and Laffer ran down nearly everyone who became an important advocate of the reforms implemented under Reagan's and Federal Reserve Chairman Paul Volcker's auspices in the early 1980s.

For Mundell, initially this meant writing and making presentations that would change minds in university economics. Indeed, the paper in which Mundell first outlined (in 1963) the basic supply-side fiscal-monetary policy mix was one of the two main citations in the award of Mundell's Nobel Prize. As time wore on, however—and as the unwelcome serial-recession, high-inflation conditions of the 1970s got entrenched and urgent—Mundell became more given to talk, as in behind-the-scenes talk with influential people at conferences, appointments, and gatherings.

Arthur Laffer was himself known well enough as a conversationalist, but in the late 1970s he began to produce written output of a significant size and scope. Shortly after Laffer moved from the University of Chicago to the University of Southern California in 1976, he set up a research consultancy (now known as Laffer Associates) that oversaw the production and dissemination of hundreds of paper-length economic studies on the major issues facing the country, assessed from a supply-side perspective. Every year from 1978 to the present, Laffer's consultancy averaged some thirty to forty such papers.

A substantial number of these papers were composed by Laffer himself, the rest by talent, often young talent, attracted to Laffer's vision and method. In the main, these papers have not only been left unconsulted by historians; they have not been made available to the public generally, beyond the members of the subscriber base to whom they were sent over the years. Yet what these papers represent is no less than the comprehensive running commentary of the implementation of the supply-side revolution on the part of the firm bearing the name of the co-founder of that revolution.

As the economic conditions of the long aftermath of the Great Recession become more and more unimpressive, we would do well to acquaint ourselves with the wisdom of supply-side economics. The economic recovery that came with putting into practice supply-side ideas was too immense and too long-lasting for us to be uninformed about it today. That there are, in storage, thirty to forty papers from Laffer Associates per year from 1978 on means that a wealth of untapped information and intelligence about real economic resilience is available to us as we try to shake the lingering effects of the Great Recession.

THE COLLECTION

The collection assembled here is an initial selection of ten papers, dating from 1980 to 2005. These ten were chosen in view of three things: their representativeness; their ability to illuminate key historical junctures over the last thirty some years; and their potential usefulness in current debates over economic policy.

Each paper is introduced (and has been lightly edited) by the editor, with comments on the historical context that prevailed when the paper was composed, along with thoughts on how the paper has aged and ripened over the years. The first selection is from eight months prior to the Reagan electoral victory of November 1980, when stagflation was starting its last huge gasp. This paper (written by Laffer) took up the monetary policy that the new Federal Reserve Chairman (Paul Volcker) should have been following, if only he could have gained the clarity.

The next, written by Warren Brookes, one of the greatest journalists in the supply-side tradition, takes us to Massachusetts, where in 1982, despite a brutal national recession, the state was enjoying bounty from having anticipated the Reagan Revolution by cutting taxes in years prior. It is then on to two pieces calling the origin of the Reagan boom as it happens. The first is from Laffer and Charles Kadlec, and the second is from George Gilder, the most lyrical voice that the supply-side tradition ever produced. Both of these papers predicted at its moment of inception what today we refer to as the Great Moderation.

The next piece dates from 1985, and is Stuart Sweet's case that the great boom, then well underway, should have been an occasion to put Social Security on sound footing. This advice was not taken, to our great detriment, but the record now shows that it was given. Moving into the 1990s, there comes Laffer's reaction to a captious new economic commentator: Paul Krugman. And then there are two pieces on economic inequality, the purported shortcoming which critics of the supply-side revolution seized upon once the enormous growth, employment, inflation, and business-formation achievements became impossible to ignore and belittle. One of these was written by Laffer and David Booth, the other by the notable supply-side advisor, congressional staff member, and historian Bruce Bartlett.

These ten were chosen in view of three things: their representativeness; their ability to illuminate key historical junctures… and their potential usefulness in current debates over economic policy.

The collection concludes with two reflections on the significance of the supply-side revolution, broadly conceived. One is again from Bartlett, from a perspective near the sunset of the Great Moderation in 2005, and the other is from Laffer, as the namesake took up, in 2004, "The Laffer Curve: Past, Present, and Future."

To be sure, books, articles, pamphlets, websites, and social-media pages devoted to diagnosing our current economic malaise have come on the scene like crabgrass since the Great Recession first got going and the recovery came in faulty. Whatever merits can be found in the sea of economic commentary with which we have had to contend since 2008, none of it can claim to be the event-by-event record of recovery as it ought to be done.

This is precisely what we are now privy to with the publication of the Laffer papers by the Laffer Center at the Pacific Research Institute, and plans are underway for more volumes from this unique source. Sluggishness, dullness, and paucity of opportunity have been this nation's economic fate for six years now since the onset of the Great Recession. Surely attendance to the stated principles of the supply-side revolution at its many moments of high achievement in our recent history can help us overcome our status quo.

The Case for a
Gold-Backed Dollar

Arthur B. Laffer
February 29, 1980

The Great Recession that has upended our world in recent years has perhaps made us forget how bad things were in the 1970s and early 1980s. Every time someone says that this is the worst recession since the Great Depression, we let the stagflation era off the hook.

The first thing that this piece by Arthur B. Laffer from early 1980—when the inflation rate was running at a stratospheric 20 percent per year—indicates is how terribly stressed the economy was in the dozen years after the U.S. effectively decided to decouple the dollar from gold in the late 1960s. The litany is brutal and unremitting, even to ears conditioned by the Great Recession to grim news.

In early 1980, interest rates were at 14 percent, up from 4 percent a dozen years prior. Unemployment had also been at 4 percent, but now was running at 6.2 percent, having tested 10 percent, a level then cleared in the last gasp of stagflation in the early 1980s. The federal government's budget deficit, well below $10 billion in the late '60s, was pushing $40 billion in 1980, en route to $74 billion the next year. Inflation was cruising at over 10 percent per year, and the dollar was in the process of skidding down by two-thirds against major currencies. Stocks were flat the whole while from the late 1960s to the early 1980s, masking a huge real decline on account of the hollowing out of the dollar's value.

Stark stuff all around.

There appeared to be a control. The U.S. first wavered in its commitment to the gold-convertible dollar in the late 1960s, and then in 1971 cut off gold redemptions once and for all. The strange and substandard times, the stagflation years, began their run.

It was only fitting, therefore, for Laffer in this piece to make a case for returning the dollar to gold. Halcyon postwar prosperity had preceded, and miserable stagflation followed, this country's loosing the dollar from gold. Here was a plan to get the gold-convertible dollar—and all the outstanding economic conditions associated with it—back again.

In February 1980, Paul Volcker had been chairman of the Federal Reserve for six months. Over this brief period of time, Volcker had striven mightily to tighten money so as to control inflation. He had set lower quantity targets, raised interest rates, and prepared credit controls. The moves were unsuccessful: the consumer price index was powering upward at a 14 percent rate the month this piece was published.

For all Volcker's valiant efforts in late 1979 and 1980, one thing remained untried and unused in monetary policy since 1971. This was gold. Even with Volcker (during the Carter presidency), there was no express gold-price targeting, no call for a new gold convertibility of the dollar, no explicit concern about this greatest of currency hedges passing $800 an ounce (from $35 nine years prior) in January 1980.

This was odd, in that, as Laffer revealed here, Volcker had made his views on gold fairly clear over the years. Namely, Volcker had always been firm that gold was not to be cashiered in the international monetary system, but rather given a principal place in that system, perhaps even a formal one.

In the early 1980s, just like today, grandees of the economics establishment pooh-poohed advocacy of gold-backed money as reactionary, unworkable, and an enthusiasm of the untutored. Whatever his private views on the matter, Volcker was probably reluctant, at the outset of his chairmanship of the Fed, to pursue a gold-oriented monetary policy, on account of prevailing opinion. Yet if that opinion would somehow begin to turn in favor of gold, it stood to reason that Volcker might change course and act on the basis of his long-held beliefs.

Thus the stakes in this piece were high. Laffer was taking it upon himself to begin the process whereby gold could regain the intellectual credibility it had unaccountably lost in the stagflation years as a monetary anchor. The readiness of the Federal Reserve to take gold seriously conceivably stood in the balance.

Laffer's path to a gold standard outlined in these pages addressed the usual criticisms against gold and made the case that a dollar backed in gold would resolve problems. For example: under the plan, the U.S. would not make the dollar convertible to gold immediately, at gold's super-high price in early 1980, but rather would announce that it was planning to do this in the near future, prompting a decline in the gold price to a permanently sustainable level. After all, the skyrocketing gold price to date reflected a worldwide attempt to hide from the precipitously declining dollar; a dollar officially committed to being strong and stable would make gold itself settle down.

As for effects, Laffer argued that a gold-backed dollar would relieve the United States from having to watch over the dollar's exchange rates with other currencies, in that a stable price of gold would be the equivalent of a stable dollar. Any fluctuation in exchange rates would by definition derive from instability on the part of foreign currencies, not the dollar.

Employment, economic growth, and rates of returns in real enterprises would go up with a dollar backed in gold—quite the opposite of what had been prevailing financially and economically in the long 1970s.

Moreover, the need to hedge against further devaluations of the dollar, devaluations with respect to foreign exchange and the price level, would evaporate with the dollar tied to gold at a fixed price. This would leave all that capital tied up in gold (and the other hedges mentioned here, including objets d'art) to migrate to other, more economically productive outlets, such as investments and the stock market. Employment, economic growth, and rates of returns in real enterprises would go up with a dollar backed in gold—quite the opposite of what had been prevailing financially and economically in the long 1970s.

The U.S. would never make the formal move to gold as Laffer suggested in this piece, whatever Volcker's inclinations at the time. We have remained on a fiat-currency system continuously since 1971.

However, and as Laffer and Charles Kadlec were able to point out in several *Wall Street Journal* articles in the two years after this piece was written, Volcker did at last adopt something close to a gold-price rule in his conduct of monetary policy as Fed chairman, at least by mid–1982. And sure enough, after 1982, in the face of the Fed's targeting of the gold price—which effectively meant Fed loosening on gold-price drops and tightening on spikes—inflation collapsed, stocks went on a historic run, employment ballooned like in nobody's memory, and growth surged (ultimately for two decades) such that the old stagflation era was put to pasture and forgotten in the face of blooming prosperity and a technological and business revolution of inordinate dimensions.[1]

We can only wonder if Laffer's advice of February 1980 had been taken—to put the dollar on gold formally, de jure, not just de facto as happened under Volcker for a time after 1982—we would have experienced the so very consequential Fed mistakes of the early and mid-2000s, when so much money was printed that a housing bubble emerged, only to be popped at the cost of the Great Recession. In February 1980, Laffer may not only have been telling this nation how to vanquish stagflation. He may also have been clueing us in about how to avert crises decades into the future.

REINSTATEMENT OF THE DOLLAR: THE BLUEPRINT FEBRUARY 29, 1980

The issue of a gold-based monetary system has again come of age. The impulse originates in the debacle of the current system in which inflation and rising interest rates have reached epidemic proportions. The threat of monetary disintegration provides fertile ground for a radical change in the world's monetary system; an early reinstatement of the dollar as a world currency convertible into gold no longer is inconceivable. The pressing issue is whether a return to a gold standard will be used to avert a financial collapse or come in its aftermath.

Restoration of a link between gold and the dollar does not, per se, guarantee stability. Done improperly, such a policy change could cause enormous dislocations to the economy. The blueprint for a successful return to dollar convertibility, presented here, includes a transition period to assure that it is the gold market, not the economy, that makes the initial adjustment inherent in a return to a gold based monetary system. "Safety valves" also are provided to minimize the chances of altercations in the gold market being forced upon the economy as a whole.

This paper makes extensive use of Federal Reserve Chairman Paul Volcker's ideas as found in the 1972 U.S. proposals to the International Monetary Fund. By virtue of his position, Volcker is key to reinstatement of the dollar.

Implementation of such a policy change would spur growth in real output, personal income, and corporate profits. Stockmarkets throughout the world would rise and interest rates fall in recognition of the benefits that would accrue to the global economy and political order from the U.S. reaffirming its responsibility to provide a stable, world numeraire.

☙❧

From Anthony Solomon's commencement address as newly appointed president of the New York Fed to Ronald Reagan's political rhetoric, the issue of a gold-based monetary system has again come of age. The current monetary system has, since its link to gold was severed, been an unmitigated debacle. Interest rates and inflation rates are hitting new highs virtually on a daily basis. Unemployment rates bottomed out quite some time ago at levels well above the "full employment level" and now are ascending even higher. At the same time, exchange rates, investment rates, and growth rates are sinking to new lows.

A brief revisitation of the economic events surrounding the full demonetization of gold and the unhinging of the dollar illustrates the extent to which the monetary system has descended. The U.S. withdrawal from the gold pool and the elimination of private dollar convertibility into gold occurred in March of 1968. The establishment of a fully inconvertible dollar began August 15, 1971. While these two dates present a false sense of precision, they are nonetheless good points of demarcation for what was actually an emerging process. When juxtaposed against the previous period, the calendar years following these dates offer a starkly vivid picture of the decline of the American economy. In 1967 the official price of gold was $35 per ounce and traded at that price in private markets. By 1970 that price had risen to $47 and currently is in the range of $625-675. This rise reflects an eighteenfold increase in some thirteen years.

Other economic indicators display similar patterns. Inflation as measured by the Consumer Price Index rose from a 3 percent annual rate in 1967 to 5½ percent rate in 1970 and then surged to the 13.3 percent rate experienced in 1979. The pattern of three-month Treasury bill rates parallels the inflation movements remarkably well. In 1967 these three-month bill rates averaged 4.3 percent. By 1970 they averaged 6.5 percent and as of the writing of this paper are in the neighborhood of 13.8 percent.

In tandem, the dollar fell in value when measured in terms of German marks, Swiss francs, and several other currencies. In 1967, four marks exchanged for one dollar as did 4.3 Swiss francs. By 1970 the ratio had become 3.6 marks and still 4.3 Swiss francs. As of February 21, the full extent of the dollar collapse could be seen in that now dollars could be purchased at a price of only 1.74 marks and 1.64 Swiss francs.

The real side of the economy has suffered as well during the monetary collapse. The rate of unemployment stood at 3.8 percent in 1967. It rose to 4.9 percent in 1970 and now resides somewhere in the range of 6.2 percent. The Dow Jones Industrial Average in dollar terms today is roughly at its 1967 level. The decline when measured in units of purchasing power has been extraordinary. Even the federal deficit has become engorged over these years. In 1967 the red ink totaled $8.7 billion; in 1970 it was $2.8 billion; and in 1979, it stood at $27.7 billion.

THE RETURN TO A GOLD STANDARD

It is hardly surprising that, whatever its merits, the current monetary system is being barraged with heated assaults. Unless quickly rectified, which seems highly unlikely, the current state of monetary chaos appears to be a fertile breeding ground for a radical alteration of our monetary system. An early return to a gold standard is no longer inconceivable. In my view, the probabilities that the U. S. will return to a convertible dollar have become high enough to justify describing the likely shape and implications of a specific program to restore dollar convertibility. Of some concern is whether the return to dollar convertibility will avert a financial collapse or come in its aftermath.

A return to a gold standard should not be embraced impulsively nor implemented by surprise. Done improperly, dollar convertibility could cause egregious dislocations to the financial markets and the economy. If the price of gold were to be set too high, for example, inflation would continue to rise. Interest rates would reach new highs. If, on the other hand, the price of gold were set too low, the price level would fall, leading to deflationary pressures throughout the economy. Moreover, if the technical aspects of the program were defective, announcement of a return to dollar convertibility could create a speculative run on U.S. gold reserves that would abort the attempt to restore gold backing to the dollar.

A properly designed program should have as its initial goal the stabilization of prices generally at or near their current level.

A properly designed program should have as its initial goal the stabilization of prices generally at or near their current level. Secondly, the program must be credible and workable. And finally, it should be designed to protect the general economy from shocks to the gold market per se, disturbances that have nothing to do with monetary policy. Stated simply, a workable system of gold/dollar convertibility must not permit the economy to experience wrenching adjustments because of changes in gold. If shocks to the gold market do occur, any responsible system must pemit the price of gold to do the adjusting. Therefore, safety valves must be included.[2]

As newly appointed chairman of the Board of Governors of the Federal Reserve System, Paul Volcker's term does not expire for almost seven years. Any radical change in our monetary order, therefore, presumably would require not only Volcker's acquiescence, but more likely his enthusiastic support.

Based upon his posturing since the late 1960s it is, in my opinion, quite conceivable that Volcker could actually lead the search for a new order. While undersecretary of the Treasury during the hectic monetary gyrations of the early 1970s, Volcker was reported to be the last to abandon the need for maintaining the dollar's convertibility into gold. In fact, it was rumored that even after the enormous dollar devaluations, Volcker expected and argued in favor of a return to convertibility.

Volcker is, in my view, the most knowledgeable high-ranking bureaucrat on monetary affairs in the United States. His history at the U.S. Treasury goes back to 1951 and covers positions such as undersecretary of the Treasury, president of the New York Fed and now chairman of the Board of Governors of the Federal Reserve System. He was one of the singlemost involved operatives in each of these positions.

Moreover, Volcker singlehandedly carried out the negotiations with the international community throughout the entire monetary reordering of the world in the 1970s. Of quite some importance, in my view, is the fact that the design of "The U.S. Proposals" presented at the Nairobi International Monetary Fund meetings in 1972 was attributed to him. As the principal U.S. representative to these meetings, then Treasury Secretary George P. Shultz, formally presented the proposal.[3]

THE BLUEPRINT

Given my perception of Volcker's native inclinations and the U.S. proposal at Nairobi, one could well imagine a reordering of the world's monetary system and the reemergence of gold convertibility in something of the following form: The U.S. would announce a double-faceted program providing for the restoration of dollar convertibility into gold. The first part of the program would allow a transition period designed to permit the gold market in particular, and financial markets in general, to adjust to dollar convertibility before its implementation. The need for such a period was widely recognized in 1972. "The U.S. Proposals" stated:

> We merely want to note that some generally acceptable transitional arrangements are necessary. This transitional problem is not unique to the proposed system. Any monetary system based upon concepts of equilibrium and convertibility will require special measures to deal with transitional problems."[4]

The second part of the program would provide the requisite technical specifications necessary to make the new monetary system workable and credible. As in 1972, the proposal outlined below visualizes

> .... a system in which disproportionately large gains in reserves for a particular country indicate the need for adjustment measures to eliminate a balance of payments surplus, just as, in any system of convertibility into reserve assets, disproportionately large losses of reserves indicate the need for adjustment to eliminate a balance-of-payments deficit.[5]

The transition phase would encompass the following policy initiatives:

- The U.S. would announce its full intention of returning to a convertible dollar at some prespecified time in the future; say three months.

- At the time of this pre-gold price fixing announcement, the U.S. also would provide the financial markets with as much potentially relevant information as could be made available. Gold and other metal stockpiles would be enumerated precisely. This would require a resurrection of the Treasury's gold budget, which was abandoned in the early 1970s.

- The U.S. could announce that during this three month interval neither the Federal Reserve nor the U.S. Treasury would intervene in the foreign exchange markets or have any net intervention in the open market. Net loans of reserves to member banks in the Federal Reserve System through the discount window would also be frozen at their current level. Stated simply, during this three month interval, the Federal Reserve and Treasury would "take a vacation" so as not to disrupt the natural forces in the private market. The monetary base would, as a result of the absence of actions, remain literally unchanged during this three month interval.

The same announcement would outline the actual exchange mechanism linking the dollar to gold. It would read something like this:[6]

- Three months hence, the Federal Reserve has been instructed to establish parity between a dollar unit of its liabilities (currency in circulation and member bank reserves) and a fixed quantity of gold at that day's average transaction price in the London gold market. This will be the official value of the dollar and price of gold. From thenceforth on:

- The Federal Reserve will stand ready to sell gold to all demander's at a price 0.7 percent higher than the official price in exchange for units of its liabilities (Monetary Base).

- The Federal Reserve will stand ready to purchase gold from all sellers at a price 0.7 percent below its official price in exchange for units of its liabilities.

- When valued at the official price, the Federal Reserve will attempt over time to establish an average dollar value of gold reserves equal to 40 percent of the dollar value of its liabilities. This average reserve (AR) will be a "Target Reserve Quantity" around which policy operates.

- A gold reserve band will be instituted whereby a reserve level equal to 70 percent of the dollar value of the Federal Reserve's liabilities would be designated as the Upper Reserve Limit and a reserve level equal to 10 percent of its liabilities would be designated as the Lower Reserve Limit.

- Once established, the Target Reserve Quantity of gold will determine the mandatory policy trigger points. Within a band of 25 percent either side of the Target Reserve level, the monetary authorities would have full discretion in exercising control over the monetary base. As long as the monetary authority maintains the official price via direct convertibility, there will be no strictures placed on actions taken to change the monetary base. Open market operations, discounting and even exchange rate interventions would be solely under the discretion of the monetary authority as long as the dollar value of the quantity of gold was between .30 and .50 of the Monetary Base; i.e., within the 25 percent band of target reserves.

- If actual reserves were, however, to fall within the range of .20 and .30 of the Monetary Base, then the monetary authority's discretion would be removed in its entirety. The monetary authority would be required to run policies such that the monetary base would experience absolutely no growth. This, in effect, means that the monetary authority would be required to offset fully any gold/dollar conversion as long as actual gold reserves fell between one half and three quarters of the target reserve level (.20 and .30 of the Monetary Base).

- If, in spite of the cessation of the growth of the monetary base, actual reserves fell between 50 percent and 25 percent of target reserves (.10 and .20 of the Monetary Base), the monetary authority would then be compelled to contract the monetary base at the rate of 1 percent per month. This means that the monetary authority must act to effectuate a decline in the monetary base of 1 percent per month, inclusive of the monetary base effects of maintaining gold convertibility. If the decline in the base due solely to gold sales were greater than, or less than, 1 percent, then open market operations would be used to limit or increase, respectively, the change in the base to the prescribed amount.

- A symmetric set of mandatory policy dicta result when actual reserves grow to between 1.25 and 1.5 of target reserves and 1.5 and 1.75 of target reserves. The monetary base rules in each of these ranges are an increase of 1 percent per month and 2 percent per month, respectively, again inclusive of all gold/dollar conversions.

- If the gold reserve protection measures fail to preserve the actual value of reserves between 0.25 and 1.75 of the target level of reserves while maintaining convertibility, all gold/

dollar conversion provisions cease. The dollar's convertibility will be temporarily suspended and the dollar price of gold will be set free for a three month adjustment period.

- During this temporary period of inconvertibility, the monetary authorities will be required to suspend all actions that would affect the monetary base. Again, the price of gold would be reset as before and convertibility would be reinstated.

Once the official price for gold is established, the actual reserves of gold held by the monetary authority would be different from the level of target reserves. If, as appears most likely for an initial move back to convertibility, the actual amount of reserves is in excess of the amounts needed for the target reserves, then this gold should be segregated and sold in a systematic manner. A reasonable solution would be to sell the entire amount in equal monthly installments over a five-year period. Quite symmetrically, if there is ever a deficiency, there should be a five-year plan to acquire gold in equal monthly amounts. The deficiency or surplus should have no bearing on the monetary authority's behavior. In the monetary authority's account for the purposes of maintaining dollar convertibility, the initial amount of gold would be the Target Reserve Quantity, or 40 percent of the Monetary Base.

With the value of the dollar defined in terms of gold, there would no longer exist any reason for the U.S. government to be concerned with the foreign exchange value of the dollar. The official policy of the U.S. should remain that the dollar would be free to seek its own level. The U.S. should neither concern itself with foreign official intervention nor with the fluctuations in foreign exchange rates. It is quite likely that many foreign governments would be quick to reestablish parity between their currencies and the dollar. With the dollar as good as gold, the attraction would be great.

With the value of the dollar defined in terms of gold, there would no longer exist any reason for the U.S. government to be concerned with the foreign exchange value of the dollar.

LINKS TO THE "U.S. PROPOSALS" OF 1972

The approach outlined above includes several key concepts put forward in "The U.S. Proposals" of 1972. First, the need for a "base" level of reserves, the "Target Reserve Quantity," was recognized. Forty percent was selected as the illustrative amount in the above proposal because it approximates the pre-1934 relationship between gold reserves and the monetary base in the U. S. within the Federal Reserve Bank system.[7]

Second, changes in the level of gold or primary reserves is used as the key policy variable:

> Reserves are more comprehensive, more reliable and more quickly available indicators than other criteria of external balance. While reserves may be distorted in the short run, no other single series provides a superior basis for analysis. In a convertibility system, reserve data are necessarily indicative of disequilibrium in the adjustment process; this has always been understood in terms of inducements to adjust for deficit countries—and the concept applies with equal logic to adjustment needs for surplus countries.[8]

The use of reserve bands also was part of the 1972 proposal, and no doubt incorporates much of Volcker's technical inputs. "Under a reserve-indicator system," says "The U.S. Proposals," "certain points would be established above and below each country's base level to guide the adjustment process and to assure even-handed convertibility disciplines." A "low point," "lower warning point," and "outer point" are recommended as trigger mechanisms for appropriate policy responses to restore equilibrium:[9]

> .... countries would not be expected to ignore imbalances blithely until their disequilibria had become so extreme as to prompt strong international concern through the indicator mechanism. Reserve

fluctuations would signal emerging disequilibria; movement to outer indicators signalling strong international concern would occur only when countries failed to make the appropriate responses as the disequilibria built up.[10]

Later, the proposal states:

The purpose of a reserve-indicator system is to provide strong incentives for countries to act in limited steps, using a variety of tools suited to their circumstances before their situation becomes so urgent as to involve international concern and action.[11]

PROBLEMS AND SOLUTIONS

The above proposal would attempt to rectify two serious defects inherent in most systems to return to gold convertibility. The original fixing price of gold no longer would be left to the vicissitudes of political pressures. With full knowledge, the market and its transactors who, with the threat of losses and the hopes of profit, would select the appropriate price for gold. This would thus avoid the necessity of making the overall economy adjust to some inappropriate price of gold. As was pointed out in the 1972 monetary proposal by the U.S.:

A decision to provide the system with too few reserves induces—and sanctions—a destabilizing and ultimately fruitless competion for scarce reserves. Creation of too many reserves pushes too great a share of the adjustment pressure onto surplus countries and facilitates world inflation.[12]

Allowing the price of gold to adjust would minimize this problem by permitting gold's original price setting to accommodate to the economy, instead of forcing the economy to adjust to a price set by government fiat.

The second criticism to which this proposal is responsive is to an explicit change in the market for gold itself. If gold became excessively plentiful or scarce due to conditions beyond the control of the monetary authority, it makes no sense whatsoever to force the economy to either deflate or inflate to accommodate an altered market for gold itself. Whenever such disturbances occur, the dollar would be defended until excessive reserves of gold were acquired or lost. At such a time, the price of gold would again be set free and allowed to adjust to the overall economy.

Another issue that invariably arises when discussing gold convertibility is the role to be played by gold coins. As a matter of practice, the issue is neither complex nor central to the workings of an effective system.

Nonetheless, if coins are to circulate and be used as money, the value of the coin when used as money must be greater than the value of the metal contained in the coin. If the value of the metal were equal to or greater than the monetary value, coins would be melted down and disappear from circulation. The value of the coin as a money need not be much in excess of the value of the metal. In fact, gold coins today have a premium of less than 10 percent unless they have other characteristics. It would seem reasonable, then, that the monetary authority would mint gold coins and place them in circulation. Counterfeiting legislation should also be enacted to guarantee the quality of circulating coins. The minting of gold coins is a natural way for the monetary authority to rid itself of gold reserves in excess of those to be held against the monetary base.

IMPLICATIONS

A policy change leading back to dollar convertibility along these lines would change dramatically the outlook for inflation, the economy, and harmony among the industrial nations.

Inflationary expectations would fall precipitously. With the monetary system hinged to the real world through gold—a surrogate for all goods and services—price stability would return in short order. Announcement of the program alone would tend to increase confidence in the dollar, leading to an incipient excess demand for dollars relative to their supply. That is a necessary condition to arresting inflation. The growth in the monetary aggregates would tend to accelerate to accommodate this excess demand for dollars. Velocity would fall such that this increase in money would be consistent with lower rates of inflation. For example, if the velocity of money measured by nominal GNP divided by M1 were to decline to its 1965 level of 4.08, the money supply at today's level of real output could expand more than 50 percent with no change in the price level.[13]

With the monetary system hinged to the real world through gold—a surrogate for all goods and services—price stability would return in short order.

Interest rates over horizons both near and far would fall. Most likely, the greatest initial adjustment would be in short term maturities. As confidence extended out over longer time horizons, longer term rates would continue to decline. The more credible the program, the more precipitous the decline in interest rates.[14]

With the threat of unexpected inflation reduced, the relative price between inflation hedges and tax avoidance schemes on the one hand, and financial assets on the other, would shift in favor of financial assets. The value of such investments as gold, silver, antiques, objets d'art, real estate, oil and other tax shelters would fall relative to stocks and bonds. An absolute decline in their price is possible, but not certain.

Once the dollar were as good as gold, demand for dollars would surge in international markets as well. The foreign exchange value of the dollar would tend to rise. Foreign monetary authorities, however, might offset this shift in demand out of their own currencies into the dollar through offsetting foreign exchange operations; i.e., selling dollar reserve assets into the foreign exchange markets in exchange for their domestic money. Such a move by foreign monetary authorities would be all to the good. By securing the value of their currencies relative to the dollar, their monetary systems, too, would be linked through the dollar to gold. Inflationary expectations and interest rates would fall in these currencies as well.[15]

Once the dollar were as good as gold, demand for dollars would surge in international markets as well.

Benefits also would accrue to the real sector of the economy. Uncertainty over the value of money both in terms of goods and the cost of financing is itself an impediment to capital formation. It is an additional, external factor outside of the control of management that increases the risk of engaging in long term investments. Moreover, the sharp reduction in the rate of inflation that would ensue with a return to dollar convertibility would diminish the illusory component of corporate profits due to undercosting of goods sold and underdepreciation of fixed assets. Effective tax rates on corporate profits would fall. Real after-tax returns would rise. Corporate economic activity and profits would expand.[16]

The stock market would rise. Two factors would be evident. First, expected future after-tax profits would be higher, because of the expansion in corporate activity and the reduction in effective tax rates. Second, the real value of these profits would more closely approximate reported profits—smaller adjustments would have to be made to correct for illusory gains. Thus, price/earnings ratios based on accounting profits would go up.

Individuals would benefit by a return to dollar convertibility for similar reasons. Resources devoted to protecting savings from the danger of unexpected changes in the value of the dollar in terms of goods; e.g., purchasing gold coins, foreign exchange, etc., would be directed toward increasing production and wealth. "Bracket creep"— the rise of nominal incomes into higher tax brackets even while real incomes remain constant—also would cease, removing the expectation of ever-increasing effective personal income tax rates without legislative relief. Employment would rise, unemployment would fall.[17]

The financial health of the government also would improve. Interest expense on the Federal deficit for fiscal year 1979 was $60 billion—the third largest budget item. A fall in interest rates, per se, would reduce the cost of financing the government debt. The expansion in the economy following a restoration of dollar convertibility also would increase the tax base—leading to an increase in revenues. In a healthy economic environment, demands for government spending decline. Higher tax revenues and lower spending reduce directly the deficit. The financial health of the Federal government would improve.

Finally, the return to dollar convertibility would reinstate the United States as central banker to the world. The importance of this change is difficult to underestimate. For almost a decade, the world has been without a numeraire, a North Star by which to guide international commerce and investment. The resulting cumulative economic inefficiencies have subtracted from the wealth of all nations. It is not too much to say that many of the political and social tensions of the era have been due, in part, to these real costs. With the dollar once again the world numeraire, these inefficiencies would be removed, and global resources freed would be employed toward productive ends.

"Bracket creep"… would cease, removing the expectation of ever-increasing effective personal income tax rates without legislative relief.

New York's position as the center of world finance would be elevated and the competitive position of U.S. banks would be enhanced, relative to London and other overseas money centers. But all Western commercial centers would gain in the absolute expansion of global wealth. Assuming most of the major trading nations of the world would link their currencies to the dollar, global inflation would be effectively arrested. Inflation's destructive impact on domestic economies would be curbed as well, although the need for global tax reforms would remain to offset the effects ot a dozen years of inflation on fiscal systems.

Transcending these not inconsequential commercial considerations, though, are the benefits that restoration of the dollar as a stable world currency would bring to world political order. Protectionist pressures in the West would be mitigated, although not eliminated. And an element of cohesion would be returned to the Western alliance, which, along with the present monetary system, threatens fracture and disintegration.

Throughout history, it has been the world's premiere economic and military power that has put its strength and responsibility behind the maintenance of a stable world currency. The United States abandoned this element of global leadership when it unhinged the dollar from gold. It is not within the capacity of any other nation or cluster of nations to take on this responsibility. The United States can signal its willingness to resume this critical role by once again placing the dollar within the disciplined framework I have outlined here.

2

The Massachusetts Miracle

By Warren T. Brookes

April 6, 1982

One of the distinguishing characteristics of the American political system is its federal structure. "Federal" in this context refers to the significant degree of power that is reserved to each of the states, as opposed to the national government centered in Washington, D.C. The classical expression of federalism is the last entry in the Bill of Rights, the Tenth Amendment to the Constitution: "The powers not delegated to the United States by the Constitution, nor prohibited by it to the States, are reserved to the States respectively, or to the people."

In terms of economic policy, federalism has made a significant difference in terms of which states have prospered and which have lagged. Because states can set up their own tax, budget, and regulatory policies, they can serve as laboratories for the range of economic policy choices, with the various results plain for all to see.

Some of the most important contributions of supply-side economics have been in the area of state policy. Arthur Laffer played an integral role in the first great supply-side triumph in the states, the passage in California in June 1978 of Proposition 13. This was a measure cutting down property tax rates, rates which had become punishing on account of being un-indexed for inflation, at a time when inflation was regularly running 8 to 10 percent per year.

Not to be outdone, Massachusetts—under the auspices of a Democratic governor and legislature—pushed through a series of laws and ballot initiatives from 1979 to 1982 that not only cut property taxes, but also lowered the capital gains tax rate and excise taxes, along with capping municipal spending.

Watching all this with amazement was the foremost journalist in the supply-side tradition not in the employ of the *Wall Street Journal*. This was Warren Brookes, whose syndicated columns (based at the *Boston Herald American*) and book (*The Economy in Mind* [1982]), remain among the most rigorous statements of supply-side principles ever produced. In his writing, Brookes stressed evidence and statistics as he weighed the merits of supply-side policies. Brookes showed time and again that however intriguing was the theory—the Laffer Curve, for example—it was hard data that brought home the urgency of the supply-side revolution.

In this piece, Brookes confirmed that the effect of Democratic Governor Edward J. King's tax-cutting was economic excellence all around. From 1979 to 1982, the unemployment rate in Massachusetts tumbled far below the national average; personal income went appreciably up as the need for welfare benefits went down; and in a classic case of the Laffer Curve, state receipts plowed forward—up by double-digit amounts in 1982, a recession year nationally.

This period—which largely preceded the implementation of the Ronald Reagan economic program for the nation as a whole—laid the foundation for what would become known as the "Massachusetts Miracle." By the mid-1980s, the Bay State was creating high-tech jobs by the thousands and served as a magnet for capital and entrepreneurs. In one of history's ironies, Governor King lost his re-election bid in 1982 to Michael Dukakis, who six years hence would be the Democratic opponent to Reagan's heir apparent George H.W. Bush in the presidential election. Dukakis based his (unsuccessful) 1988 campaign on the contention that his policies were those responsible for the Massachusetts Miracle.

California had its own tech miracle in the wake of Proposition 13, the Silicon Valley boom of the 1980s and 1990s. Today, low-tax, low-regulation states from Texas to Tennessee lure residents by the millions from places such as Illinois, Michigan, and a California forgetful of its supply-side heritage. All these states have doubled down on taxes, spending, public-sector employees, and roadblocks to doing business—though Michigan did reverse course in becoming a "right to work" state in 2012. It is one of the defining features of the present day that Americans up and move their residences to states that commit to government-limiting principles in economic affairs.

Warren Brookes noted in this piece that the state that sponsored the Tea Party of 1773 should have kept guard well enough to prevent the breakout in taxation that Massachusetts residents suffered in the 1970s. He chalked it up to faulty memory. Today, as a new political movement called the Tea Party presses on in this country, it is worth remembering that the experiences of the states—even famously liberal and Democratic ones like California and Massachusetts—have validated the supply-side solution as much as anything that has come from Washington.

OF TEA PARTIES AND TAX REVOLTS, APRIL 6,1982

First California, then New York, and now Massachusetts—the oldest of the old industrial states—is demonstrating that reductions in tax rates will restore economic growth and fiscal health. In the past two years, Massachusetts has reduced its capital gains tax rates by 60 percent, slashed property and auto excise taxes, and imposed a 4 percent cap on increases in local spending. As a result, the state's tax burden has gone from the fifth highest in 1979 to 22nd highest in 1981.

The economic—and political—effects have been more immediate and have had a greater impact than anyone anticipated. The state's unemployment rate has gone from 2 percentage points above to nearly 2 percentage points below the national average. Since 1970, the state's per capita income has expanded from 3.4 percent above the national average to an estimated 8.2 percent above. Slow growth "Taxachusetts" is now among the nation's high growth states. And thanks to the fastest growth of revenues in more than a decade, the budget has moved into surplus.

Democratic Governor King of Massachusetts is a staunch supporter of the supply-side policies which have lifted the heavy tax burden from the "Boston Tea Party" state's populace, much to the chagrin of liberals such as Senator Ted Kennedy. Yet, the decisive victory has not yet occurred. On September 21, 1982, the state gubernatorial primary will be held with Governor King confronting Michael Dukakis, the liberal candidate and ex-governor of Massachusetts. It will be a contest of tax cuts and economic growth policies on the one hand and liberal policies on the other hand. With recent polls in Massachusetts still strongly in favor of tax reductions, it is likely that the electorate will continue to support the supply-side experiment. The Massachusetts economy is a working model which points the way for a successful federal policy.

ꙍ

On March 10th, 1981, early in the Reagan Administration's quest to promote its tax-cut/budget-cut package, the prestigious *Christian Science Monitor* led its edition with the following prophetic story:

> Surprise, surprise.
>
> Massachusetts, with an economy scorched in the 1970s, now blossoms, at least compared with the rest of the U.S. In fact, a hidden message lies in the Bay State's *unexpected* departure from the national economic recession: 'Follow me ....'
>
> In 1980, the Commonwealth recorded the lowest unemployment among the top industrial states, and remains a full two percentage points below the national joblessness average ....
>
> In three areas, Massachusetts is setting a pace for the nation: *tax cuts*, energy conservation, and high technology.
>
> Last fall voters dealt a severe blow to the state's heavy-tax reputation by passing the Proposition 2½ referendum, which effectively reduces total tax levies by about 9 percent. This came after a capital gains tax reduction (of 60 percent) and the imposition of a 4 percent cap on increases in local spending which, coupled with rising taxes in the Sunbelt, help place Massachusetts closer to the national average in total tax burden.

If the 'Laffer Curve' theory of cut-taxes-and-end-stagnation works, it will be shown here.[1]

Less than one year later, on February 24th, 1982, Governor Edward J. King, a Democrat, told a public hearing of the Joint Economic Committee (JEC) of Congress that supply-side economics is alive and well, and working in Massachusetts. It is working so well, in fact, that despite federal cutbacks, and a tough recession, the Bay State will wind up its 1982 fiscal year with a modest surplus. Partly as a result, Governor King is now planning a further reduction in its burdensome income tax in 1983 and 1984 which would effectively eliminate the 7½ percent surcharge that had been put on in 1975 by his liberal Democratic predecessor (and heavily favored 1978 election victim), Michael Dukakis.

THE MASSACHUSETTS TURNAROUND

During the Dukakis Administration (1974–78), the Massachusetts tax burden (revenues from all its own sources divided by personal income) rose nearly two full percentage points to 17.6 percent. That was on top of a nearly 3 percent point rise in the prior administration of Republican Frank Sargent (Graph 1). This increase brought the Massachusetts tax burden in 1978 to a level nearly 20 percent above the average of seventeen industrial states and nearly 12 percent above the national average. During the decade, the state had risen from 25th in the nation in tax burden to fifth. It is no small wonder that, by 1978, the Commonwealth's personal income was growing at the 47th slowest rate in the nation. Since 1978, however, the state has accomplished a complete turnaround in its fiscal policies. This year, Massachusetts' tax burden is expected to fall to 14.5 percent, dropping the erstwhile "Taxachusetts" back down to the 22nd highest state in tax burden. In the process, its economy has gone from being one of the weakest of all industrial states to one of the two or three strongest economies in the country.

GRAPH 1
Massachussets Total Tax Burden

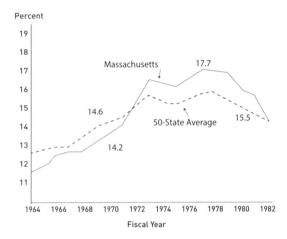

Total tax burden – state and local general revenue from our own sources as percent of total personal income.

Source: U.S. Department of Commerce; 1982 estimates by Associated Industries of Massachusetts

GRAPH 2
Unemployment Rate - Massachusettes vs. U.S.

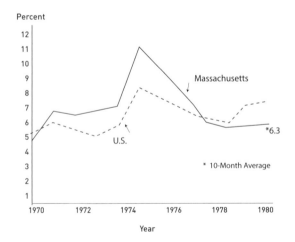

Source: Bureau of Labor Statistics

Just three weeks before his testimony, King learned that the Massachusetts unemployment rate for January, despite a cruel winter and economic recession, was at 6.9 percent, a full 1.6 percentage points *below* the national figure of 8.5 percent and the second lowest of any of the top ten major industrial states. Only Texas' rate was lower (Graph 2).

What's more, per capita personal income in Massachusetts has completely reversed its downward trend relative to the national average. Personal income had plummeted from 10 percent above the U.S. average in 1970 (when the state had a lower than average tax burden) down to only 3.4 percent above the national average in 1978. In the past two years, per capita personal income has risen back to 8 percent above the national average. For the 1980–81 period, Massachusetts was among the ten fastest-growing states.

If supply-side economists and Ronald Reagan are looking for proof that their "supply-side" tax curve works, Massachusetts provides the most glittering proof yet developed—a kind of laboratory experiment in both the negative and positive implications of tax policy.

In the process, Massachusetts' economy has gone from being one of the weakest of all industrial states to one of the two or three strongest economies in the country.

The stunning symmetry of movements in the state's tax burden and its personal income demonstrates that the economic fortunes of Massachusetts' citizens have fallen and risen again in precisely inverse proportion to the tax burden they have carried (Graph 3). During the state's pursuit of high-tax, welfare state policies, its economy fell apart—disastrously. As these policies were modified and the tax burden declined, the recovery was immediate.

The "match" between taxes and the economy is even more dramatic when applied to the unemployment rate (Graph 4). From an unemployment rate chronically 20 to 30 percent above the nation's, Massachusetts has in the last three years moved to a position of having one of the lowest unemployment rates, now some 18 percent below the national figure.

What has taken everybody by surprise in this whole scenario is the immediacy of the economy's response to lower tax burdens. There was no lag on either side of the Laffer Curve. The reason for this, of course, is that there is no lag in the reaction of the marketplace to price cuts. And since tax rates are a "price" for working, it is no accident that employment began to churn ahead the moment the price of employment began to decline.

Reinforcing this has been a reversal in Massachusetts' attitude toward welfare. In 1978, the state had one of the five highest welfare benefit levels in the nation and one of the highest levels of unemployment. But since 1978, under Governor King, welfare benefits have been allowed to fall to inflation's ravages, with only one modest cost of living adjustment. This lowered the state's relative position to 15th. Since welfare must be understood as a marginal tax on working, the lower the benefits, the lower the tax, and the less the disincentives for employment. As a result, total Massachusetts welfare caseloads have fallen by nearly 20 percent since 1979.

GRAPH 3
Massachusetts Personal Income and Tax Burden[1]
(Compared to the National Average)

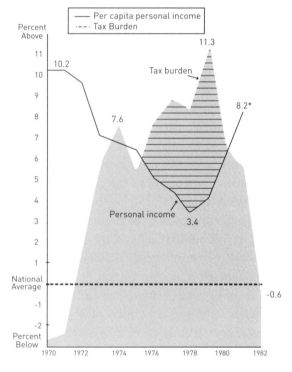

[1] *Total tax burden – state and local general revenue from own sources as percent of total personal income*
*1981/2 estimates by Associated Industries of Massachusetts
Source: US Department of Commerce

GRAPH 4
Massachusetts Tax Burden and Unemployment Rate

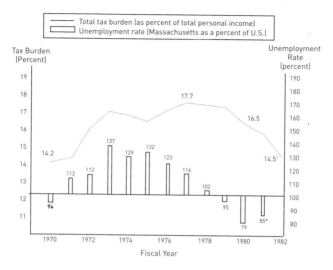

Total tax burden (as percent of total personal income)
Unemployment rate (Massachusetts as a percent of U.S.)

1 Estimates by Associated Industries of Massachusetts
* 10-month average
Source: U.S. Department of Commerce

It is no coincidence that Texas, with the lowest welfare benefit levels in the nation, also enjoys the strongest employment growth concurrently with the lowest unemployment. Similarly, as the Massachusetts benefit level has fallen (nearly 15 percent in real dollars), its own employment picture has been rejuvenated as well. This analysis is consistent with a study done in 1980 which showed that the fifteen states with the highest levels of welfare benefits had (from 1970–78) an average of one percent more unemployment than the national figure, while the fifteen states with the lowest welfare benefits enjoyed an average 1.5 percentage points less unemployment than the national average (Table 1).[2]

In fact, between 1970 and 1978, the low welfare benefit states outperformed the high benefit states by more than two to one in job growth and three to one in personal income growth. This suggests that any comprehensive view of supply-side economics cannot ignore welfare and unemployment disincentives as part of the overall "marginal tax rates" on economic growth and employment. Massachusetts has accomplished its economic turnaround by making the price of work go down sharply, not only for the average worker, but for the welfare dependent as well.

Perhaps the most startling demonstration of classical "wedge theory" that has occurred is the increase in tax revenues following the reduction in auto excise taxes. Under Proposition 2½, this tax rate was cut to $25 per $1,000 in auto value from $66 per $1,000. That is equivalent to reducing the price of a new car by $300 the first year and nearly $700 over the average term of ownership. The response by auto buyers has been immediate and powerful. While the national auto industry has been in the midst of a severe slump, new car sales in the Bay State during 1981 were *up* nearly 20 percent over 1980. This jump put Massachusetts' car dealers way ahead of their industry for the first time in three decades. In addition, the increased sales boosted sales tax revenues by an estimated $15–20 million.

TABLE 1
Welfare vs. Employment 1970–1978
(weighted averages)

	15 Highest Benefit States	15 Lowest Benefit States	U.S. Averages
Percent on Welfare (1978)	5.7	3.6	4.7
Percent Unemployed (1978)	7.0	5.5	6.0
Percent Minority Unemployment (1978)	12.3	10.6	11.9
Average Job Growth (1970-78)	10.6	46.6	21.0
Average Personal Income Growth (1970-78)	17.1	57.5	32.1

Source: Bureau of Labor Statistics, Census Data

Above all, the Massachusetts experience stands as a strong lesson that the best "social policy" for helping the poor remains a low tax and high incentive environment. The "welfare state" provides primarily for its bureaucratic defenders. Those states with the highest welfare benefits have, on average, the highest levels of minority unemployment while low benefit states have minority unemployment rates well below the national average (Table 1). As the 1981 Laffer study of Massachusetts for the Business Roundtable put it:

> (In 1980), the major expansion in its tax burden and public welfare expenditures over the decadal period cost the Massachusetts economy nearly 300,000 jobs and 11.5 percent less growth in personal income, or $5.4 billion in 1979 dollars ... an especially heavy burden for the poor and disadvantaged for whom growth and opportunity are the necessary conditions for realizing a higher standard of living for themselves and their children.[3]

GOVERNOR KING'S MESSAGE

All told, the Massachusetts turnaround is an enviable one which Governor King has understandably been broadcasting far and wide. In fact, his 1983 budget message contained a special section of statistical charts showing the relationship between the path of the state's tax burden relative to the national average and the path of its per capita personal income and unemployment rates relative to the nation, respectively. They were accompanied by a suitable spate of braggadocio:

> The Massachusetts economy is as strong as any state in America. It's been a long time since such a bold statement could be made, but in the last three years, the economy of Massachusetts has improved dramatically. Downward trends which developed early in the last decade have been reversed, and the economy has outperformed most expectations.[4]

The central theme of this budget message and of King's testimony to the Joint Economic Committee was clear:

This upward spiralling tax burden (of the early 1970s) had become a deterrent to the growth and expansion of our economy .... (Reversing that trend) has achieved an estimated savings of $2.1 billion in 1982 for the taxpayers of the Commonwealth. In 1978, the wage earner paid $177 in taxes out of every $1,000 earned. This year, the wage earner will pay $145 out of every $1,000 earned.[5]

The "real benefit" of this reduction, King testified, "is in the increase in employment opportunity. In the first three years of this Administration, 200,000 new jobs have been created. The Commonwealth has been below the national unemployment rate for twenty-eight consecutive months ... a dramatic change."[6]

Governor Hugh Carey of New York unwittingly strengthened King's testimony when, at the same hearing, Ohio Congressman Clarence "Bud" Brown reminded him: "You cut marginal tax rates by 45 percent in New York State (in 1977–79) and yet you're critical of the President's tax cuts which are only half as large on the federal level! Why is it good economic policy in Albany and not in Washington?"[7]

After muttering something about "budget cuts first," Carey did admit: "We felt that the marginal tax rate of 15 percent was confiscatory and counterproductive to attracting talent, technology and leadership to the state." Brown then reminded him that "the year before the tax cuts were enacted, the New York unemployment rate was 2.6 percent higher than the national average. After you enacted the tax cuts, the gap between New York and the national average began to drop dramatically ... so that you had, in effect, a change in your (tax) policy that stimulated the growth of the economy and it helped balance out the situation in the city of New York, didn't it?" To which Governor Carey could only reply, "That's right." At the end of this exchange, Representative Brown wondered out loud to the New York governor, "I'm trying to figure out whether you taught Jack Kemp or Jack Kemp taught you."[8]

THE POLITICAL CONNECTION

It is no small wonder that the embattled Republicans of the JEC wanted to hear King's message and that the Democrats were just as eager not to have one of their own party members bring the gospel of Reaganomics to Capitol Hill just when they have the Republicans on the run.

In fact, Senator Edward Kennedy was so incensed at the prospect of such a message that he convinced JEC Co-chairman Henry Reuss of Wisconsin to cancel the hearing entirely unless King's testimony was suppressed. But when the ten Republican members threatened to hold a separate public hearing, Reuss finally relented.

One can understand Kennedy's embarrassment. Not only has he led the national effort to debunk the Laffer Curve and Reaganomics, but he was outspokenly opposed to Proposition 2½ in Massachusetts. The liberal wing of the state's Democratic Party sees King as a positive pariah who not only backed Reaganomics wholeheartedly as a Democrat, but who now supports the "New Federalism."

No one in either Washington or Massachusetts has done more than Kennedy to impede the trend toward lower tax burdens and no one has been more emphatic in his repudiation

The liberal wing of the state's Democratic Party sees King as a positive pariah who not only backed Reaganomics wholeheartedly as a Democrat, but who now supports the "New Federalism."

of supply-side theory. To have his own state governor turn the tables this way can be very unsettling, so unsettling in fact, that the entire Massachusetts gubernatorial race for 1982 has now been revived.

Indeed, Governor King's political fortunes have posted nearly as dramatic a turnaround as the state's economy. In the November 1981 polls, King had fallen to a 65-15 deficit to his old nemesis, Michael Dukakis. King's poor showing in large part was due to his own political ineptitude and the clumsy way in which he first dealt with Proposition 2½. In addition, Dukakis's claim to the overpowering liberal constituency in the state also had contributed to King's almost certain defeat in the upcoming primaries.

Over the past two months, however, King has begun to turn this deficit around with powerful media presentations featuring the economic accomplishments of his administration and contrasting them with those of his predecessor. This effort was furthered by the governor's 1983 budget message which showed that, because of the strong economy, Massachusetts' tax revenues were growing far faster than ever before. In spite of the recession, tax revenues in 1981–82 fiscal year now are projected to finish nearly $100 million higher than even the most optimistic forecasts as late as last August (Table 2).

TABLE 2
State Revenues Soar
(Growth rates of first 5 months of fiscal 1982 over 1981)

	Senate Ways & Means Projection	Actual Performance
Total Taxes	+7.7%	+15.8%
Corporate Taxes	+5.1%	+15.2%
Income Taxes	+7.5%	+17.3%
Gasoline Taxes	+17.0%	+39.1%
Sales Taxes	+9.6%	+9.8%

Source: Department of Revenue

The pace of the revenue gains have prompted Senator Chester Atkins, Senate Ways and Means Committee Chairman (and liberal chairman of the state Democratic Committee), to abandon his prior gloomy forecasts of deficits and the need for higher taxes. Atkins now has switched, joining the emerging tax *cut* debate by offering a "fairer" tax-cut proposal of his own. In one stroke, King had moved the debate into his corner. And now Michael Dukakis is being forced to accept a television station's offer for a public gubernatorial debate on "the economy and taxes," a debate that King will surely dominate even with his wooden platform manner. In fact, the latest public opinion polls now show Dukakis with only a 15–20 point edge. One poll now shows a modest 45–30 margin, far smaller than the one Governor King overcame to upset Dukakis in 1978.

The best proof of the movement in King's direction is the startling statement by liberal U.S. Senator Paul Tsongas at the end of January that "what this state needs is a continuation of a pro-business climate." While Tsongas denied he was "tilting" to King, the message was clear: "The state economy is doing surprisingly well, considering the recession," Tsongas said, and he was not about to kick the man who was presiding over it, particularly when comparing his fiscal performance to his predecessor's in both constant and current dollars (Table 3).

TABLE 3
A Tale of Two Governors
Massachusetts State Spending, 1975–1982
(billions of dollars)

Fiscal Year	Local Aid		State Spending		Total Budget	
	Current $	1975 $	Current $	1975 $	Current $	1975 $
1975	$1.012	$1.012	$2.540	$2.540	$3.550	$3.550
1979	1.295	0.969	3.741	2.802	5.031	3.763
1982	1.912	1.051	4.472	2.462	6.383	3.514
% Changes (annual rate)						
Dukakis 75-79	6.3%	-1.1%	10.2%	2.5%	9.1%	1.4%
King 79-82	13.9	2.8	6.2	-4.3	8.3	-2.2

Source: State Budgets 1975-82

While King cannot legitimately lay claim to more than half of the tax burden reduction since 1979 (most of it came from Proposition 2½), he can prove that his administration has been fiscally responsible in creating the right climate for the trend—something Michael Dukakis will find hard to demonstrate for himself.

It was, after all, Michael Dukakis who told a radio audience on June 6th, 1978, the night that Proposition 13 passed in California, that "Massachusetts' voters are just too smart to fall for something like that!" Within four months, he had been upset in the primary, and in 1980, Proposition 2½ passed by a nearly 60–40 margin. The implementation of this measure made 1981 a year of intense political and fiscal chaos. Not only did the governor lose the initiative to his foes in the legislature, but they even outdid him in holding down the level of state spending and in supporting "bail-out" property tax relief to the cities and towns.

It is obvious that Massachusetts' voters like the change in fiscal policies that they found through the ballot box. Pollster John Becker of Becker Research reported in December 1981, that "it is significant that, despite all the emotional pronouncements, political maneuvering and the beginning of significant budget cuts in some municipalities, the ratio of opposition and support regarding Proposition 2½... has not budged one iota in the past nine months."[9]

Not only did the governor lose the initiative to his foes in the legislature, but they even outdid him in holding down the level of state spending and in supporting "bail-out" property tax relief to the cities and towns.

Becker found that among voters the tax cut measure was still ahead 53 to 45 (compared with 59–41 in the election). The idea that the measure should be "softened" was rejected by a 55 to 35 margin. Moreover, Becker and the U-Mass Poll both confirmed that, by a nearly 75 to 15 percent margin, Massachusetts' voters continue to support tax burden reduction.

Becker's findings were borne out in a series of March municipal elections in which efforts to override Proposition 2½ on local options were resoundingly defeated in 23 of 28 ballot questions by margins of up to 10 to 1. The only losses were on five separate proposals to exempt specific bond issues in three very wealthy towns.

It seems the voters now understand very well that, during the decade of the '70s, Massachusetts had become a modern paradigm for David Hume's original "supply-side" thesis. As James Ring Adams quoted Hume in a recent *Wall Street Journal* column:

> Taxes, like necessity, when carried too far, destroy industry by engendering despair; and even before they reach this pitch, they raise the wage of the laborer and manufacturer, and heighten the price of all commodities. An attentive disinterested legislature will observe the point when the emolument ceases and the prejudice begins.[10]

It is perhaps a reflection of our weak memories that the same state which began the first tax revolt with a "tea party" had to be forcefully reminded of the economic blessings of low taxes by the extraordinary "prejudice" of high ones. It remains to be seen whether the "attentive" legislature and governor who have wrought this economic turnaround will manage to stay the course in September and November, when liberal forces will mount their most serious assault against this path. Massachusetts will provide a microcosm of the national debate. At the moment, the prospects are perilous but improving; but the liberal press seems determined at this point to keep the economic debate superficial so the outcome is very much in doubt. But politics alone cannot change the economic model that has been developed, and economists and statesmen alike will have a difficult time ignoring it.

3

The Reagan Recovery

Charles W. Kadlec and Arthur B. Laffer

February 29, 1980

Ronald Reagan campaigned for and won the presidency in a recession year, 1980. As soon as the centerpiece of his economic plan—the three-year, phased-in income tax cut of 23 percent—was put into law early in his term in 1981, the United States fell into recession again.

It was a brutal recession, at the time "the worst since the Great Depression" (as we have heard so often in recent years about our own malaise). GDP dropped by nearly 3 percent in the last quarter of 1981 and the first of 1982, and then came in flat. At the end of 1982, nearly halfway through President Reagan's first term, the economy was smaller than in the recession year of 1980. Twelve million were unemployed.

These bleak statistics bear resemblance to those supervised by President Barack Obama in his first years as president in 2009 and 2010. Obama won the election of 2008 during a recession, but the economy only shrank on his taking office in 2009 and the passage of his economic plan. What growth that came thereafter was so modest that the 2007 peak was never reached in Obama's first two years, and the number of the unemployed swelled beyond previous highs, all the way to fifteen million.

But there the similarities end. For in the third and fourth years of the two presidencies, very different things in the economy ensued. Under Obama, 2011 brought timorous growth of 1.8 percent and a tiny crawl in job growth, with essentially the same thing in 2012. But under Reagan, beginning in 1983—it was morning again in America.

The first quarter of 1983 saw handsome economic growth of 5.1 percent, giving way to five consecutive quarters over 7 percent—one of the stellar runs of modern American history. This was economic growth *triple* of what we have had to be satisfied with in our own meek recovery from the Great Recession. By the end of 1984, there were six million more jobs in the economy than when Reagan had campaigned for office in 1980, on the way to seventeen million more by Reagan's departure from the presidency, after his second term, in 1989.

The secret to the success begun in 1983 was that this was when Reagan's economic plan really kicked in. Lost in all the rhetoric from over the years about the "huge" Reagan tax cut of 1981, that tax cut was actually small at the outset. It was a phased-in cut, such that the first year, 1981, there was only a 5 percent reduction in income tax rates. Another 10 percent came in 1982, and again in 1983, with 1985 bringing the permanent indexing of the tax code against inflation.

There was no way the economy was going to recover given a small tax cut in 1981, and recover it did not. In 1982, as the recession got entrenched, Reagan's opponents in Congress strove to get the president to cancel the forthcoming tax cuts of the 1981 law—the bigger installments of 10 percent and indexing. Reagan refused to budge, and the tax cuts kept on coming. When the cuts finally were of measurable size in 1983, blowout economic results occurred. The nation never looked back as the new era of prosperity begun in 1983 held through the rest of the century.

All along, from his position on the President's Economic Policy Advisory Board, Arthur Laffer had been warning Reagan that it was dangerous for the tax cut to be phased in. In the following paper from April, 1983, written by Laffer and Charles Kadlec, it was clear that the danger zone had finally passed. By early 1983, the tax cuts—of 5 percent in 1981, 10 percent in 1982, and 10 percent in 1983, then indexing—were now just about implemented. The economy was taking off, given that the government was permitting so much larger a share of wages and profits to be retained by those who earned them.

This paper, therefore, stands as one of the great prophetic statements of supply-side economics. It called the great 1980s boom at its take-off point. During the recession of 1981–82, some "Reaganites"—budget director David Stockman for example—made a volte-face because of the grim economic conditions. They said the tax cut of 1981 must be stopped in its tracks. Laffer and others held, to the contrary, that if the tax cuts outlined in the 1981 law kept on coming, an economic renaissance would occur.

Supply-side economics has always been a "policy mix," calling for tax cuts in the context of stabilizing the monetary system. The Kadlec-Laffer paper here began with a reiteration of a classic supply-side position on monetary policy. This was that the standard "targets" of monetary policy, interest rates and the quantity of money and such, have little to do with the proper conduct of monetary policy. The most important thing in monetary policy is for the Federal Reserve to meet real money demand with money supply.

The principles are as follows. *Thus a central supply-side* Given a good marginal tax cut, people *message to the Fed is to* who earn more keep a greater share *realize that when the* of their new earnings than they had *American economy is set* before. This results in a race in the *to roar, the Fed's main job* economy for new investment, new *is to finance the boom.* business creation, and new hiring. There is greater demand for money after a marginal tax cut, and it all serves the purposes of "real" expansion in the economy, as opposed to fodder for inflation and tax hedges.

The right thing for the Fed to do in such a context is to expand the money supply, without fear of inflation. Such a move might violate restrictive quantity preconceptions, derived from monetarism or what have you, but the effect will be an inflation-free boom. Thus a central supply-side message to the Fed is to realize that when the American economy is set to roar, the Fed's main job is to finance the boom.

As it turned out, beginning in 1982, the Fed stopped letting musty quantity targets and fear of inflation restrict its monetary issuance in the face of the great demand for money that stemmed from the tax cuts. Given the economic boom that then came—accompanied by the collapse in inflation—the monetary side of this paper also became prophetic.

FROM HERE TO THERE: ELEMENTS OF RECOVERY, APRIL 29, 1983

The recovery remains on track. Economic as well as political forces are working together to augment economic growth. Recovery among America's major trading partners will bolster the U.S. recovery as well. And the sole threats to economic recovery—a sharp rise in interest rates or a substantial new tax increase—also would threaten President Reagan's expected bid for reelection, lowering the possibilities of both.

At the same time, the presumed desire of Paul Volcker to be reappointed Fed chairman provides personal incentives for him to create an environment in which interest rates decline to new lows. The answer to reducing interest rates does not lie in a return to a strict quantity rule. Whether or not M1 growth rates this quarter should be above or below the first quarter's pace simply cannot be answered in any absolute sense. The appropriate growth in money depends on what happens to the demand for money. By contrast, Volcker's identification of benefits associated with stabilizing the exchange rates is a small step toward a more formalized commitment to a price rule and its promise of lower interest rates.

The most likely threat to recovery is a tax increase on oil. The point at which any oil tax is levied is as important as the tax itself. If the tax were levied solely on domestic oil production, then the burden of the tax would be borne by domestic oil producers. If the tax were levied on domestic and foreign crude oil, then the burden of the tax would be borne by domestic refineries. Only if the tax were levied on imported refined products would domestic refined product prices be elevated above the world level. In such a case, profit margins throughout the rest of the economy would be squeezed. The American consumer would import energy in "fabricated form"—foreign produced steel, automobiles, plastics or fertilizer. This would be by far the most damaging form of oil tax.

Absent such folly, however, the outlook for sustained recovery, stable prices, and lower interest rates continues to improve.

~

The outlook for sustained recovery, stable prices, and lower interest rates continues to improve. Economic as well as political forces are now working together to augment economic growth. The sole threats to economic recovery—a sharp rise in interest rates or a substantial new tax increase—also would threaten President Reagan's expected bid for reelection. Therefore, the possibilities of either have been lowered.

This link between economic and political outcomes provides personal incentives for the President to evaluate conflicting advice, and weigh different policy options in terms of expected results. This emphasis on results will diminish the power of arguments that elevate "bipartisanship" as the basis for economic policy.

MONETARY POLICY

As a result of Reagan's own political imperative, time is running out for Fed Chairman Paul Volcker to create an environment in which interest rates decline to new lows. Moreover, the presumed desire of Volcker to be reappointed chairman provides the personal incentives for him to concentrate on obtaining that result.

The fact that Volcker is being considered at all for reappointment with unemployment above 10 percent and record real interest rates can be attributed to the considerable accomplishments of monetary policy over the past year. Prices have been stabilized—the Consumer Price Index rose 3.6 percent during the twelve months ending in March 1983. And interest rates are down—yields on 30-year government bonds at the end of March were 2.7 percentage points below their year earlier level, while yields on three-month Treasury bills were nearly 5 percentage points lower. But these lower rates were all in hand by year-end. During the first quarter, interest rates climbed even as the price indices remained stable….

[I]f interest rates fail to move to new lows for the year, or if prices begin to rise, the viability of Volcker's professed standard—watching all variables and acknowledging the value of all theories—will be brought into question.

The answer to reducing interest rates does not lie in a return to a strict quantity rule. Whether or not M1 growth rates this quarter should be above or below the first quarter's pace simply cannot be answered in any absolute sense. The appropriate growth in money depends on what happens to the demand for money. An acceleration in Gross National Product (GNP) growth, for example, would increase the demand for money. Further declines in interest rates also would tend to increase the demand for money relative to GNP. Such a decrease in interest rates reduces the opportunity cost of holding assets in non-interest bearing or below-market interest bearing currency and checking accounts. Velocity would decline....

In any case, following a quantity rule assumes that velocity remains constant. As a result, the rate of increase in nominal GNP and money would be the same....

Absent a return to a quantity rule, the only option that remains is a more formalized commitment to stabilizing the price level. Such a guarantee would reduce the fear of future inflation and thereby produce lower interest rates. Volcker's identification of benefits associated with stabilizing the price of the dollar and other currencies in foreign exchange markets is a small step in this direction. Moreover, his suggestion that limited and coordinated central bank intervention to damp excessive volatility in exchange rates broaches, if only indirectly, the issue of what is an appropriate monetary standard. Coordinated intervention begs for a benchmark that identifies which country's monetary policy is either inflationary or deflationary. If exchange rates are stabilized relative to each other and such a benchmark, the result would be the return of global price stability and lower interest rates.

FISCAL POLICY

An imperative for political survival makes it a better than an even bet that the President will thwart the latest attempt to kill the third year of the tax cut, repeal indexing, and otherwise raise $30 billion in taxes for 1984.

For one thing, the benefits of the first real reduction in tax rates are now evident to all. The 3.1 percent advance in first quarter real GNP could have been almost stronger if it hadn't been for the arcane accounting procedures of Commodity Credit Corporation purchases. But even so, it occurred without the substantial build-up in inventories that marks the beginning of most recoveries. Moreover, the 1.1 percent advance in industrial production in March, the continued strength in the housing industry, and pick-up in retail sales, and March's 1.5 percent advance in the index of leading economic indicators all point to an economic recovery that is gathering momentum.

Against such a backdrop, the incessant incantation of the words "budget deficit" are nonsensical. Better than expected economic growth and lower than expected unemployment mean the worst of the budget deficit problem is already behind the economy. Absent a tax increase, the news on the deficit front can only improve in the months ahead.

Going for a tax increase now may win the President votes he might not otherwise have had in the Congress, but it will cost him votes where it now counts, among the electorate. In addition, refusal to back the Democrats proposal for a $30 billion tax increase gives Reagan a partisan issue for the campaign ahead. Finally, permitting repeal of the third year of the tax cut would be tantamount to abandoning the growth agenda that propelled Reagan into the Oval Office. There are few if any policies the President is more closely identified with than the across-the-board tax reduction now under assault.

An imperative for political survival makes it a better than an even bet that the President will thwart the latest attempt to kill the third year of the tax cut, repeal indexing, and otherwise raise $30 billion in taxes for 1984.

The economic implications of securing the tax cut are twofold. First, the current debate makes somewhat problematic half of the 10 percent reduction in personal income tax rates that took effect January 1. Repeal of the third year of the tax cut would reduce the rate reduction for 1983 to 5 percent, and thereby leave withholding schedules unchanged. Loss of half of this year's scheduled tax rate reduction would weaken the recovery.[1]

Because of this danger, the full effects of this year's reduction in tax rates have not been incorporated into economic activity. Elimination of uncertainty over the tax cut thus is equivalent to a further reduction in effective tax rates. Securing the tax cut will increase incentives and provide additional stimulus to the recovery.

Second, implementation of the July 1 change in withholding schedules carries with it an additional 5 percent reduction in personal income tax rates effective January 1, 1984. That will give the recovery a final boost at the opening of the presidential primary season.[2]

Similarly, the political imperative demands that the President block repeal of indexing. Defense of indexing the personal tax code is a sure vote getter throughout middle-class America. It is the average wage earner who faces the most rapid tax rate increases with inflation. Ironically, inflation cannot push the rich into a higher than the 50 percent maximum tax bracket. Condemnation of indexing by several of the leading Democratic presidential candidates gives Reagan a winning issue in 1984.

THE THREAT OF AN OIL TAX

The only apparent remaining fiscal policy danger to a sustained recovery is a substantial tax increase on oil. In mid-April, the price of oil was once again under pressure in the spot markets of Rotterdam. A sharp fall in the price of oil now would provide an avenue for the Administration to pursue the illusion of a non-tax tax increase—a tax increase that does not change incentives.[3]

For example, Chairman of the Council of Economic Advisers Martin Feldstein, speaking on his own behalf, and Chairman of the Federal Reserve Board Paul Volcker both have called for new oil taxes if the price of oil should drop below $25. Environmentalists, in the name of conservation, also support such a tax. Even the Reagan Administration, while opposing an immediate oil tax, has been mesmerized by the prospect of huge revenues into recommending a standby $5 oil tax commencing October 1, 1985. Under static assumptions such a tax would raise an estimated $38 billion a year in revenue. Seemingly slight differences in the manner in which an oil tax would be imposed would have sharply different implications for the oil industry, the U.S. consumer, and the path of the economic recovery.

It is widely assumed that domestic crude oil prices are the primary determinant of the prices of gasoline, heating oil, and other refined products sold in the U.S. market. This assumption provided the logical basis for controlling domestic crude oil prices throughout most of the 1970s.

This assumption is incorrect, as are the forecasts of those who used it when they asserted that decontrol would lead to higher gasoline prices. Domestic crude oil prices, by themselves, do not determine domestic refined product prices. Refined product prices in the U.S. are established in world markets without direct reference to U.S. crude oil prices. As a result, a crude oil tax will not produce anything like a proportionate increase in domestic refined product prices....

If the tax were levied solely on domestic production, as with the windfall profits tax, then the burden of the tax would be borne by domestic oil producers. Since domestic oil refineries can purchase either foreign or domestic supplies, U.S. oil producers would be unable to pass on a domestic crude oil tax. The impact of a domestic oil tax would be to lower the returns to domestic oil exploration and production relative to oil exploration and production outside of the U.S.A. Domestic oil tax, like the windfall profits tax, increases imports of foreign oil, decreases production of domestically sourced crude oil, and leaves virtually untouched the price of refined products.

If the tax were levied on domestic and foreign crude oil, then the burden of the tax would be borne by domestic refineries. A tariff on foreign oil equivalent to the domestic tax eliminates the alternative of non-taxed oil. However, it leaves unchanged the world price of refined products. As a result, domestic refineries would be able to pass on little if any of the now higher cost of crude oil to their customers. In general, refinery margins would be narrowed by the amount of the tax.

The impact of a tax on domestic and foreign crude oil would be to reduce the profitability of domestic refineries, both absolutely and relative to foreign based refineries. In the aftermath of such a tax, imports of refined products would be expected to rise while imports of crude oil and the utilization of domestic refinery capacity would be expected to decline. This result is just the reverse of what happened when the oil import fee was lifted in 1976. As then, wholesale prices of refined products would be left virtually unchanged.

Only if the tax were levied on imported refined products would domestic refined product prices be elevated above the world level. In such a case, distributors of refined products would have no choice but to pay a price equal to the world price plus the tax for their supplies. Before-tax profit margins within the domestic oil industry would rise by the amount of the tax. But profit margins throughout the rest of the economy would be squeezed.

The process of arbitrage does not stop at refined product markets, however. Domestically based manufacturing facilities that face foreign competition will find it difficult if not impossible to pass on higher energy prices to their customers. Such an overall energy tax would thus hurt those industries the most that are most intensive in the use of energy and that also face foreign competition. The domestic steel, aluminum and petrochemical industries are just three examples that come immediately to mind. To the extent that recently negotiated steel import quotas protect that industry, then those industries intensive in the use of steel, including autos, also would be affected.

Refined product prices in the U.S. are established in world markets without direct reference to U.S. crude oil prices. To put it differently, to the extent possible, the American consumer will try to obtain the cheaper foreign oil in whatever form possible. If the imports of crude oil at the world price are blocked, then foreign crude oil will be displaced by imports of refined products. If, in a similar fashion, the price of imported refined products are elevated above the world level, then energy in "fabricated form"—whether it be foreign sourced steel, automobiles, plastics or fertilizer—will be sought.

The least damaging oil tax would be one imposed only on domestic oil. It would isolate the negative effects to the owners of domestic crude oil. But if efforts to defeat such a tax fail, the oil industry can be expected to broaden the tax to include imports of oil and refined products. That would maintain profits in the oil industry, but impose yet another competitive disadvantage on American industry. A slower recovery and intensified pressure for more trade restrictions would be the inevitable result.

A WORLDWIDE RECOVERY

Absent such folly, however, the recovery will remain on track. Moreover, it is likely to pick up added support from recovery among America's major trading partners. Bull markets are now rampant from Japan and

Australia to Canada and Germany. Over the past year (as of April 26), the Dow Jones Industrial Average rose 41.0 percent to 1209.5. This advance was exceeded by stock market indices in Holland, South Africa, Sweden, and Canada. The stock market in Germany is up 32.7 percent, in Japan up 14.3 percent, and even in troubled France, it is up 8.1 percent. Moreover, with the exception of France, these gains are all the more impressive due to price stability—making them more real than has been the case in quite some time. Such gains in worldwide equity values point to a global recovery that will enhance the prospects for sustained recovery in the U.S. by reducing the threat of protectionism and easing the pressures for higher tax rates in all countries.

TABLE 1
A World-Wide Bull Market
(As of April 26, 1983)

Stock price indices	1983			Percentage change on	
	April 26	High	Low	One Month	One Year
DJIA	1209.5	1209.5	1027.0	+6.9	+41
Australia	603.0	603.0	487.8	+19.0	+19.4
Belgium	122.2	122.8	100.5	+5.4	+24.6
Canada	2321.3	2328.8	1949.8	+9.4	+47.7
France	117.8	121.0	96.1	+2.9	+8.7
Germany	952.1	957.1	727.9	+6.9	+32.7
Holland	104.7	109.2	83.5	-2.8	+41.7
Hong Kong	1028.3	1067.4	761.6	+5.0	-21.3
Italy	191.0	214.9	160.5	-9.4	-0.9
Japan	624.4	624.4	574.5	+1.5	+14.3
Singapore	932.8	932.8	712.3	+10.5	+20.8
South Africa	927.3	940.5	740.9	+13.5	+59
Sweden	1390.3	1396.9	896.2	+10.7	+146.6
Switzerland	322.0	322.0	294.1	+3.3	+24.9
United Kingdom	695.2	695.5	584.4	+6.6	+21.9

Source: The Economist, April 30–May 6

4

The Great Moderation

George Gilder

September 16,1983

Carping about Ronald Reagan's economy was getting more difficult to do by the time George Gilder wrote this piece in September 1983. Though the year Reagan campaigned for office, 1980, along with the first two years of his presidency, 1981 and 1982, had been recession years, 1983 was nothing of the sort. Economic growth was 5 percent in the first quarter of 1983; fully 9 percent in the second quarter; and as Gilder set to writing this piece in the summer, a run of three consecutive quarters at 8 percent was getting under way. There was a boom going on. The long stagflation of the 1970s and early 1980s was coming to an end.

Gilder confronted the *Washington Post* and other assailants of the Reagan recovery by making a prediction in this piece. Not only would this recovery last and come in the absence of inflation—it would usher in an American economic renaissance. Soon to come, said Gilder, was a new era in which technological industries and entrepreneurship, as opposed to the old-industrial behemoths of the Fortune 500 and a Keynesian government bent on regulation, industrial policy, and spending, would become the drivers of the economy.

Gilder's predictions would be fulfilled. A generation later, economists would speak of the "Great Moderation" of 1982–2007, where growth came in strong virtually every year, the march of government slowed, the recessions that came were few and small, and the terrors of inflation and unemployment stayed at low levels unimagined in the 1970s. By common consent, this new era was that of the computer- and Internet-centered "Information Age."

In this piece of September 1983, Gilder not only called the origin of the Great Moderation; he identified its salient characteristics.

To begin, Gilder cleared up some misconceptions that have nonetheless hung around to this day about why the Reagan policy took some time to produce recovery. The problem was one of slow implementation. At first, in 1981, the Reagan tax cuts were small. The 1981 law provided for only a 5 percent marginal income tax cut in that year, followed by cuts of twice that magnitude in each of the following two years. Moreover, monetary policy was notably tight through the first twelve months of these tax cuts. Then late in 1982, it began to relax.

As Gilder pointed out, this slow implementation was the sure origin of the "Reagan recession" of 1981–82. Had the full income tax cut come all at once, the effects actually seen in 1983 would have occurred earlier. And had the Federal Reserve been clued in in 1981 that the forthcoming tax cuts would prompt new real activities in the economy as opposed to still more inflation, it would have been comfortable with relaxing monetary policy in order to finance the boom at an earlier date. By 1983 the happy coincidence of policy—marginal tax cuts coupled with money-creation feeding real growth—was finally realized.

Even as the economy launched into a boom in 1983, there were some dislocations. Those who had invested with an eye to the perpetuation of the conditions of the 1970s and 1980s were in for a rude awakening. As Gilder stressed here, those who had gone all-in for "housing, collectibles, natural resources, farmland, gold and other investments of capital flight and inflationary fear…suddenly suffered a sharp drop in their net worth and liquidity."

In inflationary environments, investors plow money into things that cannot be readily increased in supply (above all, commodities limited by the earth's geology), in that these things will go up sharply in price given a general rise in prices. Gold and oil, for example, both went up fifteen- to twenty-fold from 1970 to 1980, even though the overall price level went up about one-and-a-half times, itself a peacetime record.

In high-tax environments, in turn, investors wait to take profits on their investments, in that selling is a taxable event. Thus in the long years of stagflation preceding the supply-side revolution, a tremendous amount of capital in the American economy was locked up unproductively in inflation hedges and tax hideouts. The result was slow growth, a capital shortage for real enterprises, and unemployment.

What happened once the supply-side policy mix kicked in in 1983 was a massive asset-shift. People got out of the inert inflation/tax hedges of the past and into stocks and bonds—titles to businesses in a word—now that the returns to enterprise could be kept, and kept in a strong currency. Cumulatively, this asset-shift reached the level of $10 trillion, by some estimates. It is again to Gilder's credit that he perceived the whole matter with clarity in September 1983 just as these great events were coming to pass.

In 1981, Gilder published a book on the economic excellence that would come to this country if only it would turn away from its ill-advised Keynesian experiment. *Wealth and Poverty* spent weeks on the *New York Times* bestseller list. But as the "Reagan recession" came in 1981 and 1982, readers began to wonder if Gilder was a false prophet. By September 1983, as he wrote the following, Gilder stood on the cusp of vindication.

THE SUPPLY-SIDE RENAISSANCE
SEPTEMBER 16, 1983

Economists from across the political spectrum have predicted that Reagan's tentative supply-side measures would result in doom and depression, collision and crunch, wild inflation and crushing deficits, soaring unemployment and runaway interest rates. But, now, when the economy is booming, unemployment dropping, inflation under control and the rich paying a record share of taxes, the puzzle is to find a new tune—one that will acknowledge the reality of a rising economy without giving credit to Reagan and supply-side policies.

Skeptics—whatever their economic or political stance—don't comprehend the origins, depth or reach of the recovery. A positive change in public sentiment has sprung from supply-side and monetary policies, combined with the technological breakthroughs of the computer age. Understanding the true relationship between the supply-side measures and our recent recessionary distress is the key to understanding the gyrations of the Reagan Administration in the last three years.

The U.S. is undergoing not a recovery but an industrial renaissance. It is a classic supply-side revival, led not by the consumer but by purchases of producer durables, especially computers and other electronic equipment, and a surge of venture capital.

The link between supply-side policies and technology dates from the capital gains tax cut of 1978 which reversed the catastrophic tax "reform" of the 1970s. The computer revolution, in turn, made possible the current economic renaissance despite a continual dearth of capital. Due in large part to the explosive advances in computer technology, the U.S. has been the only industrial country to increase manufacturing employment during the last decade. Continued technological breakthroughs and advances in manufacturing are now being fed by an acceleration in the pace of venture investment, which was nine times higher in the first eight months of 1983 than in any previous year.

The next challenge for supply-side policy should be a reduction in all tax rates to a level that penalizes neither work nor savings nor the ultimate investments of family life. Concomitantly, the Fed should restore the dollar as a secure store of value, thereby providing low and stable interest rates to a nation busy in its pursuit of the new frontiers that beckon at the fringes of man's technological prowess and understanding of the world in which he lives.

⊘⊘

Every time they wake some economist these days from deep intellectual slumber to award him the Nobel Prize, he rushes blinking and blurry-eyed to the microphones to denounce supply-side economics. Even pre-Nobel figures like Martin Feldstein, confronted by the press after his appointment as chairman of the Council of Economic Advisers, saw fit to distance himself from any "vestigal supply-side extremists" in the Administration.

For several years, other eminent economists—from Alan Greenspan on the right and Henry Kaufmann on Wall Street to MIT's Lester Thurow on the left—have been predicting doom and depression, collision and crunch, wild inflation and crushing deficits, soaring unemployment and runaway interest rates as a result of the tentative supply-side measures of the Reagan Administration.

At the end of 1982, the consensus forecast for 1983 was for growth of below 3 percent; the Administration, itself, under Feldstein's guidance, predicted 1.4 percent. Economists of many stripes, moreover, from Wall Street's Gary Shilling to James Tobin of Yale, shed tears over the alleged favors to the rich embodied in the Reagan program. The gap between rich and poor loomed ever larger in media reports.

Now that the economy is booming, unemployment dropping, productivity soaring, inflation under control, and the rich paying a record share of taxes, the chorus of economists is necessarily changing its tune. Except for a few incorrigibles like author Robert Heilbroner, they have abandoned their popular dirge of a new great depression and, except for the most devout monetarists, no longer predict runaway price increases. But with their opposition to supply-side policy as fervid as ever, they needed a new theme of analysis: some way to acknowledge the reality of a rising economy without giving any credit to Reagan administration policies.

THE SKEPTICS' VIEW

Needless to say, the economic profession has been up to the task. The *Washington Post* summed up the new theme in a lead editorial. The recovery is a temporary demand-side episode "generated by a big budget deficit that is driving up consumers' spending." Yet big deficits, the *Post* declared, "are the very medicine that Mr. Reagan always said was addictive and was getting the country into serious trouble." The *Post* pointed to the apparent dip in personal savings in the second quarter, to 3.9 percent, and to the two-year slump in quantitative business investment, and could announce the dismal failure of supply-side policy in the face of the dramatic revival of economic activity.

On the right, monetarists took a similarly skeptical stance toward the recovery. They argued that the revival was attributable to the Fed's loosening of the money supply in 1982 after tightening it to extinguish inflation in 1980. But in the monetarist vision, the economy is now running out of control as a result of excessive money creation in 1983.[1]

The initially sober recovery, according to this school, has turned into an easy-money binge that will lead to inflation and crash in 1984 or beyond. Pointing to a post-World War II record M1 growth of some 10 percent over the last twelve months (adjusted for the distortions from NOW accounts) and to a recent surge in the monetary base, these conservatives believe that the system has returned to the morbid monetary spirals of the 1970s.

None of the skeptics comprehend the origins, depth or reach of the recovery. Despite serious limitations in the Reagan program, the current resurgence is the most promising of the post-war era and constitutes not a mere cyclical revival of growth but the kind of economic renaissance long predicted by Jack Kemp and other supply-side leaders. In the light of this perspective, the monetary expansion appears not as a morbid excess of Fed policy but as a necessary response to a fully healthy shift in public demand. People have been rejecting illiquid inflation hedges in favor of the financial assets and productive investments fueling the new era of growth.

This fully positive change in public sentiment sprang from supply-side and monetary policies, combined with the technological breakthroughs of the computer age. It was enhanced by the apparently enduring political triumph of pro-business leadership and the enactment of the Reagan program. But it did not come without severe initial costs: recessionary distress that obscured the change from many economists and policy makers and led many observers to denounce supply-side economics as the cause of the problem rather than the cure.

The critics were partly correct, in that supply-side policy shaped to some extent the pattern of recessionary damage. But they had no idea of the nature of the link between the policy as enacted and its impact. To understand the true relationship between the supply-side measures and our recent troubles is the key to understanding the political and economic gyrations of the first three years of the Reagan Administration.

TAX GIMMICKS AND RECESSION

The first effect of the Reagan Administration's economic program was to target its tax incentives toward the purchase of machines and other capital equipment, while deferring the tax cuts on the earnings of the men and women who operated the machines and managed the factories and create tomorrow's businesses. Old wealth benefits the most from accelerated depreciation, investment tax credits and the like, while profits—the creation of new wealth—faced high marginal tax rates. Such tax gimmicks act, for the most part, as tax shelters for those with existing income, rather than as a spur to innovation and the creation of new enterprise.

The initial policy focus on targeting incentives toward capital investment was a mutant version of the original supply-side agenda.

The supply-side argument has never been restricted to government revenues or capital formation alone. Some of the most destructive effects of the tax binges of recent years hit labor as much as capital, family structure as much as industrial structure. Studies at the liberal think tank, Brookings Institution, and in the income maintenance experiments of the Department of Health and Human Services (formerly HEW), show that the impact of progressive tax rates on work effort and productivity are greater than indicated in earlier studies by Laffer Associates and other supply-side investigators.

The Brookings study, for example, indicated that the progressive features of the U.S. tax code reduce work effort among prime-age males by some 8 percent. Brookings computed that no less than 54 percent of the revenue raised through progressivity is lost through tax-inflicted distortions of the economy. It concluded that in terms of distortion of effort and "deadweight loss," the tax burden rises at roughly the square of its progressivity. Thus, contrary to all previous Brookings studies, the tax burden is both more progressive and more economically perverse than even supply-siders have claimed.

In making this argument, moreover, Brookings ignored the interplay of various tax disincentives and neglected the tragic entrapment of the poor and elderly who suffer marginal rates implicit in their welfare programs of close to 100 percent or more. These analyses also neglected the huge rates of family breakdown that result from tax systems which drive men out of the workforce and onto the streets, while their wives become wards of the state.[2]

Targeting tax benefits to owners of existing wealth also failed to spur the economy because those most likely to benefit from the investment shelters were immobilized by the Administration's rapid success in controlling inflation. The result was a drastic decline in the value and potential of the public's holdings of inflation hedges, tax advantages, and political entitlements piled up during the era of growing socialist ascendancy in Washington. Tax shelters are of little benefit when incomes are falling and profits collapsing.

With housing, collectibles, natural resources, farmland, gold and other investments of capital flight and inflationary fear falling from favor, those who had profited from the distortions of high taxes and high inflation of the 1970s suddenly suffered a sharp drop in their net worth and liquidity. The $2.7 trillion trove of residential housing—replete with second homes and additions, antiques and art—which had become the chief reservoir of household savings suddenly lost some 10 percent or more of its real value.

A similar misfortune befell many American corporations that had borrowed heavily to purchase real estate, natural resources, raw material inventories and other inflation hedges in response to the assaults of the 1970s. Many issued commercial paper to meet interest charges in anticipation of the rising cash flows of inflation. Without the planned-for inflation, bankruptcies multiplied and seemed to vindicate the prophets of doom.

The first outward and visible effects of the turn to the supply side were, therefore, calamitous for many households and corporations. At the same time, individuals were left awaiting their tax cuts. Hence, all the hesitation in following the apparent supply-side incentives for aggressive risk-taking and enterprise. Most entrepreneurs had little access to money. Hence, all the predictions of depression and collapse in the midst of the most positive changes in economic policy of the last several decades.

Implicit in the decline in value of the assets of capital flight, however, was a rise in the value of the assets of capital commitment—stocks. For the desire to get out of inflation hedges sprang in part from a desire to get into financial assets. In the public mind, financial assets became more valuable compared to non-financial holdings. Interest rates should have gone down. But, instead, they went up.

THE ROLE OF MONETARY POLICY

The reasons for the rise in real interest rates during 1981 and 1982 will be debated by economists for the remainder of the decade. What is incontrovertible, however, is that the high rates imposed real costs on the economy, especially those sectors most intensive in the use of credit. Among the biggest users of credit were those who had played the inflation game to the hilt, leveraging inventories and factories in anticipation of using cheaper dollars in the future to retire the debt. But those plans, too, were shattered by the combination of a sudden return to low inflation accompanied by continued high interest rates. The result was a dissolution of old collateral and a rise of distress borrowing.

Nonetheless, undetected by economists, unmeasured by government statistics, unimagined by the Federal Reserve Board or by the nation's bankers, the real wealth of the society was growing massively. New collateral for productive debt was rapidly accumulating.

That wealth and that collateral, however, consisted not of old houses but of new hopes, not of new tax dodges but of new technologies. It comprised all the revived motivations, long-term visions, revolutionary inventions, entrepreneurial ambitions, and political commitments of a supply-side economy. It was the best collateral in the world, but its chief manifestation in the realm of measurable assets was a drastic drop in the value of those assets and financial strategies that had dominated the previous decade. Its chief impediments were the delay of the personal tax cuts and the distortions born of sky-high interest rates.

Undetected by economists, unmeasured by government statistics, unimagined by the Federal Reserve Board or by the nation's bankers, the real wealth of the society was growing massively. New collateral for productive debt was rapidly accumulating.

For many long months, the nation's economy suffered in that paradox of policy. The nation's central bank—which had freely funded the nation's long flight from productive assets—refused to finance the economy's return to health. The Fed refused to recognize either the enduring significance of the drop in velocity, or the cost of continued high interest rates at a time of a drastic reduction in the rate of inflation, or the nation's dramatic but unmeasurable accumulation of the metaphysical capital of supply-side growth. Thus, even as the nation's old wealth became trapped in unproductive assets—incarcerated in bricks and mortar, gold and collectibles all dwindling in value—the new wealth was forced to await the benefits of supply-side policies and the restoration of properly functioning credit markets. All the while, the economy, thriving in the crucial domain of the public mind and entrepreneurial spirit, withered in the streets and shops and markets of the land.

Meanwhile, households and corporations slowly rebuilt their balance sheets. By mid-1982, household net liquidity—current assets over liabilities—had quadrupled in three years, to some $200 billion. Although this amount fell far short of the previous losses on durable assets, it represented a major step of adaptation to the new era. Savings rose some 20 percent as money poured into money market funds. But the velocity of money continued to decline as the public no longer felt compelled to turn over its dollars at the previous inflationary pace.

This lower velocity meant that even the Fed's begrudging expansion of the money supply could no longer finance the transaction and investment needs of a growing economy. To fulfill the promise of the 1980s, already roaring in the minds of Americans, required a dramatic and sustained surge of money growth. This the Fed finally and reluctantly delivered, in late 1982 and 1983, supposedly to prevent the collapse of banks in Brazil (and hence in the U.S.). The Fed thus finally released the national economy from the liquidity trap of the 1970s and into the renaissance of the '80s.

THE SUPPLY-SIDE, TECHNOLOGY NEXUS

To supply-side visionaries of the condition of U.S. entrepreneurship and technology, however, it has been obvious for several years that the nation needed only a change in policy to ignite a boom of technological advance, productivity growth and rising living standards. Part of the promise derived from the rapid commercial maturation of microchip technology: semiconductors proliferating in ever more consumer products at ever lower prices and in ever more fruitful forms of office and capital equipment. From home computers, video games and mobile telephones, small business consoles, point-of-sale terminals and office automation, to automobile engine microcontrollers, programmable robots and CAD-CAM tools (for computer-aided design, manufacture and engineering), the computer revolution finally and massively arrived.

This development, which was key to the shape and dynamics of the current recovery, may seem unrelated to supply-side policy. But the fact that the revolution came first to the U.S. was crucially dependent on the initial major salvo of the supply side-movement: the capital gains tax cut of 1978 engineered by the late Congressman William Steiger of Wisconsin with the important aid of the *Wall Street Journal* editorial page, the intellectual inspiration of the Laffer curve, and the prestigious support of Martin Feldstein and his National Bureau for Economic Research.

This supply-side bill, reversing a catastrophic tax "reform" of the early 1970s, came just in time. In the mid-1970s, the evaporation of venture capital had halted new high tech public offerings and gravely slowed the thrust of progress in the computer industry. In their desperation, American entrepreneurs sold their technologies to foreigners in order to continue development. Gene Amdahl, for example, America's leading computer designer, had to turn to Fujitsu of Japan for capital after he left IBM, and Richard Petritz, formerly of Texas Instruments and Mostek, sold out to the National Enterprise Board of Great Britain to get funds for Inmos, a promising semiconductor startup. In all, between 1974 and 1978, fourteen significant chip firms slipped away to foreigners during this Silicon Valley tax sale.

THE CAPITAL GAINS TAX CUT

Following the 1978 cut in the capital gains tax, however, venture capital funds, public offerings, and business starts all resumed the surging trajectory of the late 1960s and early 1970s. By the end of 1978, venture funds had risen more than fifteen-fold, from $37 million in 1977 to some $570 million in 1978. By 1981, this catalytic source of capital had reached record levels of between one and two billion dollars annually, depending on definitions in the exploding venture capital industry. Without the Steiger Amendment, it is fair to say, the current resurgence of the U.S. economy would have been much slower and the U.S. would no longer lead the world in the computer and microchip technologies that are the driving force of global economic progress.

Portents of the current recovery also emerged on the stock markets of the late 1970s. While the Dow Jones industrials remained in the doldrums, the Wilshire Index of some 5,000 public companies returned to its earlier peaks in real terms. In addition, a great transition was already under way in American patterns of employment. Jobs in office equipment and computers began a five-year surge from 50 percent of auto industry employment in 1978 to 140 percent in 1982. The industrialization of booming U.S. service firms brought huge new purchases of electronic equipment. Making capital outlays that would rise some 145 percent in real terms between 1975 and 1982, service companies prepared the way for the productivity upsurge now sweeping through American offices.

The election of Ronald Reagan brought the decontrol of oil and the renewal of hope to American business. Together with energy efficiencies spreading through the economy and the new oil and gas discoveries around the world, decontrol removed the pressure of rising fuel prices from the inflationary calculus. The enactment of Reagan's supply-side program of tax cuts—despite all delays and distortions—signaled the end of the long siege of soaring tax rates.

Even though taxes in 1981 absorbed 52 percent of all incremental GNP, the drop of the top rate from 70 to 50 reduced the capital gains tax to a ceiling of 20 percent. This new cut spurred the venture capital industry to new highs and set the stage for the stock market boom of late 1982, when the eighties first began to roar and every week saw more new stock offerings than a typical year of the mid-1970s.

The recovery began in January 1983 with the first across-the-board tax cuts not nullified by inflation and social security tax hikes. (As Arthur Laffer has long explained, tax rate reductions take place at the beginning of the year, not at their official mid-year date.) Contrary to the *Washington Post*, the recovery was not led by consumption nor did the savings vote decline in any economic sense. In fact, the estimated $600-billion rise in the value of equities provided an enormous increase in the valuation of household assets and was tantamount to a dramatic rise in their savings....

For the last fifteen years, taxes on personal savings, adjusted for inflation, never once dropped below 100 percent for the crucial top-bracket taxpayers.

At the same time, the computer revolution made possible the current economic renaissance despite a continued dearth of capital. For the last fifteen years, American capitalism has suffered from an unprecedented assault on its sources of savings and investment. For that entire period, taxes on personal savings, adjusted for inflation, never once dropped below 100 percent for the crucial top-bracket taxpayers. This assault continues today, with taxes on dividends and capital gains still exorbitant compared to all our economic rivals.

This tax problem challenged American entrepreneurs to economize on capital: to increase the efficiency of their investments. Their solution, again, was the application of knowledge-intensive gear: the computer revolution in all its many forms. Computer firms use less than one half the capital per worker of heavy industry; software firms use virtually no long term capital at all except education and knowledge. Yet recent studies at MIT indicate that these products yield twice the long term productivity gains per dollar of conventional investment.

Unfortunately, such capital economies were far less available to American heavy industry, with its highly capital intensive production processes and fierce competition from Japanese companies that combined the computer revolution with ample availability of cheap funds. But through this general shift to more efficient and knowledge-intensive activities, the U.S. economy led the world in the rapidity of its conversion to high technology during the 1970s and early 1980s.

The U.S. trade surplus with the European Economic Community, for example, steadily increased through the 1970s in high technology goods. During the recession of 1982, the surplus doubled, to some $10 billion in information technologies alone, despite billions spent on EEC industrial policies focused on this field. The result is that the U.S. now has a more capital-efficient economy than any of its competitors. Each dollar of U.S. capital spending sustains far more employment and real production than the investments of European and Asian countries.

THE U.S. LEAD IN MANUFACTURING

The U.S., in fact, is the only industrial nation that has been increasing employment in manufacturing for the last decade. Japan, for example, lost 11 percent of its manufacturing jobs during the 1970s while the U.S. gained 4 percent in this category. The EEC countries have created no net new jobs of any kind for more than a decade and have suffered deep drops in manufacturing despite floods of government money into heavy industry.

Those who revere smoke stacks and blast furnaces will balk at the notion of America's still leading the world in the creation of manufacturing jobs. Smoke stack fetishes, in fact, have snarled Europe's industry and labor in a decade of seamy obsolescence, disguised and intensified by more than $100 billion in government subsidies and "industrial policies." Smoke stack fetishism lures the media spotlight inexorably to Detroit while the U.S. moves in a mass of firms, most of them small, onto the new frontiers of the world economy.

Grit and grime and clattering assembly lines are not the essence of modern fabrication. Intel and Coleco, IBM and 3M, Rolm and Boeing are manufacturers more productive of both jobs and wealth than U.S. Steel or Chrysler. Every high technology firm, moreover, depends on a large network of producers of ordinary goods, from paper napkins to wooden pallets to transportation products. Every service, from medicine to modern dance, entails manufacturing support.

New technology does not destroy manufacturing employment. It multiplies jobs by magnifying the wealth and productivity of the nation, and by spurring the massive shift in American employment over the last five years: from auto and steel fabrication to the making of the systems of telecommunications, office management and industrial automation. During these very years that the U.S. led the world in manufacturing job creation, it also led in movement to new technologies and services.

The future looks still brighter. The venture industry raised more than $7 billion during the first eight months of 1983, a pace of venture investment more than nine times higher than in any previous year. This is the most catalytic capital in the economy. Earlier this year, the General Accounting Office (GAO) estimated that previous venture capital investments of some $209 million in a sample of seventy-two companies over the last five years directly generated 130,000 jobs, increased corporate taxes of more than $100 million, increased employee taxes of $350 million and increased exports of $900 million. By implication, the $7 billion in venture capital raised during the first two-thirds of this year may directly create some four million jobs and generate $15 billion in additional federal tax revenues. The unpredictable products and processes that will shape the prospect of the world economy are still emerging first in the U.S.

AN INDUSTRIAL RENAISSANCE

In sum, the U.S. is undergoing not a recovery, but an industrial renaissance. It began with a resurgence of venture capital and an explosion of computer sales and technology. It continued with a revaluation of financial assets and a surge in the stock markets, especially in the value of new firms and products. It was accompanied by bankruptcies, distress loans and other growing pains of an economy in transition. But, finally, the renaissance reached the domain of housing, autos and conventional consumer goods that define a recovery in the conventional GNP accounts.

Nonetheless, this is a classic supply-side revival. It should always be remembered that the recovery began in the U.S., not in France or Sweden with their bigger deficits, or in Japan and Britain with their smaller ones; not in Germany with its aggressive industrial policies and overwrought welfare state, or in any of the other countries of the world that eschewed tax cuts during the recent recession. The U.S. differs from all its rivals chiefly in its five-year, supply-side campaign and its intensely entrepreneurial high technology and venture industries.

The supply-side agenda is far from finished. Inflation has been curtailed and tax rates on entrepreneurs have been drastically reduced since the mid-1970s. At the same time, the reductions in the highest tax rates have yielded the higher revenues that Laffer predicted. In the U.S. in 1982, cuts in the top rate and on inheritances led to a dramatic surge in revenues from the rich, who paid their highest share of income taxes in eleven years. Together with an 18 percent rise in inheritance tax payments, an 11 percent surge in top bracket income tax revenues brought the total increase in payments from the rich to over $10 billion in the midst of the recession. Although some analysts ascribed the rise in tax revenues to increased penalties on failure to make quarterly estimated tax payments, this change merely shifted payments from 1982 quarterly totals to April 1983. The April to April surge in payments by the rich was nearly as great as the 1982 figures alone. These results demonstrate anew the supply-side route to "revenue enhancement."[3]

THE NEXT FRONTIER

The next frontier for supply-side policy should be to reduce all tax rates to a reasonable level that penalizes neither work nor savings nor the ultimate investments of family life. For this goal, a flat rate tax, even if, like the Bradley-Gephardt bill, it includes some progressive features, offers the greatest promise for the future. Reducing tax rates on physical capital will prove futile if the human capital on which our future depends is driven from the economy.

At the same time, the lesson of the last two years is that good tax measures can fail if they are combined with destructive monetary policies. The Federal Reserve must come to comprehend the qualitative as well as the quantitative dimensions of the U.S. economy. Easy money to finance a flight into collectibles can entrench a cancerous spiral of perverse expectations in an otherwise healthy economy. But a refusal to finance the creative investments of U.S. entrepreneurs under ever more competitive stress in the world economy can lead to stagnation and protectionism: another and equally destructive form of capital flight.

The Fed also should develop a healthy skepticism about the various indices of "inflation" offered by the government. At a time of increasing protectionism and industrial subsidies and guarantees, the U.S. will necessarily experience a continued pressure of rising prices. But while costs in key high technology industries are plummeting without any notice in government data thereby vitiating the traditional measures of inflation, the Fed should focus on exchange rates and key commodity prices in judging claims of a dangerous depreciation in the dollar's purchasing power, the only real meaning of inflation.

The value of a nation's money ultimately depends on the values of its people. Optimism and faith in the efforts of humankind are more important in fighting scarcity than any rigid rule of money. If Americans fear the future and flee to sumps and shelters of a false "security," they will deserve their distresses. But if they are seeking the challenges of enterprise, the Fed should restore the dollar as a secure store of value, thereby providing low and stable interest rates to a nation busy in its pursuit of the new frontiers that beckon at the fringes of man's technological prowess and understanding of the world in which he lives.

5

The Social Security Surplus

Stuart J. Sweet

July 15, 1985

SWEET

T oday it seems that all we hear are doomsday scenarios about the big public entitlements, Social Security and Medicare. Their "trust funds" are running out, they are soon to bust the budget, anyone older than a Baby Boomer will not see a dime of benefits. If you dig into the accounting, these scenarios do have the look of accuracy.

Hard as it may be to believe, there was once a moment in the not-so-distant past when these problems could have been averted, and a course to a much happier fate set in motion, at least with respect to that most famous (and cherished) of American benefits, Social Security.

In 1985, the United States had recently been making major changes to Social Security, a program that had barely escaped the 1970s alive. During the inflationary 1970s, a "cost-of-living adjustment" (COLA) had to be set up to hold benefits in line with prices. The COLAs themselves required such big financing that Social Security taxes kept going up, with the whole system teetering on insolvency every year.

When inflation collapsed in the early 1980s, the COLA payouts once again got manageable for the federal government. In addition, in 1983, Congress raised Social Security taxes nearly as much as had been raised cumulatively in the 1970s. Thus were payouts scheduled to be less than in the recent past, and receipts greater. The Social Security trust fund in its modern form was born.

Enter Stuart J. Sweet with the following analysis, just as that trust fund was beginning to grow. Sweet pointed out that an excellent new opportunity was emerging with respect to the long-term viability of Social Security. Traditionally, Social Security had used current receipts to pay out current benefits. Now, with the trust fund, a system could be envisioned where a good portion of receipts were set aside to pay future benefits. At some point only a few decades hence, all benefits could be paid out from the trust-fund account, and all current receipts could be placed in that account for future benefits.

In other words, the opportunity was right there to turn Social Security into a fully-funded pension system. Government administrators chafe when the "Ponzi scheme" charge is leveled at Social Security, but the charge has merit. The viability of Social Security with respect to benefits owed has always rested on the ability to bring in new money. In 1985, the United States was in position to correct this major flaw in Social Security and get the system on sound accountancy in time for the twenty-first century.

The details are all here, but the deplorable point to be made today is that the excellent opportunity outlined by Stuart Sweet a generation ago was never taken advantage of. What happened to the trust fund is, of course, that it was spent. The excess Social Security receipts were lent to government agencies, the agencies spent all the money, and the federal government was left on the hook to…the federal government. Today, Social Security is eager for new receipts to cover near-term obligations, obligations that are only getting enormous with the retirement of the Baby Boomers.

However successful were the free-market reforms of the 1980s, it is important to remember that several crucial initiatives in the direction of sound economics were *not* made at the time, and we are living with the consequences today. Perhaps the most discussed missed opportunity of the 1980s was the failure to institutionalize reform of discretionary monetary policy, which is to say the Federal Reserve. Stuart Sweet's paper from the heady days of the early Great Moderation should make us reflect that times of great prosperity, as opposed to those of crisis, are those most propitious for making government not only smaller and more efficient, but more capable of keeping its promises.

AMERICA'S GREAT OPPORTUNITY: THE INCREDIBLE SOCIAL SECURITY SURPLUS, JULY 15, 1985

The Social Security Amendments of 1983 have profoundly changed the prospects for Social Security. In calendar year 1985, Social Security is expected to post an $8.6 billion operating surplus, and the system is likely to run a stream of growing annual surpluses well into the next century.

The ultimate size and duration of the projected Social Security (OASDI) surplus is extremely sensitive to the rate of return assumed on Social Security investments. Under present law, SSA funds can be invested only in Treasury securities. If Congress grants the Trustees the authority to invest more aggressively, the higher expected rates of return promise a far greater surplus than the current SSA projections.

What will Congress choose to do with this huge windfall once it is widely recognized? An obvious choice is to dissipate the surplus by increasing Social Security benefits and/or spending more on other domestic programs. However, Congress may choose to follow either of two more constructive courses.

First, large cuts could be made in Social Security tax rates. By lowering employer costs for labor and increasing employee receipts for working, a reduction in Social Security tax rates would provide a strong, short-run stimulus to employment and economic growth. However, unless accompanied by other reforms of the system, a Social Security tax cut would lead to another cash flow crisis thirty-five to forty-five years from now.

Second, Congress could choose to let the nominal Social Security surplus grow indefinitely. One possible result of this choice is that the Social Security system could retire the entire national debt by the year 2016! A final, more radical alternative is to use the surplus, in conjunction with more aggressive investment policies, to transform Social Security into a fully funded, vested national pension system. Such an evolution would remove the economic distortions caused by the Social Security payroll tax and, by creating a large real Social Security surplus, eliminate the necessity of future Social Security tax increases. Thus, pursuit of this second alternative would lay important groundwork for lasting economic growth.

EXECUTIVE SUMMARY

The Social Security Amendments of 1983 have profoundly changed the prospects for Social Security. In calendar year 1985, the Old Age, Survivors, and Disability Insurance (OASDI) programs are expected to post an $8.6 billion operating surplus. Based upon projections made by Social Security Administration (SSA) actuaries, the system will almost certainly run a stream of growing surpluses well into the next century....

The ultimate size and duration of the projected Social Security surplus…is extremely sensitive to the rate of return earned on OASDI funds….If Congress permits…funds to be invested more aggressively, the higher expected rates of return promise a far greater surplus. [I]f the annual real rate of return is increased to approximately 4 percent, the real Social Security surplus never stops growing.

To date, policymakers have chosen to err on the side of caution…. This means that the Social Security surplus likely will be much larger than most policy makers anticipate.

What will Congress do with this huge windfall once it is widely recognized? One obvious choice is to dissipate the surplus by increasing Social Security benefits and/or spending more on other domestic programs. There are some promising signs that Congress will not choose this wasteful, profligate course.

A more likely choice is that the looming surplus will be used to justify cuts in the Social Security tax rates. Cutting Social Security taxes has much political and short-run economic appeal. Since Social Security taxes are levied on both employers and employees, they raise employers' costs for labor (i.e., wages plus employer tax payments) and lower employees' receipts for working (i.e., wages minus employee tax payments). Thus, at a given wage rate, Social Security taxes reduce the number of people employed. The large increases in Social Security taxes in recent years have increased this distortion in the labor market. Thus, a reduction in Social Security tax rates would augment economic growth and profits, especially in industries that use or are highly dependent upon low-skilled, low-wage workers.

However, simply cutting Social Security revenues to match expenditures poses a potential long-run danger. Unless such tax cuts trigger a significant increase in the Social Security tax base or are accompanied by simultaneous reforms of the present Social Security system, e.g., the gradual phase-in of later retirement ages or a reduction in the growth rate of benefits, the system will face another cash flow crisis in 2020-29 as the Baby Boom generation reaches retirement age. At that time, Social Security taxes would have to be raised up to 33 percent to make promised benefit payments.

A third alternative is to let the Social Security surplus grow. One possible result is that the Social Security system could retire the entire national debt by the year 2016. Investment managers take note; within the next thirty years, it is quite possible that all Federal debt securities will be retired.

Another possible result is that, if OASDI funds are invested aggressively, the Social Security system could be transformed from its current pay-as-you-go basis into a fully funded, vested national pension system. If payments into Social Security were related dollar-for-dollar with expected future returns at market rates, the distortive effects of today's pay-as-you-go system would vanish. Social Security payments would no longer be viewed as taxes but as personal savings. Effort would be more closely aligned with reward. Rather than choosing not to work because Social Security and other taxes are excessive, many people would enthusiastically seek employment so that they could participate in a very attractive savings program.

Such a massive reduction in effective tax rates would, itself, encourage additional economic growth that would further assure the fiscal soundness of the Social Security system. This de facto repeal of the OASDI payroll tax would be especially beneficial to the low-skilled unemployed in the inner cities and to companies that are otherwise dependent upon low-skilled, low-wage labor.

The potential evolution of Social Security into a fully-funded, vested retirement system is one of the brightest opportunities created by the future OASDI surplus.

☙❧

One achievement of the Reagan presidency goes unnoticed: Social Security has been turned into a cash cow. In calendar year 1985, OASDI is expected to run an operating surplus of $8.6 billion, and official projections now show that OASDI programs will run a stream of ever escalating annual surpluses well into the twenty-first century. In nominal dollars, the surplus is expected to grow until 2031 or later attaining an anticipated peak value of at least $12 trillion. These ever growing Social Security surpluses increase the odds that there will be major positive surprises in tax and spending policies in the years ahead as America decides the disposition of this windfall.

Congress could use it to boost spending on domestic programs by funding national health insurance or increasing Social Security benefits. On the other hand, payroll tax rates could be lowered substantially. In either case, the unified Federal budget is expected to run a decades-long string of annual surpluses retiring the entire national debt in the process. Furthermore, the prospects for major changes in the Social Security system will increase as it becomes widely known that substantial resources are available. Such changes may take surprising forms: e.g., a successful drive by working Americans in cooperation with politicians to transform Social Security into a fully funded national pension program. A fully funded, vested program will indeed emerge if Social Security is allowed by Congress to invest in the corporate equity and bond markets.

Projections of substantial Social Security surpluses are currently being made by the top actuaries of the Social Security Administration (SSA) itself. The SSA's most widely cited forecast is based on the so-called Alternative II-B assumptions. Under the Alternative II-B forecast, SSA actuaries use demographic assumptions they believe are most likely to transpire while deliberately selecting values for key economic variables that moderate the size of the surplus. Even under these conservative projections, net assets of the Social Security system will rise dramatically from only $30 billion today to a peak value 400 times this size, $12 trillion, in 2031 before declining and reaching zero in 2049 (Figure 1).

The SSA actuaries also produce a more optimistic forecast, Alternative II-A, which they believe is as likely to occur as Alternative II-B. Under Alternative II-A, the same demographic assumptions used in Alternative II-B are employed. But in place of somewhat pessimistic economic assumptions, more optimistic values are selected. The growth of Social Security assets is unbounded under Alternative II-A. Assets climb to $1.5 trillion by 2000, soar to $10.5 trillion by 2020, and are still increasing in 2060 with a value of $38 trillion (Figure 1).

Of course, a more realistic presentation of the surplus requires that values be reported in inflation-adjusted terms. In 1984 dollars, the surplus peaks in 2025 at $2.2 trillion under Alternative II-B and $6.2 trillion under Alternative II-A (Figure 2).

To date, policymakers have chosen to err on the side of caution by relying on the Alternative II-B forecast. But, since SSA actuaries consider Alternative II-A to be as likely to occur as II-B, the potential exists that the actual magnitude and duration of the future Social Security surplus will greatly exceed such conservative expectations....

FIGURE 1
Projections of Nominal OASDI Surplus
1985-2055

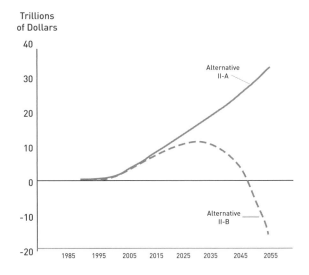

Source: *Official OASDI tables prepared as supplements to the 1985 OASDI Trustees Report*

Both II-A and II-B forecasts of future OASDI tax receipts appear to be on the low side. The main factors leading to this conclusion are the unduly conservative assumptions of no illegal immigration, low birth rates, and high long-run unemployment rates that underlie both forecasts. All of these assumptions result in underestimates of the number of future OASDI taxpayers and, hence, OASDI tax receipts. If OASDI tax receipts are underestimated, so is the projected surplus.

However, an offsetting factor is also identified. Increases in longevity will probably be greater than assumed, and, the longer the elderly live, the more benefits they will receive. If future benefit payments are underestimated, this will reduce the surplus.

Since it is likely that both future tax receipts and benefit payments are underestimated in the II-A and II-B projections, it is not immediately obvious what the net effect on the surplus will be. Nonetheless, it is the author's opinion that the underestimates of the tax receipts are greater than the underestimates of the benefit payments. Thus, if there are no changes in the current law regarding OASDI taxes, benefits, and investment strategy, the actual Social Security surplus will probably exceed the more pessimistic Alternative II-B forecast and possibly the II-A forecast as well.

FIGURE 2
Projections of Real OASDI Surplus
1985–2055

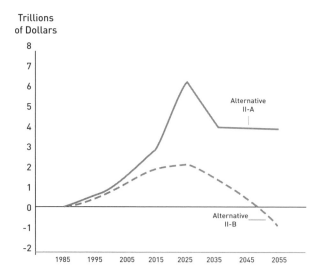

Source: *Author computations based on information from the 1985 OASDI Trustees Report and official OASDI supplementary tables.*

The potential for favorable surprises concerning Social Security is even greater than this analysis suggests. If Congress permits the OASDI Trust Funds to broaden their investment holdings to include corporate securities, a fully vested Social Security system could emerge.

A CRITICAL VARIABLE: THE REAL RATE OF RETURN

Lost in the debate over Social Security funding is a crucial issue: What is the appropriate rate of return on OASDI investments? Over the period 1995-2055, the SSA assumes a 2 percent annual real rate of return on the accumulated OASDI surplus under Alternative II-B and a 2.5 percent real rate under Alternative II-A. Depending on the investment strategy employed by the OASDI trustees, a real rate of 2 to 2.5 percent may be either optimistic or conservative.[1]

At the present time, OASDI funds must be invested only in Treasury securities. Over the past fifty years, the average annual real rate of return on Treasury bonds has been less than 0.5 percent. If the present restrictions on OASDI investments remain unchanged, history suggests that an average real rate of return as high as 2 percent is unattainable. Even when a zero nominal rate of return is used along with the other Alternative II-B assumptions, the OASDI will be in surplus until 2030 (Table 1).[2]

Alternatively, a 2 percent real rate of return is a very conservative estimate if OASDI is permitted to invest its funds more aggressively. Over the past fifty years, the average annual real rate of return on common stocks has been about 7 percent. Roughly 25 percent of the assets of state and local government employee retirement funds have been held in corporate equities in recent years. Should Congress grant the OASDI similar authority to invest in common stocks, an average annual real rate in excess of 2 percent seems attainable.[3]

The sensitivity of the size of the surplus with respect to the real rate of return earned is stunning. In a special SSA study, new forecasts were generated by varying the real rate of return from 2 percent to 7 percent while retaining all other Alternative II-B assumptions. The results show that OASDI nominal income in 2025 will be more than twice as large if a 7 percent real rate of return is earned rather than a 2 percent real rate of return (Figure 3).[4]

Of course, to obtain a higher expected real rate of return, OASDI funds will have to be exposed to greater risk. Undoubtedly, many will argue that OASDI funds should be exposed to only minimal risk since the promises they secure are "sacred." Following this reasoning, the only acceptable investments are Treasury securities.

TABLE 1
Year OASDI Surplus Will Be Exhausted Using the II-B Assumptions and Various Real Rates of Return

Real Rate	Year
-4.0%*	2030
.1%	2038
.5%	2039
1.0%	2042
2.0%	2049

A real rate of –4.0 percent corresponds to a nominal rate of zero.

Source: Author's computations based on information from the 1985 OASDI Trustees Report and official OASDI supplementary tables.

FIGURE 3
Projections of OASDI Nominal Income under Alternative II-B - At Differing Real Rates of Return
1985–2034

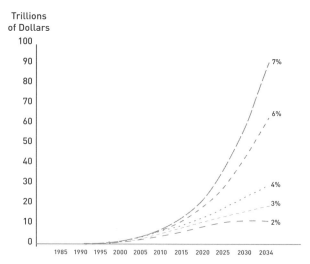

Source: Special study prepared by the Social Security Administration for Senator Steven Symms (R-Idaho).

However, this argument ignores the fact that fiscal crises have led Congress to break its "sacred" promises to Social Security recipients in the past. In 1983, faced with a projected $100 billion decline in OASDI balances over the next eight years and dissipation of the OASDI Trust Funds, Congress cut benefits by postponing scheduled cost of living adjustments (COLAs) and by making a portion of Social Security benefits subject to income taxation. Some Social Security recipients lost as much as 27 percent of their benefits as a result of these changes. Similarly, in its budget bill for fiscal year 1986, the Senate has threatened another real benefit cut by proposing the cancellation of the scheduled 1986 COLA.

Thus, exclusive investment of OASDI funds in Treasury securities does not make real promised Social Security benefits risk free. It seems very likely that the investment of some portion of OASDI funds in more risky assets, by increasing the expected real rate of growth of the OASDI surplus, will actually reduce the risk that promised Social Security benefits will be cut in the future.

Aside from greater risk, there is another important matter to consider regarding the investment of OASDI funds in corporate securities: Wouldn't this amount to the introduction of socialism through a side door? Given the magnitude of the future surplus, the potential exists for OASDI to purchase all of the shares that will be listed on the New York Stock Exchange! What is to prevent the SSA from voting its shares to make corporations pursue "social welfare" objectives as opposed to private wealth maximizing objectives?

To eliminate this danger, Congress could take the SSA out of the business of managing funds. Employer and employee contributions, instead of going to the SSA, would be sent directly to federally approved private pension fund managers. The SSA would simply compute benefits and make disbursements. As money was needed to pay benefits, the SSA would make withdrawals from the private funds.

FIGURE 4

Projections of Treasury Debt, the OASDI Surplus, and the Net National Surplus under Alternative II-B
1985–2035

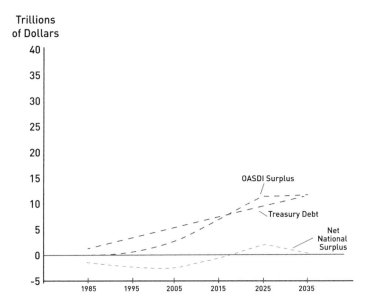

Source: Author's computations based on information from the 1985 OASDI Trustees Reports and official OASDI supplementary tables.

Private management of Social Security funds would have another clear benefit. The direct routing of Social Security contributions to private managers would deny government access to this stream of revenues and thus lower the risk that these funds will be spent wastefully.

With a competitive political process and the financial stakes so high for all voters, it is hard to imagine that the issue of the appropriate expected real rate of return on OASDI investments will go unnoticed for long. Ultimately, Congress will have to decide this issue which will largely determine the size and the duration of the future OASDI surplus.

IMPLICATIONS FOR FEDERAL DEFICITS

Since both Alternatives II-A and II-B project huge OASDI surpluses, it is important to consider how these surpluses will affect the overall balance between Federal expenditures and federal receipts. This exercise will also help to demonstrate just how large the projected OASDI surpluses are.

In 1986, it is estimated by the Congressional Budget Office that non-OASDI spending will total $724.4 billion, and non-OASDI revenue $532.3. The difference is $192.1 billion. Let us imagine that the politicians simply allow spending and taxes on non-OASDI budgetary items to remain permanently imbalanced and $200 billion apart. Let us further assume that OASDI follows the Alternative II-B pathway projected by SSA. What happens?[5]

Under the conservative II-B assumptions, OASDI will start running annual surpluses greater than $200 billion in 2001 while the "on-budget" deficit will equal only $200 billion. The result is a "unified" budget surplus. Continuing this reasoning further, the annual OASDI cash flow surplus will increasingly swamp the "on-budget" deficit. If OASDI funds are invested only in Treasury debt instruments, then OASDI will own all of them by 2016. In effect, that is the year when we eliminate the national debt. As the surpluses continue to mount, instead of a public debt, there will be a $1.9 trillion public surplus by 2025! (Figure 4)

Of course, Congress is unlikely to run $200 billion deficits indefinitely. Current negotiations make that clear. If so, the projected public surplus is accordingly understated. Should actual experience follow the Alternative II-A pathway, with only $100 billion deficits, then the national debt will be wiped out in 2008, and the public surplus will reach $8 trillion by 2025. (Figure 5)

WON'T MEDICARE DEVOUR THE SURPLUS?

Until recently, most analysts felt that looming Medicare deficits would eat deeply into the OASDI surplus. Such an argument had appeal because the Hospital Insurance (HI) fund, known as Part A of Medicare, is also financed through a payroll tax. This argument was accepted by those who believed runaway hospital cost growth would be sustained indefinitely. Even under this unlikely scenario, the OASDIHI was expected to run annual surpluses until 2009. This was true even if Medicare bankruptcy as early as 1991 was assumed.[6]

However, fiscal health probably has also been restored to the Medicare program for decades. Using the same cautious demographic and economic assumptions applied in forecasting OASDI under II-B, the 1985 Medicare Trustees Report now projects a $76 billion surplus for Medicare in 1991. The balance at year end in 1984 was $28 billion if a $12 billion loan to the OAS Fund was included. Exhaustion of the Medicare Trust Fund has been pushed back until 1998.

FIGURE 5
Projections of Treasury Debt, the OASDI Surplus, And the Net National Surplus under Alternative II-A 1985–2055

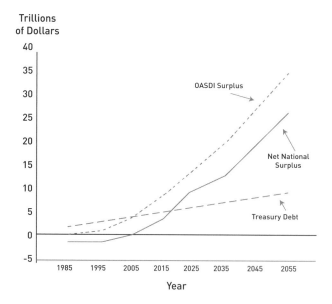

Source: *Author computations based on information from the 1985 OASDI Treasurer's Report and official OASDI supplemental tables.*

Now, the first annual OASDIHI deficit is expected in 2012 under the II-B forecast.[7] But even this projection is unduly pessimistic. The forecast that the Medicare Fund will be exhausted in 1998 ignores the sweeping changes in the incentive structure facing Medicare providers, i.e., the hospitals. As a rider to the 1983 Social Security Amendments, Congress ordered the Secretary of Health and Human Services to develop and implement a prospective reimbursement system for paying hospitals. Instead of paying hospitals all "reasonable fees" plus a mark-up, the government now pays fixed prices for curing specific illnesses. As a result, 60,000 fewer employees work in hospitals today than in 1984, a 2 percent reduction.[8]

From 1984 to 1998, using the II-B assumptions, the SSA believes expenditures by the HI fund will grow at triple the rate of consumer price inflation.

Despite the change in incentives, Health Care Financing Administration actuaries believe profligacy in hospitals will continue although in less virulent form. From 1984 to 1998, using the II-B assumptions, the SSA believes expenditures by the HI fund will grow at triple the rate of consumer price inflation.[9]

The projected real growth in HI expenditures stems from three sources. First, an increase in the number of Medicare claims as the number of people 65 or older grows. Second, as longevity increases, hospital visits per beneficiary are expected to grow. Third, the SSA believes that more real resources will be spent per case.

The growth of the HI eligible population can be projected with reasonable confidence. However, the other two premises leading to the prediction of rapid real HI expenditure growth are more contentious.

Assuming that the average admission rate will continue to grow implies that the Medicare population as a whole will be more prone to hospitalization in the future than it is today. It is likely that a growing pool of the "old old" will raise average admission rates faster than an eventually growing pool of the "young old" will lower them, but questions remain. A trend toward more out-patient care is a factor that may lower utilization.

Of far greater significance, it is illogical to assume that hospitals will receive no benefit from technological advances. Rather than spending more real resources per case, hospitals will do everything possible to spend less. For the first time in decades, hospitals make money by doing more with less. While squeezing present inefficiencies out of the system, hospitals will also implement cost saving techniques over time as they develop.

Even if there are no hospital efficiency gains, growing employment and the scheduled increase of the HI tax rate from 2.7 percent to 2.9 percent of taxable payroll in 1986 will defer the bankruptcy date for HI beyond 2015. The OASDIHI surplus is accordingly that much greater than advertised.[10]

HOW DID ALL THIS HAPPEN?

Congress made major conceptual errors when adopting the 1983 Amendments. The chief error was to view OASDI with an ongoing funding problem over the next seventy-five years. Although, on average, OASDI was going to take in 74 percent of what it was going to spend between 1983 and 2060, this masked important timing differences. OASDI should have been viewed as having three distinct phases. During phase one, OASDI lost up to $100 billion in revenue between 1982 and 1990. In phase two, lasting from 1990 to 2017, OASDI gained $2.9 trillion. Thereafter, OASDI lost altitude rapidly and tumbled into deficit in 2026. These phases are shown in Figure 6.[11]

When Congress legislated reforms to resolve the phase one insolvency threat, they carried over into phases two and three. Chief among these were three reforms.

First, Congress legislated a reduction in cost-of-living increases. Under this reform, benefit increases were delayed by six months. Thus, COLAs due in July became due the following January. This seemingly innocuous change raises vast sums of money over seventy years. This is because the next seventy-five annual COLA increases were all delayed by six months, not just the one awarded in 1984. The cumulative savings from cutting annual OASDI expenditures by approximately 2 percent every year for the next seventy-five years in this fashion is tremendous, even when only a 2 percent real rate of return is used for compounding.[12]

FIGURE 6
1982 Projection of OASDI Nominal Surplus
1985–2030

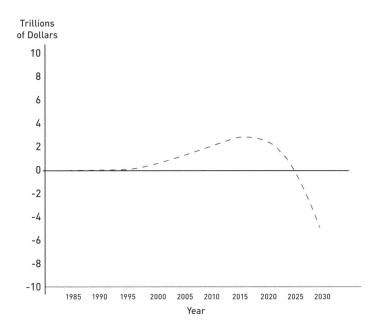

Note: The 1982 projection year of the OASDI surplus used extremely pessimistic economic assumptions of an Alternative III for the years 1982–89 and the Alternative II-B assumptions for the period 1990-2030.

Source: SSA Alternative II-B Computer Run of March 19, 1982 by Orlo Nichols.

Second, Congress decided to phase-in the taxation of OASDI benefits. Beginning in 1984, up to 50 percent of a beneficiary's OASDI income is subject to Federal income tax. Taxation begins when the adjusted gross income of a married couple exceeds $32,000 or $25,000 for single filers. The full impact of the tax occurs when adjusted gross income reaches about $60,000 for couples or $50,000 for singles. At present, only 10 percent of present retirees pay any tax on OASDI benefits.[13]

However, the taxation thresholds were deliberately established to erode over time because they were not indexed to inflation. As average

OASDI benefits and retirement incomes both increase over the years in both nominal and real terms, the percentage of beneficiaries pushed over the $32,000 and $25,000 OASDI taxation thresholds will rise.

In the third reform, Congress raised the retirement age for full OASDI benefits in two stages from sixty-five to sixty-seven. In the first stage, the basic retirement age increases by two months each year for six years in a row beginning in the year 2003. Thus by 2009, full OASDI benefits will not be awarded unless a beneficiary's age exceeds 66. The same procedure is used in 2020 to drive the retirement age up to sixty-seven by 2027. This reform also adds to the surplus.[14]

Collectively, delaying COLAs, taxing OASDI benefits, and raising the retirement age act as booster rockets on a projectile already headed for the upper atmosphere. There is now enough power to attain escape velocity.

Evidence supporting this view was presented by the Executive Director of the National Commission on Social Security Reform. On March 14, 1982, Robert Myers wrote Commission members the following:

> As is well known, the OASDI Trust Funds are expected to have significant *annual* deficits in the 1980s. Beginning in 1990, however, when a large tax-rate increase is effective, the funds have very large *annual* excesses of income over outgo, which increase from a 1982 dollars level of about $11 billion in 1990 to about $60 billion in the first decade of the next century (and, of course, much larger amounts in current dollars). The trust fund balance, in terms of 1982 dollars, increases from a *negative* (theoretical) level of about $16 billion at the beginning of 1990 and a *negative* $5 billion at the end of 1990 to a *positive* $700 billion in 2015—an amount roughly equal to the current Federal budget and about two thirds as large as the current national debt.

In January 1984, Mr. Myers began urging reductions in the OASDI tax rate hikes.[15]

THE LIKELY CONGRESSIONAL REACTION AND INVESTMENT IMPLICATIONS

Once knowledge of the surplus spreads, senators and congressmen will compete to distribute the surplus in the form of higher OASDI benefits and/or lower payroll taxes. The competition is just beginning. Congressman Edward Roybal (D-Calif.), chairman of the House Aging Committee, is already calling for a 30 percent reduction in OASDI tax rates with less than half the static revenue loss made up by completely eliminating the $39,600 ceiling on wages subject to OASDI taxes. That the chairman of the Aging Committee chooses to promote OASDI tax cuts, rather than OASDI benefit increases, provides a bullish indication of how any raid on the OASDI surplus will be distributed: most will take the form of lower payroll tax rates. Moreover, a recurring rumor in Washington is that Senate Finance Committee Chairman Robert Packwood (R-Ore.) will maneuver to have the working poor dropped from the OASDI tax rolls as part of a final tax reform package. However, the working poor would still qualify for the same OASDI benefits as they presently do.[16]

Labor-intensive industries will benefit most from the coming reductions in scheduled payroll tax rates. Look for proposals to reduce or eliminate scheduled OASDI tax rate hikes in 1988 and 1990 to enter into public debate. This issue could prove pivotal in both the Democratic and Republican presidential nomination fights and the presidential election of 1988.

Proposals to cut OASDI tax rates immediately and to reduce or eliminate scheduled future OASDI tax rate hikes will run into serious opposition from those concerned about the system's ability to honor OASDI benefit promises made to the baby boom generation in 2013 and beyond. To the extent such opposition to OASDI tax rate cuts is successful, the chances are increased that a substantial public surplus will be created. Investment managers take note: within the next thirty years, it is quite possible that all federal debt securities will be retired!

Moreover, these favorable developments are dwarfed by the growing possibility of genuine reform in OASDI. As the OASDI surplus grows in size, public pressure may well force investment into higher yielding securities. Even under Alternative II-B, more aggressive management means the development of a rapidly growing surplus in excess of that needed to pay OASDI claimants during the next seventy-five years.

The future surplus can be used today to begin the process of fundamentally reforming the Social Security system. At present, a dollar paid into Social Security will yield, at best, about one real dollar in benefits in the future. If the surplus is credited directly to the accounts of today's workers, the present pay-as-you-go system can be transformed gradually into a fully funded, vested national retirement system. Every worker could then have his payroll contributions invested to earn a positive, real rate of return. In this way, a personal retirement fund could be built up which would provide future cash flows in excess of promised Social Security benefits.

Such a transformation of the Social Security system would lower the effective tax rate on labor income and, thereby, exert a tremendous incentive effect toward higher employment. At present, many young people doubt they will receive their promised Social Security benefits in full. As a result, they view Social Security payments as pure taxes which are lost forever. This acts as a major disincentive to employment.

Suppose, instead, that Social Security contributions were credited to personal accounts which accumulated, tax free, at a market rate of return. When payments into Social Security are related dollar-for-dollar with expected future returns, the distortive effects of today's pay-as-you go system are all but eliminated. Social Security payments would no longer be viewed as taxes but as personal savings. Effort would be more closely aligned with reward. Rather than choosing not to work because Social Security and other taxes are excessive, many young, unemployed people would enthusiastically seek employment so they could earn income and participate in a very attractive savings program. The effective Social Security tax rate would be zero for all those who choose to save more than the contribution mandated by the Social Security system, and near zero for those who are forced to save more than they otherwise would have. Such a massive reduction in effective tax rates would, itself, encourage additional economic growth that would further assure the fiscal soundness of the Social Security system. This de facto repeal of the OASDI payroll tax would be especially beneficial to the low-skilled unemployed in the inner cities and to companies that are dependent upon low-skilled, low-wage labor.

Thus, the potential evolution of Social Security into a fully-funded, vested retirement system is one of the brightest opportunities created by the future OASDI surplus. By enhancing individual retirement security and increasing the reward for working, the transformation of the Social Security system would increase employment and stimulate long-run economic growth.

6

Reaganomics' Critics

Arthur B. Laffer
July 22, 1994

I n the early and mid-1990s, in particular during the first Bill
Clinton presidential term, it was fashionable to criticize the
"Reaganomics" of the 1980s for having failed to solve the
economic growth problem that had gripped the country in the 1970s.
For even though during the high period of the Reagan reforms, 1983–
89—or the "seven fat years," as *Wall Street Journal* editor and supply-
sider par excellence Robert L. Bartley put it in his 1992 book of that
name—growth was huge, some 4.3 percent per year, the performance
afterwards was not so great. The U.S. managed 1.8 percent yearly
growth in the sorry decade before 1983…and 1.9 percent in the four
years after 1989. Maybe all the Reagan Revolution was fated to amount
to was a healthy interregnum amid the new trend of low growth and
diminished expectations.

Bartley warned his readers to take heed of the story from Gen-
esis from which he drew the title of his book. In ancient Egypt, as
foretold by Joseph, seven lean years followed the seven fat years. In
modern America, from the perspective of 1992, it looked as if seven
lean years not only were going to follow the seven fat years of the
supply-side heyday, they were going to bound them on both sides, fore
and aft.

For Bartley, it was clear what the problem was in the early 1990s.
The supply-side revolution had been forsaken when Reagan exited
office in 1989. Bartley had a good case. The new president, George
H.W. Bush, at the insistence of the Democratic Congress, made two
startling moves in his first years, 1989 and 1990. He canceled a capital
gains tax cut that he had promised the electorate; and he acquiesced

to an increase in the top rate of the income tax, along with hikes in federal excises.

A recession of course came in 1990-91, and then a recovery so slow that Bush lost the presidency after just one term, to Clinton, in 1992. On taking office in 1993, Clinton raised taxes more, such that over the four years after Reagan exited office, 1989–93, growth was stuck at the meager, pre-Reagan-boom stagflation level.

It was in this context that Paul Krugman first came on the popular scene with a bestselling book called *Peddling Prosperity: Economic Sense and Nonsense in an Age of Diminished Expectations*. *Peddling Prosperity* was an attack, often personal, on supply-side economics and its advocates. It launched Krugman's career as an economic commentator.

The oddity of *Peddling Prosperity* is that it did not seek so much to shine a light on the economic deficiencies, considerable as they were, of the pre-1983 or post-1989 periods. Rather, Krugman's main purpose was to criticize the Reagan era—on its record of growth.

Laffer was at a loss to see why anyone surveying the economic landscape of 1973–93 would pick out the one period of serious growth, 1983–89, as being deficient on just those grounds.

As Arthur B. Laffer (a Krugman target in *Peddling Prosperity*) pointed out in this lively review from 1994, the only way the Reagan-era growth record (of all things) was to be minimized was through mental gymnastics. And that is what Krugman gave his readers. In *Peddling Prosperity*, Krugman went on about how growth in the 1980s was below "potential"—a wooly, outdated Keynesian concept that adds up all the capital equipment in the country and multiplies it by the hours that could be worked by the labor force.

Laffer was at a loss to see why anyone surveying the economic landscape of 1973–93 would pick out the one period of serious growth, 1983–89, as being deficient on just those grounds. Laffer was also mystified at Krugman's claim, repeated to this day, that the national "savings rate" went down in the 1980s. Perhaps the amount of money people set aside from their weekly wages was proportionately smaller in the 1980s than before—but did those savings pack a punch.

In the 1970s, as Laffer wrote here, "individuals and companies invested in tax shelters, inflation hedges and regulatory skirts, and squandered our nation's capital stock. In the 1980s under Reagan, we finally put our nation's capital stock to productive use as a direct consequence of tax rate reductions and inflation control. Our nation's capital was redirected to productive endeavors. As a consequence, the market's evaluation of the country's capital stock increased as never before….Krugman still seems to wish that we had doubled the amount of bad investments."

In the 1970s, there was a scramble to save because nothing was paying off. In the 1980s, savings easily went into profitable investments, and national wealth expanded mightily. Stocks increased fifteen-fold from the time Reagan's tax cut really started to kick in in summer 1982 until 2000.

Written just before the great 1990s take-off prompted by the Republican congressional victory in November 1994, "Time Wounds All Heels" would prove one of the last incidents in the skirmishes over whether Reagan-era growth was for real. Today we speak of the *two* great decades of growth, the 1980s and the 1990s.

TIME WOUNDS ALL HEELS, JULY 22, 1994

Paul Krugman, in *Peddling Prosperity*,[1] sets the tone in the introduction:

> There is a general rule that if you see an expert on television a lot, he or she probably isn't much of an expert—if nothing else, real experts are too busy doing research to be on that many shows. And the qualities that make for good TV are not closely related to those that make for good research. This observation is not unique to economics; for example, Stephen Hawking, whose *A Brief History of Time* was a best seller and who has been the subject of a number of adoring documentaries, is *not* the world's leading physicist. [emphasis Krugman's]

Krugman goes on to tell us that during the era of supply-side economics the U.S. economy "sprang to life." I surely wasn't aware of the fact but Krugman goes on to tell us that "a more reasonable policy would have left national income at most 3 percent higher at the end of the conservative era than it actually was." Krugman tells us that in fact the growth during the Reagan years wasn't even good growth. Supply side growth was short-term growth. Good growth according to Krugman is "potential" growth.

> From the fourth quarter of 1982 to the fourth quarter of 1989, the unemployment rate fell from 10.7 percent to 5.2 percent, a fall of 5.5 percentage points. Could this have continued? If it had gone on for another seven years, the unemployment rate would have become negative. That's even more impossible than it sounds ....
>
> What do we learn from this exercise? First we learn that potential growth does not fluctuate nearly as much as actual growth. Second, we learn that nothing much happened to potential growth in the 1980s.

As you can read from the above quote, Krugman dismisses as being irrelevant the fact that the Reagan tax cut years, 1983 through 1989, had an average growth rate of 3.6 percent per annum versus 1.6 percent for the other thirteen years since 1973. In fact, not one of those "seven fat years" experienced negative growth while seven of the other thirteen years were in the red. Krugman concludes, "The economic tides that determined political fortunes over the course of the 1980s had very little to do with administration policies." No wonder Krugman is offended by journalists.

Krugman's discussion of budget deficits leaves a lot to be desired but his conclusion couldn't be more explicit or wrong: "Reagan created a deficit, and it hurt American economic growth." But if the truth be known the official deficit as reported bears no relation to the true deficit.

Krugman proceeds to tell us all about off-budget items but then never mentions the fact that only in the federal budget are 100 percent of all capital purchases expensed counter to generally accepted accounting practices. Capital purchases in the Federal budget should be capitalized and depreciated as they are in all other budgets. In 1990 alone, the correct accounting treatment of capital expenditures would have reduced the reported deficit by almost $200 billion.

Krugman produces minute adjustments to his estimates of the growth impact of deficits during the 1980s. But then, he completely overlooks the effect inflation has had on the real value of the federal debt and thus the deficit. In 1990 for example, inflation reduced the real value of the federal debt by over $100 billion, which should be deducted from the reported deficit. Once again recognition of these facts would reduce the reported deficit by billions and billions of dollars.

Krugman seems to be unaware that state and local governments ran budget surpluses and that the federal government owned assets that increased in value over the 1980s. I could go on with more omissions each of which materially changes the official deficit as reported. The end result is that Krugman's reliance on the deficit numbers makes no sense and as a consequence his conclusions are all wrong. These adjustments to the official deficit numbers are well known in the academic literature and in fact were the research subject of the well respected Keynesian economist Bob Eisner. Eisner was president of the American Economic Association not so long ago.[2]

On a conceptual level, Krugman also never adequately explains the difference between a government that taxes away your money and a government that borrows the money from you with a promise never to repay. Crowding out is a spending phenomenon, not a deficit issue as Krugman argues. My former University of Chicago colleague Bob Barro, now an economics professor at Harvard, has done seminal work on this subject. In fact the inferences Barro draws are right while Krugman's inferences are wrong. Being wrong is forgivable. But what seems inappropriate to me is the fact that Krugman's book doesn't give Barro's perspective a fair hearing. Krugman also off-handedly dismisses people whom I consider to be serious economists such as Paul Craig Roberts and Stanford professor Martin Anderson.

We all know ahead of time what Krugman's conclusions on income distribution are going to be. Yet here his normally eloquent writing skills fail him and he leaves his readers with the sense that he is confused. He never addresses the relevant analysis done by Alan Reynolds but then out of context makes fun of Reynolds personally.

Krugman ignores a number of points essential for showing the effects of Reagan's tax policies. Let me take, for example, one fact which really does change how Reagan should be viewed when it comes to the poor and taxes. In 1981 and 1987 respectively 3.5 and 3.7 million tax returns reported adjusted gross income of less than $1,000. The shocking feature of the lowest reported income categories is that the average income of those returns was a negative $5,000 in 1981 and a negative $10,000 in 1987.

Reagan didn't tax the poor but he did tax the prosperous who feigned being poor.

Krugman must know that these negative average incomes in the below $1,000 per year income category show that for many filers there was a surplus of deductions. How else could someone have an adjusted gross income less than zero unless that person had deductions in excess of earnings? Just by looking at the negative average incomes in these categories it is clear that large, large numbers of people whose incomes are low do not fit the central casting image of poor. This "deduction effect" is present in significant proportions in all the reported low income categories.

Krugman warns us in a different context that slavish reliance on raw data is wholly inappropriate and yet by ignoring this "deduction effect" falls into his own trap. Reagan, however, knew better. In 1981, one half of 1 percent of the lowest income filers paid income taxes; yet in 1987 after Reagan's tax reforms, 20.4 percent paid income taxes. Reagan didn't tax the poor but he did tax the prosperous who feigned being poor.

Another important fact that Krugman ignores is something that everyone should know by now. The top income earners paid a larger share of total taxes in the late 1980s than they had paid in the early 1980s. Reagan jettisoned a number of tax shelters and thereby collected the taxes the high income earners should pay. It would seem to me that this aspect of supply side economics would warrant favorable mention from Krugman. It didn't get it. I could go on but what's the point. Krugman doesn't seem very interested in this genre of facts….

On the issue of investment and savings, Krugman is the victim of Keynesian accounting and parabolaffobia (a [Jude] Wanniski word for obsessive fear of the Laffer Curve). To modem Keynesians like Krugman, "national savings are the difference between national income and national consumption" and private investment is savings plus net inflows of capital from other countries.

Private savings, Krugman states,

> crashed during the 1980s from 9.1 percent of disposable income in 1980 to 5.1 percent in 1987. And, at the same time, the Reagan Administration presided over a massive increase in budget deficits: Public dissavings soon began to offset much of whatever private saving was taking place. The overall rate of national saving, public plus private, had averaged 7.7 percent in the 1970s, but was only 3 percent from 1988 to 1990.

Krugman concludes "However you measure it, investment for the conservative era was low, not high, by comparison with previous experience."

In truth savings during the 1980s was extraordinarily high—higher almost than at any time in our nation's past. Krugman's mistake is that he has Keynes' perspective on savings backwards. John Maynard Keynes made it perfectly clear in his book *The General Theory* that his focus was on short-term growth and not on potential growth. In a short term growth context aggregate demand is of the essence and investment, no matter how frivolous, is a component of aggregate demand. But misdirected investments, while they may add to aggregate demand, do not add to a nation's potential growth. What matters in the context of potential growth is the productive value of the existing capital stock, not how much society sacrificed to acquire it. The appropriate measure of a country's capital stock for potential output purposes is the market value of all productive assets. The stock market gives a pretty good picture of what the value of the nation's capital stock will be.

I can't help but feel that Krugman given his background should know better. Krugman is a Yale graduate (B.A. '74) and an MIT Ph.D. ('77) and has been awarded the prestigious John Bates Clark award ('91). There is no reason for Krugman to assume that all capital at all times is equally productive. It's not. Likewise there's no reason for Krugman to assume that all of a country's capital is being put to its best potential use. It almost never is. The appropriate concept of savings in the context of potential growth is a society's increase in net wealth. Krugman mistakenly would have us believe that producing a machine that will never be used is investment. Or, to him, finding a productive use for a heretofore obsolete machine is not investment.

Making the same mistake in a different context, he would also have us believe that a person who consumes his income precisely while his wealth rises in real terms does not save. To Krugman a person who consumes less than his income cannot go broke. Krugman just doesn't get the economics, but he does get angry.

In the 1980s, under Reagan, we finally put our nation's capital stock to productive use as a direct consequence of tax rate reductions and inflation control.

In the 1970s, individuals and companies invested in tax shelters, inflation hedges and regulatory skirts, and squandered our nation's capital stock. In the 1980s under Reagan, we finally put our nation's capital stock to productive use as a direct consequence of tax rate reductions and inflation control. Our nation's capital was redirected to productive endeavors. As a consequence, the market's evaluation of the country's capital stock increased as never before. In spite of all the evidence to the contrary Krugman still seems to wish that we had doubled the amount of bad investments.

Krugman attributes the deep recession of 1981 and 1982 to the Federal Reserve's monetary policy almost as if this view were received truth. Now it is true that a lot of people believe that monetary policy was the source of that recession but that view doesn't give the whole picture. In 1981 Reagan's first tax cut became law. But the tax cuts were phased in and did not have their major impact until January 1, 1983. People and businesses, knowing that tax rates would be lower in 1983 than they were in 1981 and 1982, postponed some of their income and income realization until 1983 and beyond. This deferral effect in my opinion was the primary cause of the recession and the tax cuts themselves were the primary cause of the subsequent longest peacetime expansion ever recorded. Money, Krugman's choice as the source of all power, chased the economy. Money didn't cause the economy.

[*Wall Street Journal* editor] Bob Bartley is right when he argues that Reaganomics began when the Reagan tax cut took effect on January 1, 1983 and lasted until the year before Bush's tax increase of 1990. The concept isn't all that deep. During the 1983-1989 period wealth in America rose enormously. The net worth of the average American family soared, pension funds reflecting future retirement benefits for American workers increased as never before and the value of the average American's home went way up. Eighteen plus million new jobs were formed. The improvement in the economic circumstances of the average black American family was greater than it was for the average white American family. Female participation rates and wage rates rose relative to their male counterparts during the seven fat years. I am at a loss to understand how denouncing these times doesn't disqualify Krugman from being a liberal.[3]

At the very outset Krugman admits to being a liberal and that "he believes in a society that taxes the well-off and uses the proceeds to help the poor and unlucky." Wanting to help the poor and unlucky is as admirable a goal as exists, but to "believe" that you can achieve that goal by paying people to be poor and by taxing them once they rise out of poverty is a pretty big leap of faith. The evidence just doesn't support his view.

But one thing can be said about the society Krugman believes in— there's no question at all that his society will hurt those who struggle to become affluent. As we have seen from the past, high marginal tax rates don't hurt the truly rich, but they do keep the poor from ever becoming rich. His society won't make anyone rich but it will keep a lot of people in poverty. And, the way I see it, it's not

> *This deferral...was the primary cause of the recession and the tax cuts themselves were the primary cause of the subsequent longest peacetime expansion ever recorded.*

very nice to use the power of the state to vent your personal prejudices against any group.

And what would Krugman have us believe if taxes and rationality don't matter? Relying on my undergraduate Yale classmate George Akerlof, Krugman concludes:

> And yet the individually reasonable decision not to cut prices in the face of a recession can have collectively disastrous results. If prices don't fall when people decide to hold more cash, then the slump in output and employment is not self-correcting. In an imperfect world, senseless things can happen to groups of people who behave sensibly as individuals.
>
> The case for an active monetary policy is now obvious.

This is Krugman's new Keynesian story. Akerlof should sue.

The real thesis of Krugman's book is the case for credentialism. And no one is more credentialed than Krugman and friends. Economics is only a side show. His regard for the public is reminiscent of the late Walter Heller's admonition that "the public has an insatiable appetite for economic charlatanism." Throughout his book he points out just how unworthy most economic commentators are.

In spite of Krugman's insensitive exposition, there is much to commend in his position. He carries it way too far, however. Take for example the exalted importance Krugman attaches to Ph.D.s, refereed publications, tenure, and professional accolades in general. Krugman never asks who judges whom in this academic process. The answer is that it's a small group of professors who give all the grades. It's those same professors who pass on Ph.D. candidates. Once again the professors ultimately recommend tenure and referee the articles for inclusion in the respected academic journals. We shouldn't be surprised to learn that successful entrants into academics are apple polishers and sycophants. I'm surprised Krugman is as adamant about the need for credentials as he is given that Keynes, Krugman's hero, didn't have a Ph.D., while my Ph.D. is from Stanford.

While Krugman's expositions of economic issues are at times truly gifted, he seeks to stifle debate. The force of his argument isn't good enough to carry the day on its own merits. Therefore, what he fails to achieve through logic and persuasion he attempts to coerce through threats and taunts.

As we have seen from the past, high marginal tax rates don't hurt the truly rich, but they do keep the poor from ever becoming rich.

Krugman's real enemies, however, are not the maligned supply-siders or the disingenuous "strategic traders" or the opportunistic policy entrepreneurs. These people could possibly be held at bay with words alone. Krugman's real problem is with markets and people. Markets just don't buy his line, and voters reject his view of the world every time they get the chance.

The economy and the electorate loved what Reagan and Volcker did. My former University of Chicago colleague and close friend Robert Mundell's tight money and tax cut policies really worked. In the seven fat years to which Robert Bartley refers, 18 plus million jobs were created, inflation fell to 4.6 percent per year, and the stock market rose from a low of 777 in 1982 to a high of 2791 in 1989. In addition the reported federal budget deficit in Reagan's last year in office was in the red by $154 billion, in spite of Reagan's enormous defense build-up.

The electorate gave supply side economics a resounding vote of confidence in 1984 and 1988. It was only after Bush proved himself a pseudo-Keynesian tax increaser that the Republicans lost the White House.

7

The Rising
Middle Class

**David Booth and
Arthur B. Laffer**
assisted by Jeffrey Thomson
September 5, 1996

Ⓐs the economic sluggishness of the early 1990s gave way to a certified boom in the latter half of the decade, criticism of America's economic performance turned to matters of inequality. Inequality had been an issue in the Reagan years of the 1980s, mainly in this form: whereas the jobs of the 1970s and before had been good, union jobs in factories and so forth, the Reagan-era new jobs, in such great number as they were, were in the likes of low-paid "hamburger flipping." But the statistics did not support this contention. Median family income, the stock metric on matters of inequality, marched up at a very nice rate over the full seven years of the Reagan expansion, 1982–89.

But then in the recession and slow-recovery years of the early 1990s, median family income did go down. It looked like the consistent progress of the American Dream over the decades was in for a hiatus, or worse.

In this piece, David Booth and Arthur B. Laffer showed that new things were indeed at play in matters of American equality and inequality in the 1990s. Specifically, family size was going down. Median family income measures the income that comes to an intact family in a household, with "median" referring to there being as many families above that level as below. If family structure is going to go through something of a revolution, this statistic will become unstable.

By 1996, when this piece was composed, the United States was beginning to experience in a statistically significant way the breakup of the traditional family, a phenomenon with which we are plenty familiar today. Fathers were starting to live separately in numbers, as single mothers proliferated. Thus were family units increasing—separate fathers and mothers each counted as a unit—while national income only increased at the historical rate of GDP growth. The demise of median family income in the face of ordinary economic progress became a stubborn fact from the first stirrings of the family crisis through the beginning of the Great Recession that began in 2008; then both GDP and particularly median family income undertook unprecedented declines.

In this piece, Booth and Laffer rally to the cause of the traditional family, insisting that public policy, as much as it is able, support, and certainly not discourage, that unit. In doing so, they placed themselves within a venerable supply-side tradition. In the latter portion of his career, in the 1980s and 1990s, Jack Kemp, the creator of the Reagan tax cut of 1981, focused on eliminating the provisions in the tax code that discouraged poor individuals from marrying or living together as husband and wife. Much of Kemp's work came to fruition in the welfare reform act of 1996. Though since that time, it must be said that the great expansion of the earned income credit has stuck those getting out of poverty with some of the highest marginal tax rates of all.

Booth and Laffer rally to the cause of the traditional family, insisting that public policy, as much as it is able, support, and certainly not discourage, that unit.

In 1992, Robert L. Bartley, the supply-side editor of the *Wall Street Journal*, wrote the following as he observed the emerging status quo: "[W]hat the statistics show above all is smaller families. In one sense, this is a sign of affluence; as a society we can now afford to live in smaller households. In another, it's a symptom of pathology; too much family splitting is bad for us, especially for children." In this piece from 1996, Booth and Laffer joined their confreres in the supply-side movement by voicing concern not over the affluence and opportunity that flowed from the tax cuts and stable money of the Reagan era, but over the strange and unwelcome results of the sexual revolution that were then coming to the fore.[1]

WHO PROSPERS FROM ECONOMIC GROWTH?
SEPTEMBER 5, 1996

During the past few years median real family income has received a great deal of attention in the never-ending political debate. According to the Joint Economic Committee, "Real median family income is a standard official measure of middle class income." The series in many ways stands at odds with most series depicting economic performance. For example, between 1970 and 1994, median real family income grew by 9.5 percent. Over the same time frame, real GDP per capita grew by 46.1 percent.

Based on these two facts alone, it is easy to jump to false conclusions, such as "the middle class has stagnated while the rich have gotten richer." Such conclusions ignore the changes in family structure over the same time period, principally the move from the two-parent to the single-parent family, from the traditional family to the "village." The number of people in the average family declined from 3.58 to 3.20, a drop of over 10 percent. From 1970-1994, median married couple real family income rose by 19.1 percent, while median single-parent real family income declined. Unfortunately, there were almost twice as many single-parent families in 1994 as in 1970.

In contrast to the modest gain in median real family income, the average family income grew by 23.8 percent and total family income grew by 64.3 percent. All of these statistics have to be used carefully when talking about economic growth.

Median family real income is biased in every which way imaginable against growth. This isn't to say that the series is without content or significance. All this means is that its interpretation has to be subtle. It is clearly one of those series that should never be used as a punch line in a political debate.

Its most common misuse has been its misuse by [Labor Secretary] Robert Reich to bash Reaganomics. In point of fact the series performed better in every which way under Reagan than under any president for which data are available.

෨෨

The airspace over Iraq isn't the only place where flack and bombers are in conflict. As the political season heats up there's going to be a lot of flack fired into the air intended to intercept incoming bombers. Some bombers are so fragile that almost any flack will pull them out of the air, and some flack is so vapid it couldn't pull down a one-engine bomber that's out of gas. Our job is to range both the bombers and the flack.

Over the past several years the data series called median real family income has appeared frequently on the public debate radar screen. Basically, this series has been used by the Clinton Administration and Secretary Robert Reich in particular to discredit the Reagan years generally and supply-side economics' trickle-down policies specifically. The seemingly poor performance of this series has been held up as proof positive that Reaganomics doesn't work for the poor even if it does line the pockets of fat cats.

THE RECENT HISTORY OF MEDIAN FAMILY INCOME

In the chart below, median real family income with all of its warts is plotted year by year from 1967 through 1994. Whatever can be culled from these data, one thing is for sure: there is no way these data can be used to demonstrate the failure of Reaganomics. The series troughs in 1982, the year before Reagan's tax cut finally takes full effect, and then rises consistently right through 1989, the last year of Reagan's policies before Bush raised taxes.

Median Family Income 1994

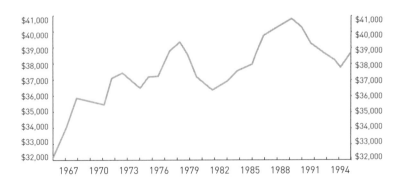

Once President Bush raised taxes the floor fell out from under median family income. In fact the series fell each and every year right up through Clinton's tax increase. This is hardly ammunition against across-the-board tax cuts.

Other periods also conform to a modestly straightforward supply-side interpretation of the economy. Nixon's wage and price controls of 1971 made it a tough year for median family income. The Carter years with all of their inflation and interventionist policies were nothing short of disastrous. But all in all these data reconfirm what we all know to be true: the Reagan years were good years for the economy.

But still there is an anomaly. Over the past twenty-four years or so there has been nothing short of an enormous divergence between traditional measures of economic performance and median family income. The behavior of median family income has in fact been fodder to critics of policies put in place over the past quarter century.

As can be seen below, median family income has grown much less rapidly than has gross domestic product (GDP) per capita in constant-dollar ("real") terms over the last twenty-four years.

Median Family Income and GDP per Capita
Selected years: 1970–1994

Year	Median Family Income (1994 $)	Index	GDP Per Capita (1987 $)	Index
1970	35,407	100.0	14,013	100.0
1975	36,177	102.2	14,916	106.4
1980	37,857	106.9	16,584	118.3
1985	38,200	107.9	17,943	128.0
1990	40,087	113.2	19,593	139.8
1994	38,782	109.5	20,476	146.1

Source: Economic Report of the President, February 1996 and the U.S. Census Bureau. National Income and Product Accounts, May 30, 1995 release.

There is an enormous 36.6 percentage point growth deficiency between median real family income and per capita real GDP growth (109.5–146.1) over the 24-year period from 1970 to 1994. And yet both data series are used frequently to make substantive judgments about the U.S. economy and the efficiency of public policy. In fact, as of late, growth in median real family income has become quite the political football.

MEDIAN FAMILY INCOME AND GDP PER CAPITA

In order to avoid the pitfalls of shedding pseudo light on non-issues, or worse yet, proving false theorems with erroneous premises, the technical reasons why these series differ are important. Arithmetically, the three ways growth in median real family income can be lower than growth in per capita real GDP are listed below:

i.)The difference between the median and the mean. The distribution of family incomes can become more skewed toward the rich, e.g., if the mean of the series is growing faster than the median this would imply that the rich are getting richer while the poor are staying poor. If true, the bulk of the gains in real income per capita would have accrued to the highest income families thus leaving the median family income virtually unchanged. It could also be caused by a disintegration of larger poor families into a larger number of poor families without anyone's income changing.

ii.)The measurement difference between family income and gross domestic product.
There could well be statistical differences arising from the differences in temporal behavior of the different components of each series between family income as measured and gross domestic product. If it were solely differences in measurements that accounted for the differential performance of the two series, then some

insights into the quality and significance of the two series would be necessary to ascertain which series or what combination of the two series was appropriate for the issues at hand. In this instance, slower growth in family income could result from family income *per se* or the share of total income going to families as opposed to other groups. And lastly,

iii.) The difference between the number of families and the number of people.

The number of people per family can decline, causing median family income to converge toward two times per capital GDP. By definition a family must have at least two people in it. Therefore, if the average family size were to fall, the process of convergence would occur, and median family income growth would be lower than growth in GDP per capita. If such were the case, then the reason median family income wasn't keeping pace with GDP per capita was simply that the number of people per family was falling.

Critics of tax cuts and supply-side policy initiatives generally latch onto the rich-getting-richer explanation as being correct. Quite simply they feel the "rich-getting-richer" observation fits more neatly into their political agenda. President Clinton, in particular, often cites the lack of real growth in median real family income as evidence that Reaganomics—"trickle-down" economics in Clinton-speak—is not working.

At the very outset of this analysis it's essential to understand exactly why two series—median real family income and GDP per capita—differ as they do. Not only is it important to know why they differ over the whole time period, but it's also important to know just why the series differ over shorter periods as well. The issues at hand and their implications are quite central to the current political debate.

i.) To range all of these differential effects we start first with the effect of using a median versus a mean. Median family income is the actual income of the family that has exactly as many families that earn less than it does and more than it does. Mean family income is total family income for all families divided by the number of families.

Interestingly enough there is quite a difference in the growth of median family income and mean family income. In the table below both series are listed for selected years from 1970 through 1994. What jumps out of the page at the reader is just how much faster mean real family income has grown than has median real family income.

Median and Mean Family Income
Selected Years: 1970–1994

Year	Median Family Income (1994 $)	Index	Mean Family Income (1994 $)	Index
1970	$35,407	100.0	$39,853	100.0
1975	36,177	102.2	40,995	102.9
1980	37,857	106.9	43,171	108.3
1985	38,200	107.9	45,375	113.9
1990	40,087	113.2	48,363	121.4
1994	38,782	109.5	49,340	123.8

Source: Statistical Abstract of the United States, 1995 and the U.S. Census Bureau.

Over the whole period mean family income has grown by 14.3 percentage points more than has the median. This difference alone accounts for over one-third of the difference between the growth in median family income and the growth in GDP per capita. This observation also lends some credence to the view that the rich have been getting richer faster than the poor have been getting richer.

Two points of interest arise out of these data. The first is that during the Reagan era—1983 through 1989—the growth in the mean on an annual basis exceeded the growth in the median by exactly the same amount as the growth in the mean exceeded the growth in the median over the whole period. If the rich were getting rich faster than the poor were getting rich, this was a general phenomenon and not one of supply-side economies or the Reagan Administration.

The other interesting observation is just how much more skewed the distribution of income has become since the tax increase of 1990.

The other interesting observation is just how much more skewed the distribution of income has become since the tax increase of 1990. For example, over the whole twenty-four year period mean income grew by 0.89 percent at an annual compound rate while median income grew at an annual compound rate of 0.38 percent over the same period. That leaves a 0.51 percent yearly differential on average.

During the Reagan years mean income grew at an annual compound rate of 2.22 percent and median income grew at a 1.70 percent per annum rate. The difference between the growth rates of the two series under Reagan was almost exactly the same as it was over the whole period, 0.52 percent versus 0.51 percent. But since Bush's and Clinton's tax increases mean income grew at a 0.50 percent annual rate while median income fell at a 0.82 percent annual rate. During the Bush and Clinton years the annual differential has been 1.32 percent, which means that income has become more skewed using this measure. I guess the harder the politicians try the more they skew the poor.

ii.) One of the surprising observations is that over this time period, there is a substantial difference in the temporal behavior of aggregate real family income and real gross domestic product.

Total Family Income and GDP
(in billions of constant dollars for selected years: 1970–1994)

Year	Total Family Income	Index	GDP	Index
1970	$2,081.4	100.0	3,388.2	100.0
1975	2,305.8	110.8	3,865.1	114.1
1980	2,603.6	125.1	4,611.9	136.1
1985	2,883.9	138.6	5,329.5	157.3
1990	3,207.5	154.1	6,138.7	181.1
1994	3,419.9	164.3	6,608.7	195.1

Source: Statistical Abstract of the United States, 1995 and the U.S. Census Bureau.

In fact, the difference here would almost be sufficient to explain the entire difference between median real family income and real GDP per capita. And, the behavior isn't explained by the number of families and the number of people. Over the period 1970 through 1994 the number of families increased by 32.7 percent and the total population of the U.S. rose by 27.1 percent. As is shown in the next section the size of the average family declined quite substantially over the period.

People in Families vs. Population
(in thousands for selected years: 1970–1994)

Year	Number of People in Families	Index	Population	Index
1970	186,973	100.0	204,982	100.0
1975	192,358	102.9	215,891	105.3
1980	198,417	106.1	227,622	111.0
1985	205,292	109.8	238,416	116.3
1990	210,241	112.4	249,845	121.9
1994	221,802	118.6	260,564	127.1

Source: Statistical Abstract of the United States, 1995 and the U.S. Census Bureau.

iii.) Even a cursory look at the data, however, shows that the lack of growth in family income is due in large part to a decrease in family size as a consequence of the break down of the traditional two-parent family. While we don't have data on the effect changes in family size have had on median family income, we do have comparable data for mean family income. In fact, holding family size constant, mean family income would have grown by 38.5 percent from 1970 to 1994. The differential gap between per capita GDP growth and mean family income would have been narrowed by about 15 percentage points. From these data it is clear that the rising economic tide has raised most boats.

Combining the number of families and average family size and then comparing this total with the overall population yields another perspective on what's happening to the two series. While the number of families had been growing somewhat faster than the overall population, the decline in the average family size more than offset the increase in the number of families. As a consequence, the number of people covered by the series median real family income has not kept pace with the overall population.

POLICY IMPLICATIONS

If increasing the growth of median real family income relative to the growth of per capital real GDP is the objective, then the policy implications are clear. Tax and entitlements policies should be changed to encourage the traditional two-parent family and altered so as not to discourage family cohesiveness.

With over sixty-eight million households and over 265 million people in the U.S. today, the issue of who benefits most from economic growth is difficult to measure. At a first pass, the following table shows how the decline in family size has contributed to the significantly slower growth of family income:

Adjusting Family Income for the Change in Family Size (all data in 1994 dollars)

Year	Average Family Size	Average Family Income	Income Per Capita (2)/(1)	Index
1970	3.58	$39,853	$11,132.1	100.0
1975	3.42	40,995	11,986.8	107.7
1980	3.29	43,171	13,121.9	117.9
1985	3.23	45,375	14,048.0	126.2
1990	3.17	48,363	15,256.5	137.0
1994	3.20	49,340	15,418.8	138.5

Source: Economic Report of the President, February 1996.
Statistical Abstract of the United States, 1995.

What is truly striking is the precipitous decline in the average family size over the twenty-four year period from 1970 to 1994. Families averaged almost 0.4 people less in 1994 than they did in 1970. Adjusting family incomes for the changes in size explains a little over one-third of the 36 percentage-point differential between income and GDP growth rates. Partially as a result of the decrease in family size, the number of families increased by 33 percent between 1970 and 1994. Population over this same period increased by 27 percent. That median incomes could rise in the midst of such an explosion in the numbers of families is an indication that the benefits of GDP growth are widespread.

From 1970 through 1994, the growth in median family income is high for families with both parents and negative for families with one parent.

CHANGES IN THE FAMILY

One logical follow-up question is why has average family size declined so dramatically over the last quarter of a century? Part of the reduction in family size is due to an increase in single-parent households, a trend which adversely affects median family incomes. From 1970 through 1994, the growth in median family income is high for families with both parents and negative for families with one parent. In fact, growth in married couples' median family income from 1970 through 1994 is almost ten percentage points higher than the growth in median family income for all families.

Married-Couple and Single-Parent Median Family Incomes

(All figures in 1994 dollars, except index)

| Year | Married Couples | Index | Single Parent Heads-of-Household: | | | |
			Male-Headed	Index	Female-Headed	Index
1970	$37,735	100.0	$32,338	100.0	$18,276	100.0
1975	39,204	103.9	34,268	106.0	18,048	98.8
1980	41,671	110.4	31,547	97.6	18,742	102.5
1985	42,835	113.5	31,158	96.4	18,814	102.9
1990	45,237	119.9	32,935	101.8	19,199	105.1
1994	44,959	119.1	27,751	85.8	18,236	99.8

Source: Statistical Abstract of the United States, 1995

Unfortunately for the children involved, the trend is away from married-couple families. Single-parent families are a bigger percentage of the population and have ever younger heads of households.

As can be seen below, the number of single-parent families has increased from 15 percent of all families to 31 percent of all families since 1970. If the percentages had not changed, the median income of families with children would be 10 percent higher.

Distribution of Family Households with Children
(Percent)

Year	Married Couple	Male Head	Female Head
1970	85%	1%	11%
1975	n/a	n/a	n/a
1980	77	2	18
1985	74	3	21
1990	73	3	22
1994	69	3	23

Source: Statistical Abstract of the United States, 1995.

Thus, by taking into account the reduction in family size and the shift toward single-parent families, the difference between GDP per capita and median family income growth has been greatly reduced. Given the 33 percent increase in the number of households, it would have been hard to have expected a more egalitarian outcome.

President Clinton argues that the slow growth in median family income is evidence that trickle-down economics does not work. A better conclusion is that economic growth has been strong enough to offset the trend towards single-parent families.

... economic growth has been strong enough to offset the trend towards single-parent families.

Thus, the ways median household or family income statistics are usually reported ignore recent trends in family structure. They also ignore the relative performances during the various sub-periods. Clinton's accusations aimed at Reagan's tax cuts and trickle down economics are misplaced. Trickle-down economics has not caused family disintegration. And in fact, when so-called trickle-down economics was in effect median family income grew at its highest rate.

What caused the break-up of the two-parent family? The answer is complex, but the policy implications are clear: We need a tax code and an entitlements program that promote the two-parent family unit.

The Question of Inequality

8

Bruce Bartlett

July 13, 2005

I n 2003, the economy of the United States began to show the kind of life that had been characteristic of it in the 1980s and 1990s. From the spring of 2003 until the spring of 2005, when Bruce Bartlett wrote the following piece on the rising clamor over inequality, the rate of economic growth was 3.6 percent per year. This was akin to the healthy pace of growth that had prevailed in the great Reagan and Clinton expansions of the previous decades.

The 3.6 percent growth of 2003–05 (which continued at a slightly reduced rate for two more years) was notable for marking a happy end to the extended spate of sluggishness that had gripped the American economy following Clinton's last year in office, 2000. From the final quarter of 2000 through the spring of 2003, the American economy experienced both a mild recession and a weak recovery, such that growth totaled only 1.2 percent per year over that span. Now came three times this number—3.6 percent.

The origins of the good growth lay in President George W. Bush's push to pass into law a serious set of marginal tax cuts. This was not accomplished in 2001, when as he took office, Bush compromised with Congress to shave all of 0.5 percent off the top rate of the income tax. In May of 2003, Bush achieved a rescheduled tax cut that took the top rate down 3.6 points all at once. A clear correlation came about between significant tax cuts and the end of economic sluggishness.

All well and good: the economy was taking off. But as Bartlett discussed here, as recovery powered forward from 2003 to 2005, there also came hand-wringing over the problem of economic inequality. Before 2003, critics had blamed Bush for growth below the standards set in the 1980s and 1990s. Now that that kind of growth was in place, the criticism shifted to apparent problems in how wealth was being concentrated among the classes.

All this had a familiar ring, as Bartlett recounted. In the 1980s, in the face of the whopping growth of the Reagan years, the easiest route for criticism to take was to point out inequalities. Then even under the mediocre growth of President George H.W. Bush in the early 1990s, that criticism intensified, only to abate, oddly, during the strong-growth Clinton years.

Bartlett accomplished two main things in this essay. The first was to point out that inequality statistics are notoriously easy to misconstruct, massage, and misinterpret. Bartlett went over an incident from 1992, when MIT economist Paul Krugman was first making a name for himself as a public intellectual. Krugman put together an inequality dataset that appeared to show that during the Reagan-Bush years, incomes for the well-off skyrocketed while gains for the lower classes remained minimal.

The Krugman research did not do well at the level of professional review by other scholars. But it did transfix the *New York Times*, which made a tremendous mistake in reporting the rich's recent gains. Taking a cue from Krugman, the *Times* reported that 60 percent of all new income was going to the rich, when it should have reported that the rich's *rate* of income-increase was 60 percent greater than that of the rest of the population, which itself was considerable. The false impression was given that the rich were hoarding almost all the new economic growth for themselves. The Bill Clinton presidential campaign ran with the bad numbers, and the *Times* altered the story without acknowledging the mistake, ultimately to the disfavor of the paper's own public editor.

The other point that Bartlett was at pains to make in this piece is that despite all the politically-inspired noise around economic-equality datasets, the conclusion that level heads invariably must draw is that all classes of Americans have consistently improved their standard of living over the last several generations, and in particular during the presidencies of Reagan and the two Bushes. Moreover, at the level of aspirations, as indicated by polls, a great proportion of this nation's inhabitants (through 2005) remained fully confident that the American dream was alive and well.

In recent months, the mainstream media have suddenly taken an extraordinary interest in the distribution of income and wealth. *The New York Times* and *Wall Street Journal* launched multi-part series on the subject, and the *Los Angeles Times*, *Christian Science Monitor* and *Business Week* chimed in as well.

The conclusion of all these reports is the same: the rich are getting richer than ever and the chances are falling that anyone not born into wealth will ever achieve it. Sometimes explicitly and sometimes as subtext, it is asserted that the Bush tax cuts have worsened the distribution of income and made the non-rich worse off.

During the Clinton years, little was heard of growing inequality, even though all the same trends that had so alarmed liberals in the 1980s actually accelerated despite a major tax increase on the rich in 1993.

We have been through all of this before. In the 1980s and early 1990s, there was a concerted effort by liberal interest groups, like Citizens for Tax Justice and the Center on Budget and Policy Priorities, and their willing accomplices in the media, to paint Ronald Reagan's tax cuts as responsible for increasing income and wealth inequality. This effort reached a peak in 1992 and was partially responsible for the defeat of George H.W. Bush.

During the Clinton years, little was heard of growing inequality, even though all the same trends that had so alarmed liberals in the 1980s actually accelerated despite a major tax increase on the rich in 1993. Now with another Republican in the White House, it is time to turn the inequality machine back on....

The problem for the Democrats is that the American people don't believe in class warfare. They don't hate the rich because they are rich. On the contrary, they want nothing more than to emulate them. And many Americans believe that they have a good shot at joining the ranks of the rich. The data confirm that such hopes and expectations are not unrealistic.

The data presented in the *Times* and *Journal* series are selective and that which contradicts their thesis is ignored. The purpose of this report is to bring together some of the data and studies that give a different and more optimistic picture of income and wealth distribution in America today.

The data show that although income distribution has indeed become more unequal, the real standard of living of all income groups has risen and there is a high degree of mobility both up and down the income ladder. As a consequence, most people believe that their living standard has improved, large percentages believe they are living better than their parents and also that they have a good shot at becoming rich themselves. For this reason, they consistently reject policies like the estate tax that are designed solely to soak the rich.

BASIC DISTRIBUTION DATA

The principal income distribution data…come from the Census Bureau's Current Population Survey and are updated annually for the previous year each fall. The latest data are for 2003 and show the bottom quintile (20 percent) of households receiving 3.4 percent of aggregate income, compared with 49.8 percent for the top quintile and 21.4 percent for just the top 5 percent of households.

Over time, the share going to the bottom quintile has fallen and the share going to the top quintile has risen. However, these figures need to be interpreted with caution.

Although income distribution has indeed become more unequal, the real standard of living of all income groups has risen and there is a high degree of mobility both up and down the income ladder.

First, the data are for pretax money income only. Thus, they exclude the effect of taxes and in-kind government transfers such as housing subsidies and food stamps.…The effect of including these factors significantly raises the share of income going to those in the bottom three quintiles and reduces the share going to the top two quintiles. In short, the official data… exclude much of what we do as a society to equalize the distribution of income, making the poor appear poorer than they are and making the rich appear richer than they are.

Second, the focus on income shares tends to lead people to assume that the economic pie is fixed, so that the gains of the rich necessarily make the poor worse off. But...the real income of every income class has risen over time. For example, in 1967 the income share of the bottom quintile was 4.0 percent versus 3.4 percent in 2003. But the average real income of households in that quintile has risen by 32 percent since 1967 despite their falling share of aggregate income.

...the real income of every income class has risen over time.

Obviously, the reason for this is that real aggregate income has risen markedly over time, improving the standard of living of all Americans. In other words, the pie is bigger. The best summary measure is the median household income—the income level at which exactly half the people are above and half are below. This figure has risen by 30 percent in real terms since 1967.

Another factor that is often overlooked is that while there are the same number of households in each quintile, there aren't the same number of people per household in each quintile. There are, in fact, considerably more individuals in the top quintile, because there are more intact families with children in the top quintile and many single-person households in the bottom. In 2002, 24.6 percent of the total population was in the top quintile, versus 14.3 percent in the bottom. When the quintiles are adjusted to put the same number of people (not households) in each quintile, the bottom quintile's share of total income rises to 9.4 percent and the top quintile's share falls to 39.6 percent.[1]

Another way of looking at the data is [to focus on] the percentage of households by income classes defined by fixed dollar amounts adjusted for inflation. From time to time, reporters will look only at the middle [ranks] and conclude that the middle class is disappearing because the percentage of households with an income between $25,000 and $75,000 has fallen. They simply assume that it is because more of such people have become poor.

These reporters make two mistakes. First is not always realizing that the figures are adjusted for inflation. Second is failing to
note that the percentage of households with a lower class income
(under $25,000) has also fallen. In 1967, 36.6 percent of households
made less than $25,000 (in 2003 dollars). In 2003, only 29 percent
fell into this category. In short, the only reason why there are fewer
people making between $25,000 and $75,000 is because more of
them are rich. In the aggregate, the percentage of the population
with an income under $75,000 fell from 91.8 percent in 1967 to
73.9 percent in 2003.

To see how clearly this is good news, imagine how wonderful
it would be if the percentage of those making less than $75,000
was zero. It would mean that 100 percent of the population was
making more than that. Therefore, it is unambiguously positive that
the percentage of households making more than $75,000 has risen
from 8.2 percent in 1967 to 26.1 percent in 2003.

Another failing of the standard Census data is that they exclude wealth. This is important because many people in the bottom
quintile may be retired, with low incomes but substantial assets and
often living in a home that they may own free and clear with no
mortgage. It also includes people who may temporarily have a low
income, because of a job loss or other short-term setback, and may
be borrowing or selling assets to maintain consumption at their permanent income level. Such people are not really poor in any mean-
ingful sense.

This point is illustrated in [the table below], which shows
that the consumption of those in the bottom quintile greatly exceeds their cash income. By contrast, the expenditures of those in
the top quintile are well below their income because they are saving
and investing, thereby adding to the national seed corn, so to speak.
This saving and investment will raise productivity and wages in the
long run, thus benefiting society as a whole. If the rich didn't save
so much, we would all be poorer.

Income and Expenditure by Quintile, 2003

	Lowest	Second	Middle	Fourth	Highest
Average Expenditures	$18,492	$26,729	$36,213	$50,468	$81,731
Average Income	$8,201	$21,478	$37,542	$61,132	$127,146
Difference	+$10,291	+$5,251	-$1,329	-$10,664	-$45,415

Note: These data are for "consumer units" that approximate households, but are not precisely the same as the Census Bureau's definition.

Source: Bureau of Labor Statistics, Consumer Expenditure Survey.

This table also makes the point that consumption is far more equal than income. The ratio of income between the top and bottom quintiles is 15.5 to one, but the ratio of consumption is just 4.4 to one. Insofar as consumption defines our standard of living, there is clearly much more equality than is evident only from the income data.[2]

It should also be noted that the material well-being of even those officially classified as poor is in some respects better than the rich of an earlier era and of most middle class Europeans today. For example, according to the Census Bureau, of those living in the lowest decile (10 percent) of households, 91 percent own color televisions, 74 percent own microwave ovens, 55 percent own video cassette recorders, 42 percent own stereos, and 21 percent own computers. A recent Swedish study found that the average European only lived about as well as the residents of America's poorest state, Mississippi.[3]

CLASS IN AMERICA

Despite the best efforts of liberals to incite class warfare in the 1980s, they never had much success. Poor people didn't seem to be particularly outraged by the great wealth of the Warren Buffetts and Bill Gateses of the world. Rather than punish them, most people wanted instead to emulate them.

In traditional European society, where wealth historically was based on land that was mostly owned by titled aristocrats, there was virtually no hope of rising above one's station at birth. According to economist Angus Maddison, the rate of growth of real per capita GDP was just 0.13 percent per year from the birth of Christ to 1820 in Europe. During that whole long period, real per capita GDP only went up 2½ times. Consequently, century after century, the vast majority of people necessarily lived in the same social and economic class to which all their parents and ancestors had been born.[4]

But all this began to change with the Industrial Revolution and incomes started to rise sharply—seven times faster than their historical rate between 1820 and 1870, according to Maddison, which almost doubled per capita GDP during that fifty-year span. Suddenly, there were opportunities for smart, entrepreneurially-minded people to make fortunes without having to own vast amounts of land. Manufacturing became the new basis for wealth and it was open to anyone with ambition, even if they were born without a title in front of their name.

The aristocrats responded by putting down the industrialists and entrepreneurs as *nouveau riche*. Such people might have money, but they had no class, the aristocrats charged. Unfortunately, this still happens and access is denied to the newly rich by institutions like country clubs that are controlled by those with "old money," which is always portrayed as superior in some way. In places like Palm Beach, it may still confer status to have inherited one's wealth, rather than having earned it oneself. But most Americans have far more respect for those who create wealth than for *rentiers*.

Observers of America like Alexis de Tocqueville have long noted the essential classlessness of American society in contrast to Europe. A key reason is the great mobility of income and wealth. De Tocqueville's mid-nineteenth century observation is still valid today:

> It is not that in the United States, as everywhere, there are no rich; indeed I know no other country where love of money has such a grip on men's hearts or where stronger scorn is expressed for the theory of permanent equality of property. But wealth circulates there with incredible rapidity, and experience shows that two successive generations seldom enjoy its favors.[5]

Even Karl Marx recognized that America was an unusually mobile society, which made the soil unfertile for revolution. Said Marx, "The function of a wages labourer is for a very large part of the American people but a probational state, which they are sure to leave within a longer or shorter term."[6]

Recognizing that mobility undermines their efforts to incite class warfare, liberals have lately taken to saying that mobility may have been high in the nineteenth century, but it is much less so today. They also argue that mobility has fallen especially sharply over the last generation. Typical is this over-the-top comment from *New York Times* columnist Bob Herbert:

> Put the myth of the American Dream aside. The bottom line is that it's becoming increasingly difficult for working Americans to move up in class. The rich are freezing nearly everybody else in place, and sprinting off with the nation's bounty.[7]

Not surprisingly, Herbert offered no evidence in support of his conclusion except his own paper's series on inequality. However, a careful examination of the available data shows no evidence of a decline in mobility since the 1960s and the level of mobility remains very high.

Before examining the available data, it should be noted that to really calculate mobility, one needs access to data on the same specific individuals and families over time. The annual Census data tell us nothing about mobility because they are just snapshots of income at a moment in time. The principal source of mobility data is the Panel Study on Income Dynamics (PSID) at the University of Michigan, which has been tracking several thousand families since the 1960s. The second major source is a special Census program started in the 1980s called the Survey of Income and Program Participation (SIPP).[8]

The first longitudinal study based on PSID data was published in 1984…. It show[ed] that between 1971 and 1978, 44.5 percent of those in the lowest quintile the first year had risen to a higher quintile seven years later. Twenty-two percent were now in the second quintile, 9.5 percent were in the middle quintile, 7 percent were in the fourth quintile, and 6 percent had risen all the way to the top quintile.

Conversely, 51.5 percent of those in the top quintile fell to a lower quintile. Mobility, after all, must work in both directions. More than 29 percent fell to the fourth quintile, 14 percent were now in the middle quintile, 4.5 percent dropped to the second quintile, and 3.5 percent now found themselves in the bottom quintile.

The Wall Street Journal editorial page immediately recognized that these data were "explosive." They completely destroyed the implicit liberal argument that the same people were in the top or bottom quintiles year after year. Were this the case, it would be hard not to support governmental efforts to redistribute income. But since we now had hard evidence that this was not the case, the logic of redistribution collapsed. Said the *Journal*:

> Therein lies the justification for free enterprise as a whole. Under what other system do we see families so unequal at the start leaping up and crashing down, reflecting varying drives and talents? This is equality, not of result, but of opportunity.[9]

In 1989, the first mobility data from SIPP became available.... Over just a one-year period from 1984 to 1985, a remarkable 18.2 percent of those in the bottom quintile had risen to a higher one, and 19.5 percent of those in the top quintile had fallen to a lower one. Subsequent studies in 1990 (data for 1985—86) and 1991 (for 1987–88), confirmed that even over a single year, there is a considerable amount of income mobility.[10] Commenting on the first three years of Census mobility data in 1991, I had this to say in a *Wall Street Journal* article:

> This dynamic movement by people up and down the income scale explains why the American people have never sympathized with class warfare. They know instinctively that those who are on top today could easily be down and out tomorrow, and that a little luck and hard work can turn today's poor into tomorrow's rich.[11]

POLITICAL CLASS WARFARE

Nevertheless, the income distribution issue heated up going into the 1992 presidential election. A particularly inflammatory contribution appeared in the *New York Times* on March 5, 1992. Based on research by then-MIT economist Paul Krugman, *Times* reporter Sylvia Nasar made an astonishing claim in a major front-page article. Said Nasar:

> An outsized 60 percent of the growth in after-tax income of all American families between 1977 and 1989—and an even heftier three-fourths of the gain in pretax income—went to the wealthiest 660,000 families, each of which had an annual income of at least $310,000 a year, for a household of four.

> While total income for all 66 million American families expanded by about $740 billion in inflation-adjusted dollars during the Carter-Reagan years, the slice belonging to the top 1 percent grew to 13 percent of all family income, up from 9 percent.[12]

Had the top 1 percent of families actually gotten 75 percent of the aggregate gain in pretax income over a 12-year period, it would indeed have been big news. With the remaining 99 percent of families dividing up just 25 percent of the total gain, the vast majority would certainly have seen a decline in their living standards over this period.

In fact, the data were completely wrong.... Although those in the top quintile did especially well between 1977 and 1989, the average real income of every quintile rose over that period. Those in the bottom quintile saw an increase of 6.9 percent and the median income went up 13.9 percent. Such results would be impossible if the *Times* report was correct.

Krugman said that his analysis was based on Congressional Budget Office data.[13] His results came partially from the peculiar way CBO calculated income that differed greatly from standard Census Bureau methods. In any case, a Treasury Department effort to replicate Krugman's results from this source was unsuccessful. The CBO itself also found significant errors in Krugman's calculations.[14]

Krugman himself made repeated efforts to explain himself that only succeeded in raising new questions about his methodology. An analysis by the Council of Economic Advisers found that Krugman's methods simply made no sense at all, despite Krugman's own corrections to his original calculations reported in the *New York Times*.[15]

All of this could be chalked up to the sort of angels-on-the-head-of-a-pin debate so beloved of academics if it hadn't had important political implications. The March 5 *New York Times* article had a major impact on Bill Clinton's campaign strategy, causing him to ratchet up his attacks on George H.W. Bush for worsening the distribution of income. Here is what another article by Sylvia Nasar had to say about the fallout from her own report:

> Governor Clinton, the likely Democratic presidential nominee, had been searching for months for facts to illustrate his claim that America's middle class benefited little from 12 years of Republican rule. The explosion of riches at the top struck him as a perfect vehicle. Not only did the widening gap between the rich and the rest of Americans conflict with traditional notions of democracy, but it also went right to the pocketbook sources of middle-class discontent.

> "He was reading the paper that morning and went crazy," said Dee Dee Myers, the campaign's press secretary, referring to a *New York Times* article in March that reported on the wildly disproportionate gains of the top 1 percent. "The story proved a point he had been trying to make for months, so he added the statistic to his repertoire."

> "The L.A. riots underscore the problem," she added.[16]

Only subsequently was it learned that all this debate was based on a reportorial mistake. It turned out that the early edition of the *New York Times* available in Washington and seen by Bill Clinton and me was incorrect. The final version distributed in New York City was changed in significant ways. If one now goes to the *New York Times* archives and calls up the March 5 article, this is how it reads, with changes in caps:

> An outsized 60 percent of the growth in THE AVERAGE after-tax income of all American families between 1977 and 1989—and an even heftier three-fourths of the gain in AVERAGE pretax income—went to the wealthiest 660,000 families, each of which had an annual income of at least $310,000 a year, for a household of four.
>
> While THE NUMBER OF AMERICAN FAMILIES GREW FROM 52 MILLION TO 66 MILLION AND TOTAL INCOME EXPANDED BY $583 BILLION inflation-adjusted dollars during the Carter-Reagan years, the slice belonging to the top 1 percent grew BY $190 BILLION, GIVING THEM 13 percent of all family income, up from 9 percent.[17]

It turned out that Krugman and/or Nasar had thoroughly misread the data. The top 1 percent had not come close to getting three-fifths of the aggregate real income gain of the 1980s. What happened is that someone confused rates of change with absolute changes. The average real income of the top 1 percent may have risen 60 percent faster than for the rest of the population, but this doesn't mean they got 60 percent of the total income gain. There were too few of them for that possibly to have been the case.[18]

No correction ever appeared in the *Times*, despite efforts by Congressman Dick Armey (R-TX) and others to get one. The *Times* simply altered the article without ever acknowledging that it had made an error, even though it was apparent that people like Bill Clinton were repeatedly citing the incorrect original report on the campaign trail. According to former *Times* ombudsman Daniel Okrent, the practice of fixing a story without issuing a correction is sufficiently well known at the paper to have a term for it called "rowback."[19]

Unfortunately, the *Times* rowback of its March 5 report only became known long after the fact. After all, how often would one have any reason to compare the Washington edition and the New York edition of the same article the same day and notice something had changed? To this day, how these changes came about and who made them is a mystery.[20]

After the election of Bill Clinton, the *Times* lost interest in whether the rich were getting richer, even though the same trends that it found so alarming when Republicans were in the White House actually accelerated. Indeed, as [census data] indicates, the rich got richer even faster on Clinton's watch than they had on Reagan's. The share of aggregate income going to the top 5 percent of households rose by 2.5 percent between 1980 and 1988, but increased by 3.5 percent from 1992 to 2000.

After the election of Bill Clinton, the Times *lost interest in whether the rich were getting richer, even though the same trends that it found so alarming when Republicans were in the White House actually accelerated.*

Indeed, by 1995 the *Times* was defending the ultra-rich against populist attacks. In an article for the *New York Times Magazine*, *Times* editorial writer Michael Weinstein even defended Michael Milken's $500 million paycheck in 1987. Weinstein also correctly pointed out that confiscating the pay of every corporate CEO would do little to improve the distribution of income because there aren't enough CEO's to make a difference.[21]

Even Sylvia Nasar, author of the controversial 1992 article, appears to have had a change of heart. By 1999, she was celebrating wealth and offering sympathy for the 70-hour workweeks of rich investment bankers. A key reason is income mobility. Said Nasar, "Most ordinary Americans...seem to feel that, whatever has happened to the income distribution, opportunities abound—and not just for the rich."[22]

INCOME MOBILITY

Although the *New York Times* may have helped elect Bill Clinton by distorting the facts about income distribution, research continued to show a high degree of mobility in the U.S. In June 1992, the U.S. Treasury Department released a study based on tax records that are unavailable to private researchers. It looked at tax filers in 1979 and then compared the same filers in 1988. It found that 85.8 percent of those in the lowest quintile the first year were in a higher quintile in the second year, including 14.7 percent who rose all the way to the top quintile....

Although the Treasury study was criticized because it wasn't adjusted for age, family size and other factors, the liberal Urban Institute essentially confirmed the results almost immediately. Utilizing the PSID database, it again found a large degree of mobility, with about half of households rising up out of the bottom quintile and the same percentage falling from the top quintile in the 1970s and 1980s....

Even more important, the Urban Institute study totally contradicted the Krugman/*New York Times* argument that only the rich benefited from economic growth in the 1970s and 1980s. It found that those in the bottom quintile achieved the largest real income gains and those in the top quintile obtained the smallest gains. The former saw income growth of 72 percent from 1967 to 1976 and 77 percent from 1977 to 1986, while the latter saw gains of just 6 percent and 5 percent, respectively....Subsequent research continues to show income mobility on the same order of magnitude as earlier studies....

Contrary to the view presented in recent newspaper reports, there is no reason to believe that the rate of mobility should rise infinitely over time. If it did, then eventually the distribution of income would be purely random. To complain that the rate is not higher today than it was in the past is akin to complaining that baseball batting averages aren't higher today than a generation ago. There is no reason to think they should be any higher.

Lastly, it should be noted that wealth mobility is of a similar order of magnitude to income mobility. Over a ten-year period, about 40 percent of those in the top decile move down and 60 percent of those in the bottom decile move up....

CONCLUSION

At the risk of beating the issue to death, this study has [discussed] data from every study I could find that measured income or wealth mobility over the last two decades. I have presented comprehensive data because the issue of mobility seems to be controversial, with unusually strenuous efforts by some of our major newspapers to prove that mobility is falling. But there is simply no evidence in the data or most academic studies showing this to be the case.

However, the strongest data against the stagnation thesis comes from polling. At the end of the day, what really matters is not some economist's opinion, but people's perceptions of their own economic status. In short, if people believe that their economic fortunes are improving, then they are. In this case, perception is reality.

[Survey] data from 1964 to 2005 in which people were asked what economic class they grew up in or lived in as a child and what class they belonged to today...consistently show that a high percentage of people lived in a higher income class than the one that their parents lived in. And the latest data report the strongest improvement, with 20 percent fewer people living in the lower or working classes today compared to their childhood, and 20 percent more people living in the middle or upper middle classes. There has been no change in the percentage of people living in the upper class.[23]

[Then there are] data on what people said when they were asked about their own chances of becoming rich. Contrary to the impression conveyed by the *New York Times* and other recent media reports, an overwhelming 80 percent of people believe it is possible, up from 57 percent in 1983.

I don't know why there is such a concerted effort to discredit the idea of mobility lately or to play up the existence of income and wealth inequality. When last we saw such a campaign in the mainstream media, it was clearly driven by an effort to discredit Reagan's tax cuts and defeat George H.W. Bush. Today I suspect that the motive may be to rescue the estate tax, which Republicans have been working to abolish for some years. For technical reasons relating to Senate rules, permanent repeal could not be enacted in 2001 and the estate tax is eliminated only for the year 2010, reappearing the following year as if nothing had happened.

Earlier this year, the House of Representatives voted in favor of permanent repeal and a vote is expected in the Senate this summer. Since 60 votes will be necessary, the outcome will be close. The liberal strategy appears to be to try and keep the estate tax in some form, even if it means sharply raising the exempt amount and cutting estate tax rates. Liberals know that it will be much easier to raise estate taxes in the future if the tax remains in effect in some form. It will be much harder to reinstate if it is abolished permanently.[24]

A secondary reason is to begin to lay the groundwork for 2008, giving the Democratic candidate an issue to run on that was successful once before. Although the American people are not as susceptible to being swayed by class warfare as Europeans, they can be influenced by a sustained liberal campaign and an inadequate conservative response, as was the case in 1992.

9

The Impact of
Supply-Side Economics

Bruce Bartlett
November 11, 2003

By any reckoning, supply-side economics was one of the most consequential developments in economic policy in the twentieth century. Indeed, it is reasonable to say that since the New Deal of the 1930s, supply-side economics, as put into practice in the Ronald Reagan administration of the 1980s, has been the biggest thing to hit American economic policy in the entire eight-decade era since the response to the Great Depression.

Yet very little history has been written about supply-side economics. The histories written of the New Deal, even those produced in its immediate aftermath, would fill a small library; and the number of professional historians in the United States is huge—the American Historical Association, a professional body, counts 20,000 of them. But even now, four decades after the event, the books written about the supply-side revolution by members of the historical profession stand in number at only one or two.

It is an adage in historical scholarship that most historians will fall in love with their topic. Surely one of the reasons that historians, so many of them liberal or progressive, have shied away from treating the great supply-side revolution with the due it deserves is that they fear having to compliment it.

Bruce Bartlett was one of the central figures in the implementation of supply-side economics in the late 1970s and early 1980s. He was a staff member for several Members of Congress and congressional committees where the supply-side revolution was taking hold. Crucially, in 1977, Bartlett became an assistant to the greatest of the supply-side U.S. Representatives, Jack Kemp. In that capacity, Bartlett helped to compose the first version of the central piece of supply-side legislation, the Kemp-Roth tax cut.

Bartlett was also a historian, having earned degrees in history from Rutgers and Georgetown. In the 1970s, while in his twenties, he published historical studies of Pearl Harbor and Keynesianism. And in 1981, just as the revolution he had helped into being on Capitol Hill was getting underway, Bartlett put out the first comprehensive history of supply-side economics, a book that remains a standard to this day, *Reaganomics: Supply-Side Economics in Action.*

Some two decades later, in 2003, when he wrote the following piece, Bartlett identified the disturbing trend: the historical profession had declined to tell the story of supply-side economics. There were no serious books on the subject from any of the credentialed historians. Consequently, all sorts of cheap information about supply-side economics and its heyday under Reagan was floating about: the supply-siders guaranteed greater revenues from any tax cut; supply-side economics had little if any academic standing; supply-side economics had no history of bipartisanship—and so forth.

Even now, four decades after the event, the books written about the supply-side revolution by members of the historical profession stand in number at only one or two.

On two counts, in 2003, Bartlett was prepared to correct these wrongs. First, he was there when supply-side economics first germinated in Congress. He knew the real history and was prepared to testify to it. And second, he was trained as a historian—he had the qualifications, ability, and publication record to sweep away the misinformation and get across what was correct with authority.

The following piece remains an essential entry in the historiography of supply-side economics. The first of its accomplishments was to set down the extensive history of the "Laffer curve" concept that has come to be synonymous with supply-side economics in so many minds. Here Bartlett not only showed that Arthur Laffer's famous diagram of 1974, which suggested the possibility of increased governmental revenues given a tax cut, built on a long and eminent tradition in economics on just this theme. He also showed that the Laffer curve as such soon entered into the lexicon of the top economics journals and stayed there. The Laffer curve, that badge of supply-side economics, has become one of the major items in the toolkit of economics as it is practiced in its advanced form today.

Bartlett also took the opportunity here to address common charges made against supply-side economics—that its advocates guaranteed immediate revenue gains from any tax cut, that it lacked for bipartisanship. In parrying these claims, it emerges that Bartlett's ability to quote from the record of the 1970s and early 1980s remains unrivaled by any commentator, journalist, or scholar. A key point that Bartlett stressed here is that supply-siders had long insisted that it was not federal revenues, but total government revenues—including those of the states—that would rise given tax cuts. Events confirmed this point very well during the economic boom of the 1980s.

Perhaps superficially appearing as esoteric, Bartlett's argument about inflation and the federal deficit in the 1980s is very important. It remains an argument that has been completely missed by all the critics of supply-side economics who cite the large budget deficits of the 1980s as an indictment of the Reagan economic plan. Bartlett revealed here that it was the *collapse in the inflation rate* in the early 1980s—unquestionably a singular good for the American economy, given that that rate was over 10 percent for three straight years, 1979-81—that underlay the large deficits of the mid- and late 1980s.

As Bartlett explained, the collapse in inflation after 1982 shut down the odious "bracket creep" of the stagflation era, whereby increases in income that kept pace with inflation were subject to higher and higher rates of income tax. In the 1980s, therefore, it was not so much the tax cuts that limited an increase in federal receipts, but the welcome stability of the price level that kept a lid on the tax take.

By the time the original supply-sider, Arthur Laffer's mentor Robert A. Mundell, won the Nobel Prize in 1999, the moment had come for students, scholars, and critics to start delving into the substantial history of supply-side economics. But strange to say, that field remained all Bruce Bartlett's own well into the twenty-first century.

SUPPLY-SIDE ECONOMICS: "VOODOO ECONOMICS" OR LASTING CONTRIBUTION? NOVEMBER 11, 2003

In the mid-1970s, a new term began to appear in discussions of economic policy: supply-side economics. It was controversial from the very beginning. Indeed, even Republicans like George H.W. Bush referred to it as "voodoo economics." Nevertheless, it was embraced by Ronald Reagan and formed the basis for the 1981 tax cut and many of Mr. Reagan's other policies.[1]

Not much is heard about supply-side economics these days. Many economists view the prosperity of the 1990s as refutation of it. Whereas supply-side economics was based on tax cuts that led to large budget deficits, it is often said, growth in the 1990s was triggered by the 1993 tax increase, which led to lower deficits and eventual surpluses.

Indeed, in certain quarters, supply-side economics is viewed as nothing but an elaborate trick played on the American people. Like the alchemists of old, who said they could make gold from lead, the supply-siders promised increased revenues from lower tax rates, knowing full well that this is impossible. Former Senator Daniel Patrick Moynihan (D-NY) has argued forcefully that supply-siders never expected higher revenues and simply made the whole thing up. David Stockman, Director of the Office of Management and Budget under President Reagan, said more or less the same thing.[2]

The Moynihan/Stockman charge is a serious one, implying intellectual dishonesty on the part of many prominent economists, including myself. I was a part of the supply-side movement starting in 1977, when I joined the staff of Congressman Jack Kemp (R-NY), one the earliest and most vocal advocates of supply-side economics. As the most junior member of the group, I had the opportunity to observe all of the key players at close hand during the formative period of the development of supply-side economics.

The basics of supply-side theory had already been formulated when I came on the scene. Much of the early work had been done by economists Paul Craig Roberts, who preceded me on Kemp's staff, and Norman Ture, a private economist long affiliated with the National Bureau of Economic Research. Another key player was Jude

Wanniski, an editorial writer for the *Wall Street Journal*, who came to supply-side economics through the work of economists Robert Mundell and Arthur Laffer.[3]

I believe that an examination of what these and other supply-siders said and wrote during the critical period of 1974 to 1981 shows that there was a much firmer foundation to their work than is commonly believed. A lot of serious research underlay supply-side economics, much done by economists who would have rejected the supply-side label.

Although it is only one aspect of supply-side economics, the Laffer Curve has come to represent what it was all about, in the minds of most people. It simply makes the indisputably true point that neither a zero percent tax rate nor a 100 percent tax rate collect any revenue; the former because there is no tax and the latter because no one will earn taxable income, knowing that the government will confiscate all of it.

The Laffer Curve implies that there is some point between zero and 100 percent that will maximize revenue. If rates are above this point—in the prohibitive range—then a tax rate reduction could theoretically raise revenue. A more important lesson of the Laffer Curve is that there are always two tax rates that will collect the same revenue—a high rate on a small base and a low rate on a large base.

A more important lesson of the Laffer Curve is that there are always two tax rates that will collect the same revenue—a high rate on a small base and a low rate on a large base.

Obviously, there are massive problems with translating a pedagogic device like the Laffer Curve into something that will predict the actual impact on revenues of any particular tax change. Whether something like the 1981 Reagan tax cut would raise revenue and over what period of time could only be answered by careful empirical analysis.

No such analysis was ever done. Every official document and statement ever released by the Reagan Administration made clear that the 1981 tax cut would lose large revenues. Moreover, its estimates were comparable to those of independent analysts such as the Congressional Budget Office.

In the words of Bill Niskanen, a member of the Council of Economic Advisers under President Reagan, "Supply-side economics.... does not conclude that a general reduction in tax rates would increase tax revenues, nor did any government economist or budget projection by the Reagan Administration ever make that claim."[4]

Nevertheless, the charge continues to be made that the American people were deluded into thinking that the 1981 tax cut would not increase the federal deficit. The rest of this paper tries to answer the question of what the supply-siders really thought about the effect of tax changes on revenues, what were their sources of information and inspiration, and whether their work was based on serious analysis or built on the quicksand of wishful thinking. I pay special attention to what was said during the period leading up to passage of the 1981 tax cut.

INTELLECTUAL ROOTS

It will come as a surprise to many people that the intellectual origins of supply-side economics can be traced to a fourteenth century Muslim philosopher named Ibn Khaldun. In his masterwork, *The Muqaddimah*, he wrote about the rise and fall of empires. He argued that high taxes were often a factor in causing empires to collapse, with the result that lower revenue was collected from high rates. As Khaldun wrote:

> It should be known that at the beginning of the dynasty, taxation yields a large revenue from small assessments. At the end of the dynasty, taxation yields a small revenue from large assessments.[5]

It may seem implausible that this ancient philosopher could have exercised any direct influence on 1970s American policymakers. However, there is a paper trail. In 1971, the *Journal of Political Economy* published an article about Khaldun by Jean David Boulakia, which quoted the passage above. Robert Mundell had been editor of the JPE until just before this article appeared and was responsible for accepting it for publication. On September 29, 1978, the *Wall Street Journal* published a long passage from *The Muqaddimah*. It was probably this excerpt that caught Ronald Reagan's eye. He referred to Khaldun by name during an October 1, 1981, press conference.[6]

Another unlikely influence was Jonathan Swift, the famous satirist and author of *Gulliver's Travels*. In a 1728 article, he noted the negative effect of high tariff rates on government revenue. His catchy phrase, "in the business of heavy impositions, two and two never make more than one," influenced many eighteenth century thinkers regarding the deleterious effect of tax rates on revenue, including David Hume, Adam Smith and Alexander Hamilton.[7]

These eighteenth century thinkers unquestionably were influential in the development of supply-side economics. Supply-siders often drew parallels between their views on tax cutting and those of the Founding Fathers.

Smith's work, in particular, was well known to all supply-siders, as well as to the Founding Fathers. The following quote from *The Wealth of Nations* is especially apt: "High taxes, sometimes by diminishing the consumption of the taxed commodities, and sometimes by encouraging smuggling, frequently afford a smaller revenue to the government than what might be drawn from more moderate taxes."[8]

The Founding Fathers also found inspiration in the work of political philosopher Montesquieu, who wrote in *The Spirit of the Laws* (1748): "Liberty produces excessive taxes; the effect of excessive taxes is slavery; and slavery produces a diminution of tribute."[9]

Another influence on supply-siders was nineteenth century economist Jean-Baptiste Say....As Say put it:

> The encouragement of mere consumption is no benefit to commerce; for the difficulty lies in supplying the means, not in stimulating the desire of consumption.... It is the aim of good government to stimulate production, of bad government to encourage consumption ....

[And] as [Say] wrote [further]:

> Taxation, pushed to the extreme, has the lamentable effect of impoverishing the individual, without enriching the state.... The diminution of demand must be followed by diminution of the supply of production; and, consequently, of the articles liable to taxation. Thus, the taxpayer is abridged of his enjoyments, the producer of his profits, and the public exchequer of its receipts.... This is the reason why a tax is not productive to the public exchequer, in proportion to its ratio; and why it has become a sort of apophthegm, that two and two do not make four in the arithmetic of finance. Excessive taxation...extinguishes both production and consumption, and the taxpayer into the bargain.[10]

Interestingly, one of the clearest statements of the Laffer Curve ever made was from the famous American statesman John C. Calhoun. While serving in the U.S. Senate in 1842, he made the following observation about the revenue effects of tariffs:

> On all articles on which duties can be imposed, there is a point in the rate of duties which may be called the maximum point of revenue—that is, a point at which the greatest amount of revenue would be raised. If it be elevated above that, the importation of the article would fall off more rapidly than the duty would be raised; and, if depressed below it, the reverse effect would follow: that is, the duty would decrease more rapidly than the importation would increase. If the duty be raised above that point, it is manifest that all the intermediate space between the maximum point and that to which it may be raised, would be purely protective, and not at all for revenue....[A]ny given amount of duty, other than the maximum, may be collected on any article, by two distinct rates of duty—the one above the maximum point, and the other below it.[11]

In the twentieth century, a number of economists wrote about the limits of taxation from the point of view of revenues. An early contribution was by Edwin Cannan, who posited a version of the Laffer Curve by pointing out that a 100 percent tax rate would raise zero revenue. In the 1930s, no less a personage than John Maynard Keynes argued that lower tax rates can sometimes increase government revenue. As he wrote in *The Means to Prosperity* (1933):

> Nor should the argument seem strange that taxation may be so high as to defeat its object, and that, given sufficient time to gather the fruits, a reduction of taxation will run a better chance than an increase of balancing the budget. For to take the opposite view today is to resemble a manufacturer who, running at a loss, decides to raise his price, and when his declining sales increase the loss, wrapping himself in the rectitude of plain arithmetic, decides that prudence requires him to raise the price still more—and who, when at last his account is balanced with nought on both sides, is still found righteously declaring that it would have been the act of a gambler to reduce price when you were already making a loss.[12]

During World War II, there was much discussion of the limits of taxation, focusing mainly on labor supply. In the postwar era, Colin Clark (1945) argued that excessive taxes become inflationary above 25 percent of GNP.[13] In *Human Action* (1949), Austrian economist Ludwig von Mises pointed out that high taxes can be self-defeating in terms of revenue:

> The true crux of the taxation issue is to be seen in the paradox that the more taxes increase, the more they undermine the market economy and concomitantly the system of taxation itself.... Every specific tax, as well as a nation's whole tax system, becomes self-defeating above a certain height of rates.[14]

In 1960, political scientist C. Northcote Parkinson, famous for his "law" about work expanding to fill the time for its completion, put forth a second law about expenditures rising to meet income. In *The Law and the Profits*, he suggested that there were diminishing returns once taxes reached 20 percent of national income.[15]

Contemporary academic economists also noted the disincentive effects of high tax rates on government revenue. For example, in a 1973 article, Richard B. McKenzie wrote:

> The main purpose of this paper is to demonstrate that not only may statutory and effective rates differ, but that it is distinctly possible on theoretical grounds that statutory rate increases may result in lower tax collections for some groups (i.e., lower effective rates). Furthermore, I submit that this perverse effect is most likely to occur among the rich, and it may even occur when work incentives are unaffected.[16]

In short, the ground was well plowed long before the first supply-sider showed up, making the case that excessive tax rates can lose government revenue and that, conversely, lower rates can, under certain conditions, raise revenue.

HISTORICAL ROOTS

It was not just theoretical discussions about lower tax rates raising revenues that influenced supply-side thinking. We were also aware of actual experience, most especially in the U.S. during the 1920s and 1960s. Herb Stein's *Fiscal Revolution in America* (1969) was an invaluable resource on the history of these episodes. Indeed, Jude Wanniski has said that Stein's discussion on pp. 9-10, regarding the belief by politicians in the 1920s that lower tax rates might raise revenue, was the first he ever heard of this idea. We were also aware of evidence at the state and local level and in foreign countries.

The federal income tax came into being permanently in 1913 with a top statutory rate of just 7 percent. However, due to the extraordinary revenue demands of World War I, tax rates were sharply increased. By war's end, the top rate had risen to 77 percent.

Although Republican presidents of the 1920s got most of the credit for reducing wartime tax rates, the initiative actually began in Democrat Woodrow Wilson's Administration. Indeed, in his 1919 State of the Union Address, President Wilson used supply-side arguments to urge tax rate reduction. As he said:

> The Congress might well consider whether the higher rates of income and profits taxes can in peace times be effectively productive of revenue, and whether they may not, on the contrary, be destructive of business activity and productive of waste and inefficiency. There is a point at which in peace times high rates of income and profits taxes discourage energy, remove the incentive to new enterprise, encourage extravagant expenditures and produce industrial stagnation with consequent unemployment and other attendant evils.[17]

Treasury Secretary Andrew Mellon, who served continuously through the administrations of Warren G. Harding, Calvin Coolidge and most of Herbert Hoover, spearheaded the tax reduction effort. By 1929, he managed to get the top statutory rate down to just 24 percent. In his book, *Taxation: The People's Business* (1924), Mellon made plain his belief that high tax rates on the wealthy lowered government revenue and that lower rates would raise revenue. As he put it:

> The history of taxation shows that taxes which are inherently excessive are not paid. The high rates inevitably put pressure upon the taxpayer to withdraw his capital from productive business and invest it in tax-exempt securities or to find other lawful methods of avoiding the realization of taxable income. The result is that the sources of taxation are drying up; wealth is failing to carry its share of the tax burden; and capital is being diverted into channels which yield neither revenue to the Government nor profit to the people.[18]

The evidence strongly indicates that the tax cuts of the 1920s did indeed raise revenue among those most affected by the rate reductions. Historian Benjamin Rader concluded, "Despite sharply reduced tax rates for upper income groups...the wealthy paid a larger share of the federal tax burden at the end of the decade than at the beginning." The latest study confirms this conclusion:

> Though the marginal tax rates were cut much more for the highest income taxpayers, the effective burden of taxation shifted away from the lower-income taxpayers toward the higher-income taxpayers. The resulting decline in tax avoidance, in conjunction with economic growth, led to some increase in personal income tax receipts despite the huge tax cuts from 1921 through 1926. Thus, the tax rate cuts worked much as Mellon and other early "supply-side" supporters had argued that they would.[19]

Of greater relevance to the supply-siders was the experience of the Kennedy tax cut. Jack Kemp was already drawing parallels to his early tax proposals, such as the business-oriented Jobs Creation Act, and Kennedy's when I joined his staff. Norman Ture was an important link to the Kennedy experience because he worked for Wilbur Mills, chairman of the House Ways and Means Committee, during the time of the Kennedy tax cut.[20]

The evidence strongly indicates that the tax cuts of the 1920s did indeed raise revenue among those most affected by the rate reductions.

In August 1976, Kemp received data from the Congressional Research Service on the estimated revenue loss from the Kennedy tax cut. By comparing these revenue loss figures with actual revenue increases from the 1960s, Kemp concluded that the Kennedy tax cut increased federal revenue.[21]

Kemp's point was more of an assertion than hard evidence, since he had no data on what aggregate revenues were expected to be in the absence of the Kennedy tax cut. Interestingly, however, Walter Heller, chairman of the Council of Economic Advisers under Kennedy, soon made the case for him. In testimony before the Joint Economic Committee on February 7, 1977, he was asked by Senator Jacob Javits (R-NY) to comment on Kemp's analysis of the CRS memo. I was in the hearing room when Heller gave this response:

> What happened to the tax cut in 1965 is difficult to pin down, but insofar as we are able to isolate it, it did seem to have a tremendously stimulative effect, a multiplied effect on the economy. It was the major factor that led to our running a $3 billion surplus by the middle of 1965, before escalation in Vietnam struck us. It was a $12 billion tax cut, which would be about $33 or $34 billion in today's terms. And within one year the revenues into the Federal Treasury were already above what they had been before the tax cut.... Did it pay for itself in increased revenues? I think the evidence is very strong that it did.[22]

Heller was later embarrassed to have provided the supply-siders with the proof they lacked and tried to take it back.[23] But as a witness to the event, there is no reason to think he was not stating a sincere belief. Indeed, a review of statements by Kennedy, his advisers and supporters at the time clearly indicates their expectation that the tax cut would in fact raise federal revenue. Kennedy said in his Economic Club of New York speech on December 14, 1962:

> It is a paradoxical truth that tax rates are too high today and revenues are too low, and the soundest way to raise the revenues in the long run is to cut the rates now.[24]

During floor debate on September 24, 1963, Wilbur Mills, manager of the Kennedy tax cut in the House of Representatives, said, "There is no doubt in my mind that this tax reduction bill, in and of itself, can bring about an increase in the gross national product of approximately $50 billion in the next few years. If it does, these lower rates of taxation will bring in at least $12 billion in additional revenue." Contemporary analyses by the Council of Economic Advisers,

Lawrence Klein, and Arthur Okun suggest that Mills was definitely in the ballpark with his estimate.[25]

Once the impact of the Kennedy tax cut became a political issue in the late 1970s, further analyses were undertaken. Data Resources, Inc., and Wharton Econometric Forecasting Associates were contracted to study the impact of the Kennedy tax cut. After reviewing these studies, the Congressional Budget Office drew the following conclusion:

> The effect of the 1964 tax cut on the federal deficit has been a matter of controversy.... The direct effect of the tax cut was to reduce revenues by some $12 billion (annual rate) after the initial buildup. The increase in output and later in prices produced by the tax cut, according to the models, recaptured $3 to $9 billion of this revenue at the end of two years. The result was a net increase in the federal deficit of only about 25 to 75 percent of the full $12 billion.[26]

Thus, while the Kennedy tax cut may not have paid for itself immediately, there is overwhelming evidence that the federal government did not lose nearly as much revenue as it expected, owing to the expansionary effect of the tax cut on the economy. Consequently, Ronald Reagan was really not too far off when he asserted that the Kennedy tax cut paid for itself.[27]

...while the Kennedy tax cut may not have paid for itself immediately, there is overwhelming evidence that the federal government did not lose nearly as much revenue as it expected, owing to the expansionary effect of the tax cut on the economy.

The real importance of the feedback argument has to do with how much additional federal borrowing is necessitated by tax cuts. If it leads to higher real interest rates, it is plausible to argue that they could offset much of the beneficial impact of tax cuts on growth. However, in this respect, it is also important to know whether a tax cut increased private saving. If saving expands, it is reasonable to include this in revenue feedback estimates.

In a 1981 article, Michael K. Evans argued that the Kennedy tax cut raised saving by more than the total amount of the tax cut. That is, households saved more than 100 percent of the tax cut. Therefore, one can conclude that the Kennedy tax cut did not put any upward pressure on interest rates due to an increase the federal budget deficit. Supply-siders often made this point with regard to the Reagan tax cut when questions were raised about its impact on federal borrowing and interest rates.[28]

The experience with taxes at the federal level was confirmed by that at the state and local level, where relatively easy opportunities for moving to other jurisdictions magnified the economic impact of tax changes. Ronald Grieson, for example, concluded that Philadelphia's income tax was so high that it was reducing city revenues below what lower rates would have brought in.[29]

It should be noted that supply-siders were well aware of the effects of tax reduction efforts in other countries, especially Germany and Japan, as well as the negative effects of high taxes in countries like Britain and Sweden. There is strong evidence that multiple tax reductions played a key role in the rapid recovery of Germany and Japan after the war, and that tax revenues rose steadily in both countries. There is also evidence that high taxes hampered growth in Britain and Sweden. Interestingly, when Britain cut tax rates after the election of Margaret Thatcher in 1979, there was a sharp increase in the share of taxes paid by the wealthy.[30]

KEYNESIAN BREAKDOWN

The rise of supply-side economics cannot be understood outside the intellectual climate of the time in which it originated. A critical factor was the breakdown of the Keynesian consensus. Since World War II, the economics profession and economic policymaking in Washington had been dominated by Keynesian theories, which viewed federal budget deficits as stimulative and monetary policy as largely irrelevant. Inflation was not considered a serious problem in the Keynesian model, because it could not arise as long as there was significant unused capacity.

Thus, the 1974–75 recession presented something of a crisis for the Keynesians. The federal budget deficit was huge, but appeared to have no stimulative effect. Inflation was shooting through the roof, but so was unemployment (i.e., unused capacity). Increasing the deficit to lower unemployment was not viable, nor was cutting the deficit to lower inflation. The Keynesians were, so to speak, "between a rock and a hard place." The result was that economic policy effectively was impotent.

By the late 1970s, it was common to hear policymakers complain that the Keynesian model offered them no way out of the problem of rising inflation and unemployment.

By the late 1970s, it was common to hear policymakers complain that the Keynesian model offered them no way out of the problem of rising inflation and unemployment. For years, they had been led to believe that there was a conceptually simple trade-off between the two—more of one would cure the other. All politicians had to do was figure out which way the political winds were blowing; tightening monetary and fiscal policy when inflation was the bigger political/economic problem, and loosening when unemployment rose to politically intolerable levels. This relationship was codified in the Phillips Curve [i.e., an inverse relationship between inflation and unemployment].

Although there are no references to anything like the Phillips Curve in Keynes' writings, since he was primarily concerned with deflation rather than inflation, it gradually became a central feature of Keynesian economics in the postwar era. Thus the obvious failure of the Phillips Curve became a deathblow to Keynesian economics. By 1976, even a Labour government in the land of his birth explicitly rejected Keynes as a useful guide to current economic problems. That year, British Prime Minister James Callaghan had this to say to his fellow Labourites:

> We used to think that you could just spend your way out of a recession and increase employment by cutting taxes and raising government spending. I tell you, in all candor, that that option no longer exists and that it

only worked on each occasion since the war by injecting bigger doses of inflation into the economy, followed by higher levels of unemployment, as the next step.[31]

In terms of economic theory, the monetarists, led by Milton Friedman, did the heavy lifting in discrediting the Keynesian model. When the 1976 Nobel Prize in economics was awarded to Friedman, in large part for his work attacking some of the central tenets of Keynesian economics, it was widely interpreted as a repudiation of Keynesian economics by the economics profession. Friedman used the opportunity of his Nobel lecture to pound nails into the coffin of the Phillips Curve.

The burgeoning Public Choice school also had a role in burying Keynes. In *Democracy in Deficit: The Political Legacy of Lord Keynes* (1977), James Buchanan and Richard Wagner accused Keynesians of responsibility for the vast postwar growth of government, by removing the stigma of budget deficits. Deficits, they argued, created a fiscal illusion, fooling voters into thinking they could get more from government at no additional cost in terms of taxes. In a review of their book, however, Roberts noted

> In terms of economic theory, the monetarists, led by Milton Friedman, did the heavy lifting in discrediting the Keynesian model.

that in the long-run deficits usually lead to higher taxes, which often erode the tax base and result in still larger deficits.[32]

The Rational Expectations school played a part as well in undermining the foundations of Keynesian economics. From the point of view of supply-siders, a key element of their critique related to econometric models. These models were often used to evaluate public policies and almost universally had Keynesian underpinnings. This tended to bias public policy in favor of Keynesian policies, even after they were generally discredited.

The most important area in which this mattered was for revenue estimating. This issue was especially a problem after enactment of the Budget Act of 1974, because no tax bill could even be considered in Congress unless there was provision for it in the annual budget resolution. This meant that Congress needed to know in advance the precise revenue loss expected from a tax cut before it could be voted upon. Although revenue estimates had been done for many years previously, they had never been an essential requirement for consideration of tax legislation.

Historically, revenue estimates for Congress have been done by the Joint Committee on Taxation, which has existed since the 1920s, although Treasury estimates were often used. These estimates were usually done by accountants for perhaps one or two years out. But by the 1970s, economists had replaced the accountants, and computers started to be used in lieu of adding machines. Moreover, the Budget Act required 5-year revenue estimates, which increased the need for economic forecasts upon which to base such estimates. The Congressional Budget Office was created to provide the macroeconomic forecasts upon which the JCT based its revenue estimates.

Thus CBO's estimate of the macroeconomic effect of tax changes became critically important in determining their net revenue impact. Such estimates were based upon commercial econometric models, such as those of Data Resources, Wharton and Chase Econometrics. However, as noted, these models were largely based on Keynesian assumptions. This tended to make the budgetary cost of tax cuts high relative to equivalent government spending programs, and biased the legislative process in favor of temporary tax cuts designed to stimulate consumption against supply-side tax cuts, such as marginal tax rate reductions.

An example of how this worked in practice can be seen in one of the CBO's earliest studies, which looked at various fiscal options for reducing unemployment. Because of the Keynesian underpinnings of the models used to evaluate these alternatives—spending drives growth in the Keynesian model, while saving is a drag on it—increased government spending appeared preferable to tax cuts. Direct spending created more jobs per $1 billion increase in the deficit than tax cuts, because all of the former was assumed to be spent while some of the latter was saved. In political terms, therefore, supply-side tax cuts were at a disadvantage compared with Keynesian-style public service jobs programs. Permanent tax rate reductions were also deemed more costly and less effective than temporary tax rebates.[33]

Paul Craig Roberts was among the first supply-siders to recognize that the breakdown of the Keynesian system and the creation of a new congressional budget process created an opportunity to promote the supply-side approach to fiscal policy. Given the constraints of the econometric models and the budget process, it suddenly became very important to be able to show that certain types of tax cuts did not increase the deficit as much as direct spending programs.[34]

Traditional tax-writers, such as Senator Russell Long (D-LA), chairman of the Senate Finance Committee, now found themselves at a disadvantage relative to the appropriators. The CBO gave spending programs the benefit of a Keynesian multiplier in calculating their economic effects. But tax cuts were calculated by the JCT on a static basis, as if they had no

Paul Craig Roberts was among the first supply-siders to recognize that the breakdown of the Keynesian system and the creation of a new congressional budget process created an opportunity to promote the supply-side approach to fiscal policy.

macroeconomic impact whatsoever. Long was no supply-sider, but he had been around a long time and seen a lot of tax changes and their effects at close hand. His experience told him that there was something to the supply-side argument that tax cuts would not lose as much revenue as static forecasts said they would. During a 1977 hearing, he had this to say:

> Revenue estimates have a way of being very, very far off base because of the failure to anticipate everything that happens.... Now, when we put the investment tax credit on, we estimated that we were going to lose about $5 billion.... Instead of losing money, revenues went up in corporate income tax collections. Then we thought it was overheating the economy. We repealed it. We thought that the government would take in more money. But instead of making $5 billion, we lost $5 billion. Then, after a while, we thought we made a mistake, so we put it back on again. Instead of losing us money, it made us money. Then, after a while, we repealed it again and it did just

exactly the opposite from what it was estimated to do again by about the same amount. It seems to me, if we take all factors into account, we wind up with the conclusion that taking the investment tax credit alone and looking at it by itself, it is not costing us any money. Because the impression I gain from it is that it stimulates the economy to the extent, and brings about additional investment to the extent, that it makes us money rather than loses us money.[35]

Long responded by commissioning Michael K. Evans, an experienced econometric modeler, to build a supply-side model for the Senate Finance Committee....

CAPITAL GAINS AND THE TAX REVOLT

In the midst of these developments, an important legislative fight took place that highlighted both the weakness of the Keynesian approach to fiscal policy and the failure of standard revenue-estimating methods to account for the supply-side effects of tax changes. It involved a cut in the long-term capital gains tax rate. Almost simultaneously, a huge political battle arose in California over Proposition 13, a voter initiative to cut property taxes. Its successful enactment on June 6, 1978, overwhelmingly demonstrated the potency of the so-called tax revolt, which dramatically altered the political dynamics for tax legislation in Washington.

The roots of the capital gains controversy dated back to 1969, when the maximum long-term tax rate was increased from 25 percent to 35 percent. On April 13, 1978, Congressman William Steiger (R-WI) introduced legislation to reduce the top rate back to 25 percent. The ensuing debate was extremely important to the development of supply-side economics for two reasons. First, a number of respected economists, such as Martin Feldstein, argued vigorously that a cut in the capital gains tax rate would almost immediately recoup the static revenue loss through a combination of unlocking and increased investment.

Second, the obvious expansionary potential of a capital gains tax cut clearly illustrated the supply-side argument that tax rate cuts could be stimulative, by increasing incentives, without any Keynesian impact on disposable income. Thus the 1978 capital gains debate was seminal in the development and acceptance of supply-side theories by mainstream economists.

Of course, the idea that cutting the capital gains tax might not reduce federal revenue was not a new one. Harley Hinrichs had concluded that "investors' elasticity to capital gains rate changes may exceed unity, thus allowing rate cuts without impairing Treasury revenues." Also, it had been long recognized that capital gains are a unique form of income, because taxpayers have the freedom to decide when and whether to realize gains for tax purposes. When rates are high they encourage a lock-in effect that reduces revenues, as investors hold on to potentially taxable gains. Therefore, a rate reduction may result in a rapid unlocking effect that could cause revenue to rise quickly.[36]

[Prop. 13's] successful enactment on June 6, 1978, overwhelmingly demonstrated the potency of the so-called tax revolt, which dramatically altered the political dynamics for tax legislation in Washington.

Feldstein was outspoken in his conviction that the Steiger bill would actually increase federal revenue almost immediately, and testified before Congress to that effect. The basis of his testimony was a paper that circulated on Capitol Hill as a National Bureau of Economic Research working paper in June 1978.[37]

In the midst of the capital gains debate, an equally important political debate was taking place in California that also had important implications for supply-side economics. It showed there was real political power behind the idea of cutting taxes, and that it was not just an "inside the beltway" issue. Proposition 13 also helped unite the supply-siders with more traditional elements of the Republican Party on fiscal policy.

In the 1950s and 1960s, the roles of the major parties switched on taxes. Under Dwight Eisenhower, the Republican Party, which had been the tax cutting party from the 1920s through the 1940s, became the party of "fiscal responsibility." The balanced budget became the sine qua non of Republican fiscal policy. At the same time, under John F. Kennedy, the Democratic Party, which had been the party of high taxes, became the spearhead for tax rate reductions.

Republicans in Congress mostly opposed the Kennedy tax cut. Republican President Richard Nixon raised taxes to balance the budget in 1969, and Republican President Gerald Ford torpedoed every effort to cut tax rates on his watch because it would increase the deficit. Even Ronald Reagan raised taxes as Governor of California in order to balance the budget. It was only due to the defeat of Ford in 1976 and massive Republican losses in Congress in 1974 and 1976 that the party once again became receptive to tax cutting.

Still, there was resistance among both Republican politicians and conservative economists to cutting taxes without simultaneously cutting spending. It was often said that the "true" burden of government is what it spends, not what it taxes. Hence, tax cuts without spending cuts do nothing to reduce the burden of government and thus cannot be expected to have any stimulative effect, in the view of conservatives. Supply-siders also saw spending as burdensome, but believed that the excess burden of taxation—the output that is discouraged over and above the tax take—was greatly underestimated in the conservative fiscal model.

Proposition 13 showed dramatically that voters instinctively believed that cutting taxes unilaterally was an effective way of cutting government waste.

Geoffrey Brennan and James Buchanan addressed the spending problem by arguing that the political dynamics in a democracy make it extremely difficult, if not impossible, to cut spending without tax cuts. Tax increases simply fueled additional spending, while tax cuts put pressure on legislatures to cut spending. Therefore, the best way to limit the size of government is by denying it revenue to spend.[38]

Proposition 13 showed dramatically that voters instinctively believed that cutting taxes unilaterally was an effective way of cutting government waste. Subsequent analysis shows that they were largely correct. Proposition 13 led to no significant reduction in vital government services, contrary to predictions of its opponents, but did limit spending growth. Indeed, Proposition 13 did almost nothing to reduce the size of government in California.[39]

After Proposition 13, there was a noticeable change in tone among previous Republican critics of big federal tax cuts. They began trying to rationalize tax cuts within a traditional fiscal responsibility framework. Herb Stein, for example, explicitly rejected any significant growth effects from tax rate reductions, but supported them anyway because taxes were too high and politicians were unresponsive to voter concerns about continually rising taxes and spending. Conservative columnist George Will, citing Alan Greenspan, made much the same point. Irving Kristol explained the changing attitude among conservatives this way:

> They have learned the lesson of Proposition 13, which is that tax cuts are a prerequisite for cuts in government spending. The politics of the budgetary process is such that a cut in any particular program will provoke intense opposition from a minority, and only indifference from the majority. In such a case, it is unreasonable to expect politicians to pay the high political costs involved. They can only cut when they are seen to have no alternative.[40]

Milton Friedman made the point succinctly in one of his *Newsweek* columns. "I have concluded that the only effective way to restrain government spending is by limiting government's explicit tax revenue—just as a limited income is the only effective restraint on any individual's or family's spending."[41]

The point is that the supply-siders were not just counting on revenue reflows to avoid the growth of budget deficits if their proposed tax cuts were enacted into law. They were well aware that tax cuts would set in motion political forces leading to spending cuts. They did not set forth their own proposals for such cuts because they understood that their critics would focus on them to the exclusion of all else. Instead, they adopted the Proposition 13 model of putting the burden on those who were concerned about deficits to find ways of reducing expenditures.

In short, contrary to the Moynihan/Stockman view, the idea that supply-siders thought spending cuts were unnecessary for budget balance is untrue. They just thought balancing the budget was not an especially important goal, although limiting the size of government was. However, spending would only be cut if taxes were cut first. Ronald Reagan made the point explicitly in a nationally televised address early in his presidency:

> There were always those who told us that taxes couldn't be cut until spending was reduced. Well, you know, we can lecture our children about extravagance until we run out of voice and breath. Or we can cure their extravagance by simply reducing their allowance.[42]

Academic research suggests that the Reagan approach was the right one. Alesina et al. report that direct taxes are often cut during successful fiscal adjustment programs. Becker, Lazear and Murphy argue that to the extent tax cuts force spending cuts, their positive economic impact is multiplied. Moreover, tax increases seldom improve fiscal balances. This is consistent with research showing that higher taxes generally lead to higher spending, rather than deficit reduction.[43]

MUNDELL, LAFFER, AND THE JEC

Certainly the two best-known academic economists involved in the origins of supply-side economics were Robert Mundell, winner of the 1999 Nobel Prize in economics for his work on international economics, and Arthur Laffer, famed as originator of the "Laffer Curve." In the critical developmental stage of supply-side economics, the Joint Economic Committee of Congress became a powerful institutional supporter.

Both Laffer and Mundell came to supply-side economics primarily through their interest in international monetary policy. They, like all economists from the 1970s, were deeply concerned about the problem of "stagflation"—rising inflation and slow growth. Laffer and Mundell, however, saw the roots of stagflation as arising from final abandonment of the gold standard in 1971. In their view, once the gold link to the dollar was broken, there was no longer any effective brake on government's ability to inflate at will.

Inflation then interacted with the tax system to sharply raise marginal tax rates. Workers receiving pay increases were pushed up into higher tax brackets, even though they might not have received any real increase in purchasing power; corporations found that depreciation allowances based on historical cost were inadequate to replace old equipment, while taxes were assessed on illusory inventory profits; and investors found that much of their capital gains simply represented inflation, but were taxed as if they were real.

Therefore, a two-prong strategy was needed to end stagflation, Laffer and Mundell said. First, money growth needed to be sharply tightened, preferably by targeting the price of gold and reestablishing a de facto gold standard. Second, tax rates needed to be cut in order to restore incentives and increase the demand for money. Mundell first spelled out this tight-money-and-tax-cuts policy mix in a 1971 paper published by Princeton's International Finance Section:

> Monetary expansion stimulates nominal money demand for goods, but, without rigidities or illusions to bite on, it does not lead to real expansion. But growth of real output raises real money demand and thus abets the absorption of real monetary expansion into the economy without inflation. Tax reduction increases employment and growth and this raises the demand for money and hence enables the Federal Reserve to supply additional real money balances to the economy without causing sagging interest rates associated with conditions of loose money. Monetary acceleration is inflationary, but tax reduction is expansionary when there is unemployment.[44]

At this time, Mundell was at the University of Chicago, where Laffer was teaching in the business school. Their mutual interest in international monetary issues brought them together and Laffer absorbed Mundell's ideas. In 1974, Laffer organized a conference sponsored by the American Enterprise Institute on the problem of worldwide inflation. This was the first opportunity many Washington policymakers had to hear about what came to be called supply-side economics.[45]

Although most of the AEI conference dealt with monetary issues, Mundell reiterated the point made in his 1971 paper about the vital role of tax cuts in the fight against inflation. This was important because the Keynesian view that fiscal deficits caused inflation was widespread. Indeed, it is not now remembered, but when Reagan, Kemp and others first began pushing for big tax cuts in the late 1970s, the principal attack against them was that such a policy would be massively inflationary.[46]

Among those in attendance at the AEI conference was Jude Wanniski, then an editorial writer for the *Wall Street Journal*. He was fascinated by the discussion and immediately wrote an article for the *Journal* explaining the Laffer-Mundell worldview. He later expanded the analysis in an article for *The Public Interest*. Interestingly, his discussion of the tax side of their work only appeared in a footnote, which was the first place Laffer explained his famous curve in print....[47]

In 1974, Laffer organized a conference sponsored by the American Enterprise Institute on the problem of worldwide inflation. This was the first opportunity many Washington policymakers had to hear about what came to be called supply-side economics.

Wanniski later went on to write the first book about supply-side economics, *The Way the World Works* (1978). He also wrote many unsigned editorials for the *Wall Street Journal* spelling out various aspects of supply-side theory. And he helped many supply-siders, such as Arthur Laffer and Paul Craig Roberts, get published in the *Journal*, thereby raising their visibility and stature as economic commentators. Indeed, when Wanniski left the *Journal* in 1978 to found a private consulting firm, Roberts was hired by the *Journal* to replace him on the editorial page staff.

Adding important institutional support to the growth of supply-side economics at this time was the Joint Economic Committee of Congress, under the leadership of its chairman, Senator Lloyd Bentsen (D-TX). The JEC was created by the Employment Act of 1946 as the congressional counterpart to the Council of Economic Advisers. The great economist Paul Douglas, famous for the Cobb-Douglas production function, was among the committee's previous chairmen. Other well-known economists, such as DRI founder Otto Eckstein, had served on its staff.[48]

In the 1960s, the JEC had been known as a hotbed of Keynesian economics. So the intellectual collapse of that school hit the committee hard. This led to much soul-searching on the part of both its members and staff. By the late 1970s, the JEC was ready to make a complete break. In a number of hearings and staff studies, the JEC began placing increasing emphasis on the role of supply in the economy, concluding that inadequate incentives for saving and investment lay behind the national economic malaise.

By 1980, the JEC was a full-blown advocate of supply-side economics, despite having a majority of liberal Democrats, such as Senators Edward Kennedy (D-MA) and George McGovern (D-SD). Its annual report that year was entitled, "Plugging in the Supply Side." Chairman Bentsen summarized the committee's new view in his introduction:

> The 1980 annual report signals the start of a new era of economic thinking. The past has been dominated by economists who focused almost exclusively on the demand side of the economy and who, as a result, were trapped into believing that there is an inevitable trade-off between unemployment and inflation.... The Committee's 1980 report says that steady economic growth, created by productivity gains and accompanied by a stable fiscal policy and a gradual reduction in the growth of the money supply over a period of years, can reduce inflation significantly during the 1980s without increasing unemployment. To achieve this goal, the Committee recommends a comprehensive set of policies designed to enhance the productive side, the supply side of the economy....[49]

The JEC's conversion to supply-side economics was extremely important in adding respectability and bipartisanship to the idea. For example, it led Leonard Silk, economics columnist for the *New York Times*, to write sympathetically about the new philosophy:

> A major change is on the way in economic theory and policy; that change will involve a deeper integration of

supply-side and demand-side economics, and an integration of thinking about both the long and short run. The change is long overdue.[50]

Even after Ronald Reagan had taken office and liberal Congressman Henry Reuss (D-WI) replaced the more conservative Bentsen as chairman of the JEC, it remained skeptical of old-fashioned Keynesianism. Said Reuss in 1981, "We have learned from our mistakes in the past. We've given up blind pursuit of Keynesian demand acceleration." Supply-side economics was important in depriving demand-side economics of "an undeserved primacy," he added.[51]

KEMP-ROTH

It was in this atmosphere that Congressman Kemp and Senator William Roth (R-DE) introduced the legislation that defined supply-side economics. It grew out of a desire by Kemp to duplicate the Kennedy tax cut by having a pure, across the board individual income tax rate reduction, without the many corporate provisions that had been the central features of his earlier tax efforts.

Work on the legislation began in early 1977. It was my job to figure out exactly what it meant to "duplicate" the Kennedy tax cut, given that the rate structure had changed dramatically in the years since 1964, when the Kennedy tax cut was rammed through Congress by Lyndon Johnson. Working together with Bruce Thompson from Roth's office, Pete Davis of the Joint Committee on Taxation and the rest of the group, we eventually decided to reduce the top statutory rate from 70 percent to 50 percent and the bottom rate from 14 percent to 10 percent. We felt that this was roughly comparable to Kennedy's reduction in the top rate from 91 percent to 70 percent and the bottom rate from 20 percent to 14 percent.

It took about a year before the Kemp-Roth proposal began to get widespread attention. Interestingly, the idea that it would stimulate growth enough to pay back some of the static revenue loss was not especially controversial at first. Indeed, Bert Lance, Jimmy Carter's Office of Management and Budget Director, had testified shortly before Kemp-Roth was introduced to that effect:

My personal observation is that as you go through the process of permanent tax reduction, that there is an awfully good argument to be made for the fact that the revenues of the Government actually increase at a given time. I think it has been proven in previous circumstances. I have no problem in following that sort of thing.[52]

When the Congressional Budget Office reviewed the Kemp-Roth legislation, it estimated that feedback effects would recoup between 14 percent and 19 percent of the static revenue loss the first year, rising to between 26 percent and 38 percent in the fourth.[53]

This is consistent with what the supply-siders themselves thought would happen. Contrary to popular belief, none of them ever said that there would be no revenue loss at all. Clearly, there would be large revenue losses in the short-run. But they thought the net revenue loss would be much less than the static estimates predicted.

Although supply-siders certainly thought there would be increases in economic growth, increased investment and labor supply from marginal tax rate cuts, this was not by any means the only way they expected revenues to be recouped. They anticipated many changes in behavior that would have the effect of increasing taxable income.

Among the most important areas where expansion of the tax base was anticipated was from a shrinkage of the so-called underground economy.

...supply-side economics...grew out of a desire by Kemp to duplicate the Kennedy tax cut by having a pure, across the board individual income tax rate reduction, without the many corporate provisions that had been the central features of his earlier tax efforts.

I vividly remember reading Peter Gutmann's pathbreaking 1977 article, which estimated that the underground economy equaled about 10 percent of recorded GNP. Although not motivated solely by tax evasion, high tax rates unquestionably contributed heavily to its growth. Hence, tax rate reduction would cause some underground economic activity to move above ground, so to speak, and become taxable.[54]

Supply-siders further anticipated that workers would alter their compensation so as to increase the taxable portion of their wages. In particular, tax-free fringe benefits would be somewhat less attractive relative to cash wages. There is considerable evidence that rising tax rates in the 1970s were behind much of the growth in fringe benefits such as health insurance.[55]

Investors were also expected to alter their portfolios in ways that would raise taxable income. For example, with lower rates, the value of tax losses and other deductions, such as for Individual Retirement Accounts, would no longer be as valuable. Home ownership, with its many tax advantages, would no longer be as appealing relative to renting. And taxable dividends and interest would become more attractive compared with more lightly taxed capital gains and tax-free municipal bonds. All of these factors were expected to have a powerful effect on raising taxable income even in the absence of any growth effects from lower tax rates.

Finally, supply-siders believed that spending would fall automatically to some extent if expansionary tax cuts were enacted. They saw much government spending for such things as unemployment compensation and welfare as costs of slow growth that would be much smaller as employment rose. Hence, the impact on the deficit from something like Kemp-Roth would include both the revenue reflows and the automatic reduction in spending for cyclical spending programs. That is why Laffer always emphasized the impact of Kemp-Roth on the deficit and not just on revenues. In his first formal statement on Kemp-Roth in 1978, he said:

> Kemp-Roth would partially redress the counterproductive structure of current tax rates leading to a substantial increase in output, and may well, in the course of a very few years, reduce the size of total government deficits from what they otherwise would have been.[56]

Laffer also always talked about the effect of revenue reflows on all levels of government, including state and local governments. This was a valid point because state and local governments tend to run budget surpluses in the aggregate. Hence, higher revenues in that sector would add to national saving. In 1978 testimony, Laffer had this to say along these lines:

> As I look at the Roth-Kemp bill, it cuts tax rates across the board over three years by approximately 30 percent.... On the federal level, there is quite a reasonable chance that within a very short period of time, a year or two or three, that not only will the cut in taxes cause more work, output and employment, but the incomes, profits, and taxes, because of the expansion of the tax base, would actually increase. It is very clear to me that a cut in these tax rates, along the lines you suggested, sir, would increase state and local revenues substantially. There is no ambiguity there. Any increase in incomes, productivity and production will increase state and local revenues substantially. If you take the government as a whole, it is likely that revenues will increase.[57]

Laffer pulled these various points together in a 1979 academic paper, in which he included higher federal revenues, higher state and local government revenues, lower government spending, and higher private saving in the reflows expected from tax rate reductions. As he wrote:

> The relevant question is not whether revenues actually rise or not but whether a change in tax rates is "self-financing." Therefore, one should focus not only on the specific receipts for which the rates have been changed but also on other receipts, on spending, and on savings. Other receipts must rise if a rate is reduced. The expansion of activity will elicit a greater base upon which all other unchanged rates will obtain greater revenue. Government spending at all levels will fall because of lowered unemployment, reduced poverty, and thus less welfare. Likewise, government employees will require less in real wages because with lower tax rates the same real wages will yield greater after tax wages, and so on.

Finally, a cut in tax rates will yield greater savings in order to finance any deficit. Using a broader interpretation these tax rates and revenue positions should refer basically to the self-financing nature of tax rate changes.[58]

Laffer never made a precise estimate of the economic or revenue impact of the Kemp-Roth bill or the Reagan tax cut in 1981. The closest he ever came to saying that the Reagan tax cut would be self-financing was in a 1981 academic paper, where he said:

It is reasonable to conclude that each of the proposed 10 percent reductions in tax rates would, in terms of overall revenues, be self-financing in less than two years. Thereafter, each installment would provide a positive contribution to overall tax receipts. By the third year of the tax reduction program, it is likely that net revenue gains from the plan's first installment would offset completely the revenue reductions attributable to the final 10 percent tax rate cut. It should be noted that a significant portion of these revenues would accrue to state and local governments, relieving much if not all of the fiscal stress evident in these governmental units as well.[59]

These vague statements about relatively fast reflows from across the board tax rate reductions, however, contrast with more detailed estimates done by Norman Ture and Michael Evans that explicitly included supply-side effects. Ture's estimate of Kemp-Roth in 1978 saw substantial revenue losses, net of feedback, even ten years after enactment, when revenues would still be $53 billion (in 1977 dollars) below baseline. Evans' figures were very similar, showing a current dollar increase in the deficit in 1987 of $61 billion.[60]

Interestingly, among the strongest supporters of Kemp-Roth in Congress was then-Congressman David Stockman (R-MI). Later, after serving as director of the Office of Management and Budget, he broke with the supply-siders and became obsessed with budget deficits. But in the 1970s, he would often speak on the House floor and in committee in favor of passing an across-the-board tax rate reduction and against tax increases for the purpose of reducing budget deficits. For example, on March 1, 1978, he said:

> A tax increase to achieve budget balance would be even less appropriate. Such a move would "crowd-out" output just as surely as more pump priming will "crowd-out" investment. Mr. Speaker, these considerations make clear that the time is ripe for implementing the only new fiscal policy idea that has been proposed in decades: A deliberate across-the-board reduction in marginal tax rates for the purpose of reducing the burden of government on the productive sectors of the economy.[61]

In testimony before the Senate Finance Committee on July 14, 1978, Congressman Stockman explicitly refuted the charge that Kemp-Roth would lead to large deficits and inflation:

> These charges are based on a total misunderstanding of what Kemp-Roth is all about. We are not merely advocating a simple tax cut, an election-year gimmick. Instead, we view this measure as just one policy step in a whole, new fiscal policy program based on the supply side of the economy; based on the idea of getting more labor, capital, innovation, risk-taking and productivity into the economy by removing government barriers and deterrents, the most important of which, I would suggest to the committee today, is the rapidly rising marginal tax rates that Congressman Kemp has just discussed.... I would like to suggest to the committee that if this proposal that we are making is properly looked at, that these scare stories about these horrendous fiscal results, the deficits, cannot be validated at all. If you understand that we are substituting tax cuts and an incentive, supply-side approach for pump priming and

demand stimulus, it can clearly be done with a large surplus produced within less than four years.[62]

There were many other occasions as well where Stockman defended unilateral tax cuts. Having worked with him closely at the time, I never heard the slightest concern from him that the basic supply-side message was not sound. And this was long before there was even the remotest prospect of Ronald Reagan being elected, or of Stockman becoming his OMB director. In fact, it is worth remembering that Stockman actually supported John Connally during the primaries, endorsing Reagan only after Connally dropped out of the presidential race. Therefore, one can conclude that he was not merely posturing about tax cuts in hopes of getting a cabinet appointment.

REAGAN AND AFTER

In 1980, Ronald Reagan essentially adopted the Kemp-Roth bill as his principal campaign economic issue. After taking office, one of his first actions was to send a proposal to Congress on February 17, 1981, requesting passage of a tax cut closely modeled on Kemp-Roth. It showed a loss in revenue of $53.9 billion the first year, rising to $221.7 billion by 1986. No revenue feedback was assumed.[63]

Interestingly, old-time Keynesian economists were more optimistic about the potential revenue reflows of the Reagan tax cut than was the White House. For example, Richard Musgrave of Harvard, dean of America's public finance economists, testified before the Joint Economic Committee in early 1981 that the Reagan plan would likely recoup 18 percent of the static revenue loss through increased demand and another 30 percent to 35 percent through increased supply.[64] Gardner Ackley, chairman of the CEA under Lyndon Johnson, compared Reagan's plan favorably to Kennedy's:

> I think the response to the proposed Reagan tax cuts would be similar to that of the Kennedy tax cuts. I think, yes, in a general way, taking the tax cut part by itself, independently of everything else. I think we would find a response of aggregate demand very substantially

to a tax cut, and this would tend, as it did following 1963, to stimulate additional production and employment and investment. It would do so again today. The results of that would be beneficial.[65]

Laffer testified that he thought it would take ten years before the Reagan tax cut would pay for itself, a view he said was consistent with what he had said about Kemp-Roth. Interestingly, Joseph A. Pechman of the Brookings Institution was largely in agreement with Laffer's assessment. Speaking at the same congressional hearing, he said:

> I was pleased to hear that Arthur Laffer did not exaggerate some of the things that have been attributed to the supply-side economists. What he told us was that, if you reduce taxes or increase the net return to saving and to labor, there will be an increase in the incentives to work and to save. I think every economist, regardless of his persuasion, would agree with that.[66]

Again, David Stockman spoke forcefully about the need for tax rate reduction to accompany budget control. Because of bracket creep and still-high inflation rates, future revenue projections always tended to show budget balance within reach a few years out. But spending always increased by a greater amount. Hence tax reduction was essential to holding down the growth of spending, which was the Reagan Administration's goal, not budget balance. As Stockman told the Senate Finance Committee at his confirmation hearing:

> Mr. Chairman, it is my very strongly held belief that if we fail to cut taxes then we have no hope, over the next three or four years of bringing the budget into balance, and of closing this enormous deficit that we face again this year. Of course, there are those who will show you a paper projection, a computer run, and will try to demonstrate that if we can keep the rate of inflation high and allow the tax rates on businesses and individuals to continue to creep up, we will then

automatically, by fiscal year 1983 or 1984, have a balanced budget. But that is pure mythology. That is only a computer projection. That is only a paper exercise that would never come true in the real world. We have had those forecasts made every year for the last four or five, but as we have moved down the path toward the target year, these balanced budgets have seemed to disappear like the morning haze. There are reasons for that. The primary reason is that the tax burden today is so debilitating that it prevents the economy from growing, and without a growing economy we simply cannot hope to achieve a balanced budget.[67]

Even long after he had broken with the Reagan Administration over the problem of budget deficits, Stockman conceded that the tax cut was not really the cause of deficits, because all it did was offset tax increases that would have resulted automatically from inflation. In his 1986 book, *The Triumph of Politics*, Stockman wrote:

The Carter revenue estimates assumed the greatest sustained period of income tax bracket creep in U.S. history. But when you started with an inflation-and-bracket-creep-swollen revenue level and trotted it out four or five years into the future, fiscal miracles were easy.

With high inflation, the Reagan program amounted to little more than indexing the fiscal status quo; the Kemp-Roth tax cut simply offset bracket creep.

In fact, a number of analysts pointed out that the Reagan tax cut was not big enough to fully offset bracket-creep. The *New York Times* even attacked it for this very reason. Subsequent analysis confirms that the Reagan tax cut did little more than effectively index the tax system, keeping aggregate revenues from rising as a share of income.[68]

With the emergence of large budget deficits after passage of the Reagan tax cut in 1981, the issue of its supply-side effects was answered in the minds of many. The simple cause-and-effect relationship seemed obvious: a tax cut is enacted and deficits emerge. Therefore, the tax cut caused the deficits.

Lawrence Lindsey was the first to calculate the effect of the Reagan tax cut on revenues after the fact, taking into account the economy's actual performance, as opposed to projections based on forecasts and assumptions. His initial effort concluded that on net the tax cut induced reflows of about 25 percent of the static revenue loss through behavioral effects. An estimate by some CBO economists came to similar conclusions. Lindsey's final calculation was that reflows paid for about a third of the direct cost of the tax cut, including both Keynesian demand-side effects and supply-side effects. In his words:

... tax reduction was essential to holding down the growth of spending, which was the Reagan Administration's goal, not budget balance.

> So who was right about the effect of tax changes on the economy, the Keynesians or the supply-siders? The answer is both, at least in part. The Keynesians were right in claiming that such a substantial reduction in rates would powerfully boost demand, a point the supply-siders never denied but perhaps underestimated. The demand-side revenue feedbacks and the combined behavioral feedbacks (supply-side and pecuniary) turned out to be roughly equal. On the other hand, the revenue results vindicate the supply-siders' most important claim: The tax cut produced quite large changes in taxpayer behavior. That claim, strongly confirmed by results, ran directly counter to Keynesian theory and most Keynesian predictions. The combined supply-side and pecuniary effects recouped well over one-third of ERTA's estimated direct cost, a very powerful response.[69]

Feldstein came to a similar conclusion: "The evidence suggests that the reduction in tax rates did have a favorable effect on work incentives and on real GNP, and that the resulting loss of tax revenue was significantly less than the traditional revenue estimates would imply."[70]

So if the tax cut was too small to fully offset bracket creep and feedback effects recouped much of the static revenue loss, then where did the huge budget deficits come from? Obviously, a lot came from higher spending on defense and other programs. But Paul Craig Roberts argues that most of it came, ironically, from the enormously greater success against inflation than anyone thought was possible.[71]

Remember, the conventional wisdom said that even without additional demand stimulus in the form of a tax cut, it would take many years to get inflation down from its double-digit level in 1980 to the low single digits. Indeed, a simple Okun's Law calculation would have suggested the need for something like another Great Depression to bring inflation down to tolerable levels.[72]

Since taxes are assessed on nominal incomes, not real incomes, the fall of inflation from 12.5 percent in 1980 to about 4 percent in 1982 and throughout the 1980s simply collapsed the expected tax base. In essence, the Reagan Administration was counting on inflation coming down fairly slowly—even though it was frequently attacked for being far too optimistic on this score—which would increase revenues from bracket creep even as tax rates were cut. When inflation came down far faster than anyone inside or outside the administration thought possible, revenues inevitably came in far lower than expected as well.[73]

Lindsey's final calculation was that reflows paid for about a third of the direct cost of the tax cut, including both Keynesian demand-side effects and supply-side effects.

To put this effect into perspective, the Carter Administration's last budget forecast 12.6 percent inflation in 1981 and 9.6 percent in 1982. It further estimated that each one-percentage point decline of inflation below forecast would reduce revenues by $11 billion. With actual inflation (CPI) coming in at 8.9 percent in 1981 and 3.8 percent in 1982, this suggests that lower than expected inflation alone added $41 billion to the deficit in 1981 and $64 billion in 1982. That is equal to half the deficit in those years.[74]

It has been argued that budget deficits offset all of the stimulative effect of the 1981 tax cut. This extreme view, however, isn't shared by most economists. Even many of Ronald Reagan's political opponents concede that bringing down inflation so rapidly, at far less economic cost than was previously imaginable, was a remarkable accomplishment. Moreover, the rebound of growth and productivity in the 1980s, after the malaise of the 1970s, was at least in part due to the stimulative effect of the tax cut.[75]

When inflation came down far faster than anyone inside or outside the administration thought possible, revenues inevitably came in far lower than expected as well.

In 1989, Paul Samuelson admitted, "The latter half of the 1980s, historians will recognize, has been an economic success story." Even Bill Clinton's Council of Economic Advisers conceded that the 1981 tax cut had been a major factor in stimulating growth. "It is undeniable that the sharp reduction in taxes in the early 1980s was a strong impetus to economic growth," it said in the 1994 *Economic Report of the President*.[76]

CONCLUSION

One of the main reasons why so little is heard about supply-side economics anymore is because so much of what the supply-siders were trying to accomplish was achieved. That is, many of the supply-side propositions that were highly controversial when first made in the 1970s, are now accepted as conventional wisdom among professional economists. For example:

- A vast number of studies now conclusively show that taxes and the size of government are critical determinants of economic growth. Although elasticities vary, almost all studies show that higher taxes and bigger government reduce growth.

- The welfare cost of the U.S. tax system is now generally considered to be very high. In the 1970s, this simply was not a matter economists gave much thought to.

- The economic cost of tax progressivity is now considered to be far higher than previously thought, encouraging efforts to institute a flat rate income tax system.

- The Laffer Curve is a frequent topic of discussion in academic journals. Although most articles are critical, the fact that the idea is taken seriously shows a significant change in the intellectual climate over the last twenty-five years.

- It used to be said commonly that labor supply was insensitive to changes in tax rates. Today, it is generally conceded that labor supply is much more responsive than previously believed.

- International organizations, such as the World Bank and International Monetary Fund, now often find tariff rates in developing countries to be in the prohibitive range. That is, tariff rate reductions are estimated to raise revenue. Similar views are expressed with regard to taxes as well.

- Even critics of supply-side economics concede that tax cuts may produce substantial revenue reflows, lowering their net cost, and that tax increases may produce negative reflows, increasing their net cost. Some liberals now label their own policies as "supply-side."[77]

Perhaps the best evidence that supply-side economics has entered the mainstream is Robert Mundell's Nobel Prize. Although his Nobel citation does not mention any of his relevant work in this area, it would be naive to think that the Nobel Committee was unaware of it, since Mundell was often referred to as a supply-side "guru" in the popular press. It is also well known that the committee thoroughly researches all aspects of a candidate's life and work before making an award. Therefore, it is reasonable to assume that the committee was well aware that giving Mundell the Nobel Prize would recognize his work in supply-side economics.

Supply-siders can also claim a piece of 1995 Nobel Prize winner Robert Lucas. In a neglected 1990 paper, he virtually declared himself to be a born-again supply-sider:

I have called this paper an analytical review of "supply-side economics," a term associated in the United States with extravagant claims about the effects of changes in the tax structure on capital accumulation. In a sense, the analysis I have reviewed here supports these claims: Under what I view as conservative assumptions, I estimated that eliminating capital income taxation would increase capital stock by about 35 percent.... The supply-side economists, if that is the right term for those whose research I have been discussing, have delivered the largest genuinely free lunch I have seen in twenty-five years in this business, and I believe we would have a better society if we followed their advice.[78]

For myself, I have always found Joseph A. Pechman's presidential address to the American Economic Association in 1989 to be a profound admission of how far supply-side economics had joined the mainstream. Pechman virtually defined the mainstream on the economics of taxation for a generation of economists. In innumerable books and papers, he argued forcefully for a highly progressive tax system on a Haig-Simons income base. So it must have been painful for him to make the following concession:

> The federal income tax has been under attack by the economics profession for more than a decade. The attack comes from two directions: supply-siders who believe that progressive income taxation impairs economic incentives, and more traditional economists who would substitute a progressive expenditure tax for the income tax.... Today, it is fair to say that many, if not most, economists favor the expenditure tax or a flat rate income tax. This group has joined the opponents of progressive taxation in the attack on the income tax.[79]

Of course, supply-side economics still has its critics. Gerard Baker, economics columnist for London's *Financial Times*, recently referred to "quack theories about supply-side tax cuts." However Floyd Norris, a columnist for the *New York Times*, was more sympathetic:

> Two decades ago, the supply-siders performed a valuable service. They persuaded a popular new president,

who had been elected as a fiscal conservative, to slash taxes and claim that no budget deficit would result. Lower tax rates, they said, would miraculously bring higher tax revenues. That proved to be wrong. But it was a good idea nonetheless. The United States was going through painful economic times, and the tax cut provided real relief for the majority who were not to be victims of the cutbacks that were needed to make American businesses more competitive. The economic stimulus helped to end a severe recession.[80]

In closing, I will quote from Congressman Richard Gephardt (D-MO), former Minority Leader of the U.S. House of Representatives and someone not given to praising Republican economic policies. So it is revealing that even he now believes that cutting taxes may actually raise government revenue. In an interview on *Meet the Press* on Sunday, January 27, 2002, Gephardt had this to say about tax cuts:

> The purpose of tax cuts is not just to have a tax cut for a particular time. It is to get the economy to grow. If you can get the economy to grow, you will start having more money coming into the government. It's a synergistic process that moves both the budget forward and the economy forward.[81]

In politics, that's called an endorsement.

10 | The Laffer Curve

Arthur B. Laffer
January 6, 2004

T he most famous idea pertaining to the Ronald Reagan revolution in economic policy of the 1980s remains the "Laffer Curve." No economic doctrine of modern vintage (at least since World War II, when people started talking about "Keynesianism") has gained so much public currency as the Laffer Curve.

The Laffer Curve is a simple theoretical diagram, a bell curve—the most common curve in all of statistics—that compares tax revenues that are gained under all tax rates between 0 percent and 100 percent. At one end (the 0 percent tax rate), tax revenues are zero, and at the other (the 100 percent rate), tax revenues are also zero, because no one chooses to earn money when the government confiscates every penny. In between there is a bulge. And at one point, that bulge peaks—implying that any tax rate increase beyond it will result in lower revenue.

The curve's originator, the economist Arthur B. Laffer, recalled in this piece from 2004 that as a young professor in the 1960s and early 1970s, he had used the curve often in the classroom, as a teaching tool. Then in December 1974, he sketched the curve on a restaurant napkin before two high staffers of the Gerald Ford administration, Donald Rumsfeld and Richard B. Cheney, along with his friend, *Wall Street Journal* editorialist Jude Wanniski.

Over the years, the Laffer-curve-on-a-napkin story has become something of an urban legend. A great many people have referred to it as some sort of notorious incident. The first time it was mentioned in print was in 1978, when Wanniski discussed the 1974 meeting in his bestselling book, *The Way the World Works.*

In the piece before us, Laffer made a point akin to that of Bruce Bartlett's in another entry in this collection. This is that any number of economists from over the ages, from Ibn Khaldun in the fourteenth century to John Maynard Keynes in the twentieth, had already expressed the concept behind the Laffer Curve. But thanks to Wanniski (not to mention the clarity Laffer brought to the underlying concept), it bears Laffer's name. And as Ronald Reagan's advisor Martin Anderson once said, "In the academic world of economists, one of the rarest, most treasured honors is to have your name associated with a curve....It must have been especially galling to other economists when they realized how easy it would have been to do it themselves, if only they had thought of it."[1]

The twentieth century provided three major test cases for the Laffer Curve. These were the big tax cuts of the 1920s, the 1960s, and the 1980s.

The twentieth century provided three major test cases for the Laffer Curve. These were the big tax cuts of the 1920s, the 1960s, and the 1980s. In each of these examples, all rates of the income tax were cut considerably, with the top rate coming down by a quarter or more. As the numbers reported here show, real revenue not only grew all three times, but put to shame the revenue-results of the periods immediately preceding the tax cuts.

Yet government revenues are not even the real story. Rather, the remarkable growth in economic output and employment that accompanied each of these tax cuts are the statistics that leap off the page. In the starkest example—that of Ronald Reagan's 1980s—economic growth averaged about 4 percent higher per year after the tax cut than before. And the record from the states and from other nations confirms the American experience.

In the late 1970s, when the Laffer Curve first became famous, liberal lions including Senators George McGovern and Edward M. Kennedy expressed interest in tax cuts, on the grounds that the Laffer Curve relationship revealed a way to fund the big-government state. That assumption was not quite correct, in that embedded in the Curve is the concept that however much revenues might increase on account of a good tax cut, the benefits to the private economy—to the "real" as opposed to the governmental sector—are even greater. The swells in government receipts in the wake of the tax cuts of the twentieth century found more than their match in the real-economy booms that accompanied them.

THE LAFFER CURVE: PAST, PRESENT, AND FUTURE
JANUARY 6, 2004

The story of how the Laffer Curve got its name isn't one of the *Just So Stories* by Rudyard Kipling. It began with a 1978 article published by Jude Wanniski in *The Public Interest* entitled, "Taxes, Revenues, and the 'Laffer Curve.'" As recounted by Wanniski (associate editor of the *Wall Street Journal* at the time), in December of 1974 he had been invited to have dinner with me (then professor at the University of Chicago), Don Rumsfeld (chief of staff to President Gerald Ford) and Dick Cheney (Rumsfeld's deputy and my former classmate at Yale) at the Two Continents Restaurant at the Washington Hotel in Washington, D.C. (just across the street from the Treasury). While discussing President Ford's "WIN" (Whip Inflation Now) proposal for tax increases, I supposedly grabbed my napkin and a pen and sketched a curve on the napkin illustrating the trade-off between tax rates and tax revenues. Wanniski named the trade off "The Laffer Curve."

I personally don't remember the details of that evening we all spent together, but Wanniski's version could well be true. I used the so-called Laffer Curve all the time in my classes and to anyone else who would listen to illustrate the trade-off between tax rates and tax revenues. My only question on Wanniski's version of the story concerns the fact that the restaurant used cloth napkins and my mother had raised me not to desecrate nice things. Ah well, that's my story and I'm sticking to it.

THE HISTORICAL ORIGINS OF THE LAFFER CURVE

The Laffer Curve, by the way, was not invented by me; it has its origins way back in time. For example, the Muslim philosopher, Ibn Khaldun, wrote in his fourteenth century work *The Muqaddimah*:

It should be known that at the beginning of the dynasty, taxation yields a large revenue from small assessments. At the end of the dynasty, taxation yields a small revenue from large assessments.

A more recent version of incredible clarity was written by none other than John Maynard Keynes:

When, on the contrary, I show, a little elaborately, as in the ensuing chapter, that to create wealth will increase the national income and that a large proportion of any increase in the national income will accrue to an Exchequer, amongst whose largest outgoings is the payment of incomes to those who are unemployed and whose receipts are a proportion of the incomes of those who are occupied, I hope the reader will feel, whether or not he thinks himself competent to criticize the argument in detail, that the answer is just what he would expect—that it agrees with the instinctive promptings of his common sense.

Nor should the argument seem strange that taxation may be so high as to defeat its object, and that, given sufficient time to gather the fruits, a reduction of taxation will run a better chance than an increase of balancing the budget. For to take the opposite view today is to resemble a manufacturer who, running at a loss, decides to raise his price, and when his declining sales increase the loss, wrapping himself in the rectitude of plain arithmetic, decides that prudence requires him to raise the price still more—and who, when at last his account is balanced with nought on both sides, is still found righteously declaring that it would have been the act of a gambler to reduce the price when you were already making a loss.[2]

THEORY BASICS

The basic idea behind the relationship between tax rates and tax revenues is that changes in tax rates have two effects on revenues: the arithmetic effect and the economic effect. The arithmetic effect is simply that if tax rates are lowered, tax revenues per dollar of tax base will be lowered by the amount of the decrease in the rate. And, the reverse is true for an increase in tax rates. The economic effect, however, recognizes the positive impact that lower tax rates have on work, output, and employment and thereby the tax base by providing incentives to increase these activities. Raising tax rates has the opposite economic effect by penalizing participation in the taxed activities. The arithmetic effect always works in the opposite direction from the economic effect. Therefore, when the economic and the arithmetic effects of tax rate changes are combined, the consequences of the change in tax rates on total tax revenues are no longer quite so obvious.

The diagram at right is a graphic illustration of the concept of the Laffer Curve—not the exact levels of taxation corresponding to specific levels of revenues. At a tax rate of 0 percent, however, the government would collect no tax revenues, no matter how large the tax base. Likewise, at a tax rate of 100 percent, the government would also collect no tax revenues because no one would be willing to work for an after-tax wage of zero—there would be no tax base. Between these two extremes there are two tax rates that will collect

The Laffer Curve

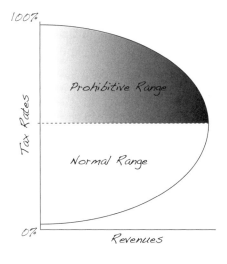

the same amount of revenue: A high tax rate on a small tax base and a low tax rate on a large tax base.

The Laffer Curve itself doesn't say whether a tax cut will raise or lower revenues. Revenue responses to a tax rate change will depend upon the tax system in place, the time period being considered, the ease of moving into underground activities, the level of tax rates already in place, the prevalence of legal and accounting-driven tax loopholes, and the proclivities of the productive factors. If the existing tax rate is too high—in the "prohibitive range" shown above—then a tax-rate cut would result in increased tax revenues. The economic effect of the tax cut would outweigh the arithmetic effect of the tax cut.

Moving from total tax revenues to budgets, there is one expenditure effect in addition to the two effects tax-rate changes have on revenues. Because tax cuts create an incentive to increase output, employment and production, tax cuts also help balance the budget by reducing means-tested government expenditures. A faster-growing economy means lower unemployment and higher incomes, resulting in reduced unemployment benefits and other social welfare programs.

Over the past 100 years, in the U.S. there have been three major periods of tax-rate cuts: the Harding/Coolidge cuts of the mid-1920s, the Kennedy cuts of the mid-1960s, and the Reagan cuts of the early 1980s. Each of these periods of tax cuts was remarkably successful in terms of virtually any public policy metric.

Prior to discussing and measuring these three major periods of U.S. tax cuts, three critical points have to be made: one regarding the size of tax cuts; another regarding their timing; and, lastly, one regarding their location.

Size of Tax Cuts

People don't work, consume or invest to pay taxes. They work and invest to earn after-tax income and they consume to get the best buys—after tax. Therefore, people are not concerned *per se* with taxes but instead their concern is focused on after-tax results. Taxes and after-tax results are very similar but have crucial differences.

Using the Kennedy tax cuts of the mid-1960s as our example, it is easy to show that identical percentage tax cuts, when and where tax rates are high, are far larger than when and where tax rates are low. When Kennedy took office in 1961, the highest federal marginal tax rate was 91 percent and the lowest rate was 20 percent. By earning a dollar pre-tax, the highest-bracket income earner would receive nine cents after tax (the incentive), while the lowest-bracket income earner would receive 80 cents after tax. These after-tax earnings were the relative after-tax incentives to earn the same amount (one dollar) pre tax.

By 1965, after Kennedy's tax cuts were fully effective, the highest federal marginal tax rate had been lowered to 70 percent (a drop of 23 percent or 21 percentage points on a base of 91 percent) and the lowest tax rate was dropped to 14 percent (30 percent lower). Now by earning a dollar pre tax the person in the highest tax bracket would receive 30 cents after tax, or a 233 percent increase from the 9 cents after-tax earned when the tax rate was 91 percent and the person in the lowest tax bracket would receive 86 cents after tax or a 7.5 percent increase from the 80 cents earned when the tax rate was 20 percent.

The higher tax rates are, the greater will be the economic (supply-side) impact of a given percentage reduction in tax rates.

Putting this all together, the increase in incentives in the highest tax bracket was a whopping 233 percent for a 23 percent cut in tax rates—a 10-to-one benefit/cost ratio—while the increase in incentives in the lowest tax bracket was a mere 7.5 percent for a 30 percent cut in rates—a one-to-four benefit/cost ratio. The lessons here are simple: The higher tax rates are, the greater will be the economic (supply-side) impact of a given percentage reduction in tax rates. Likewise, under a progressive tax structure, an equal across-the-board percentage reduction in tax rates should have its greatest impact in the highest tax bracket and its least impact in the lowest tax bracket.

Timing of Tax Cuts

The second and equally important concept of tax cuts concerns the timing of those cuts. People in their quest to earn what they can after tax not only can change how much they work, but they also can change when they work, when they invest, and when they spend. Lower expected tax rates in the future will reduce taxable economic activity in the present as people try to shift activity out of the relatively higher taxed present period into the relatively lower taxed future period. People tend not to shop at a store a week before that store has its well-advertised discount sale. Likewise, in the periods before legislated tax cuts actually take effect, people will defer income and then realize that income when tax rates have fallen to their fullest extent. It has always amazed me how tax cuts don't work until they actually take effect.

When assessing the impact of tax legislation, it is imperative to start the measurement of the tax cut period after all the tax cuts have been put into effect. As will be obvious when we look at the three major tax cut periods and even more so when we look at capital gains tax cuts, timing is of the essence.

Location of Tax Cuts

As a final point, people can also choose where they earn their after-tax income, where they invest their money, and where they spend their money. Regional and country differences in various tax rates matter as we will see when we look at state and country effects of tax changes.

THE HARDING/COOLIDGE TAX CUTS

In 1913, the federal progressive income tax was put into place with a top marginal rate of 7 percent. Thanks in part to World War I, this tax rate was quickly increased significantly and peaked at 77 percent in 1918. Then, through a series of tax-rate reductions, the Harding/Coolidge tax cuts dropped the top personal marginal income tax rate to 25 percent in 1925.

FIGURE 1
The Top Marginal Personal Income Tax Rate,
1913-2003
(when applicable, top rate on earned and/or unearned income)

Note: The PIT is currently being lowered through a multi-year phase-in. The long-term capital gains tax rate is now 18% for those assets held for at least 60 months and purchased after 1/1/01. For that reason, the capital gains rate shown above won't drop to 18% until 2006.

Source: Data through 1988 from Joseph Pechman, "Federal Tax Policy," more recent data from various sources including tax code.

While tax collection data for the National Income and Product Accounts (from the U.S. Bureau of Economic Analysis) don't exist for the 1920s, we do have total federal receipts from the U.S. budget tables. During the four years prior to 1925 (the year the tax cut was fully enacted), inflation-adjusted revenues declined by an average of 9.2 percent per year (Table 1). Over the four years following the tax-rate cuts, revenues remained volatile but averaged an inflation-adjusted gain of 0.1 percent per year. The economy responded strongly to the tax cuts, with output nearly doubling and unemployment falling sharply.

TABLE 1
A Look at the Harding/Coolidge Tax Cut

		Before and After: Federal Government Receipts (in $billions, fiscal year U.S. budget data)			
			Federal Government		
	Fiscal Year	Revenue	yr/yr % change	Inflation-Adjusted Revenue	yr/yr % change
4-Year Average Before Tax Cut	FY1920	$6.6		$6.6	
	FY1921	$5.6	-16.2%	$6.2	-6.1%
	FY1922	$4.0	-27.7%	$4.8	-23.0%
	FY1923	$3.9	-4.3%	$4.5	-6.0%
	FY1924	$3.9	0.5%	$4.5	0.0%
			-12.6%		-9.2%
4-Year Average After Tax Cut	FY1925	$3.6	-5.9%	$4.2	-8.2%
	FY1926	$3.8	4.2%	$4.3	3.3%
	FY1927	$4.0	5.7%	$4.6	7.8%
	FY1928	$3.9	-2.8%	$4.5	-1.7%
			0.2%		0.1%

Before and After: Revenue, Output and Employment
annual average rate over four-year period
before and four-year period after the tax cut

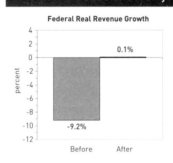

Federal Real Revenue Growth

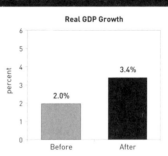

Real GDP Growth

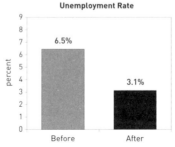

Unemployment Rate

In the 1920s, tax rates on the highest income brackets were reduced the most, which is exactly what economic theory suggests should be done to spur the economy.

But those income classes with lower tax rates were not left out in the cold: The Harding/Coolidge tax-rate cuts did result in reduced tax rates on lower income brackets. Internal Revenue Service data show that the dramatic tax cuts of the 1920s resulted in an increase in the share of total income taxes paid by those making more than $100,000 per year from 29.9 percent in 1920 to 62.2 percent in 1929 (Table 2). And keep in mind the significance of this increase, given that the 1920s was a decade of falling prices and therefore a $100,000 threshold in 1929 corresponds to a higher real income threshold than $100,000 did in 1920. The consumer price index *fell* a combined 14.5 percent from 1920 to 1929. In this case, the effects of bracket creep that existed prior to the federal income tax brackets being indexed for inflation (in 1985) worked in the opposite direction.

TABLE 2
Percentage Share of Total Income Taxes Paid
By Income Class: 1920, 1925 and 1929

Income Class	1920	1925	1929
Under $5,000	15.4%	1.9%	0.4%
$5,000-$10,000	9.1	2.6	0.9
$10,000-$25,000	16.0	10.1	5.2
$25,000-$100,000	29.6	36.6	27.4
Over $100,000	29.9	48.8	62.2

Source: Internal Revenue Service

Perhaps most illustrative of the power of the Harding/Coolidge tax cuts was the increase in GDP, the fall in unemployment and the improvement in the average American's quality of life over this decade. Table 3 demonstrates the remarkable increase in American quality of life, as reflected by the percentage of Americans owning items in 1930 that previously had only been owned by the wealthy (or by no one at all).

TABLE 3
Percentage of Americans Owning Selected Items

Item	1920	1930
Autos	26%	60%
Radios	0%	46%
Electric lighting	35%	68%
Washing machines	8%	24%
Vacuum cleaners	9%	30%
Flush toilets	20%	51%

Source: Stanley Lebergott, Pursuing Happiness: American Consumers in the Twentieth Century. *(Princeton: Princeton University Press, 1993), p. 102, 113, 130, 137.*

THE KENNEDY TAX CUTS

During the Depression and World War II the top marginal income tax rate rose steadily, peaking at an incredible 94 percent in 1944 and 1945. The rate remained above 90 percent well into President John F. Kennedy's term in office, which began in 1961. Kennedy's fiscal policy stance made it clear he was a believer in pro-growth, supply-side tax measures. Kennedy said it all in January of 1963 in the *Economic Report of the President*:

> Tax reduction thus sets off a process that can bring gains for everyone, gains won by marshalling resources that would otherwise stand idle—workers without jobs and farm and factory capacity without markets. Yet many taxpayers seemed prepared to deny the nation the fruits of tax reduction because they question the financial soundness of reducing taxes when the federal budget is already in deficit. Let me make clear why, in today's economy, fiscal prudence and responsibility call for tax reduction even if it temporarily enlarged the federal deficit—why reducing taxes is the best way open to us to increase revenues.

Kennedy further reiterated his beliefs in his *Tax Message to Congress* on January 24, 1963:

> In short, this tax program will increase our wealth far more than it increases our public debt. The actual burden of that debt—as measured in relation to our total output—will decline. To continue to increase our debt as a result of inadequate earnings is a sign of weakness. But to borrow prudently in order to invest in a tax revision that will greatly increase our earning power can be a source of strength.

President Kennedy proposed massive tax-rate reductions which passed Congress and went into law after he was assassinated. The 1964 tax cut reduced the top marginal personal income tax rate from 91 percent to 70 percent by 1965. The cut reduced lower-bracket rates as well. In the four years prior to the 1965 tax-rate cuts, federal government income tax revenue, adjusted for inflation, had increased at an average annual rate of 2.1 percent, while total government income tax revenue (federal plus state and local) had increased 2.6 percent per year (Table 4). In the four years following the tax cut these two measures of revenue growth rose to 8.6 percent and 9.0 percent, respectively. Government income tax revenue not only increased in the years following the tax cut, it increased at a much faster rate in spite of the tax cuts.

Kennedy's fiscal policy stance made it clear he was a believer in pro-growth, supply-side tax measures.

The Kennedy tax cut set the example that Reagan would follow some seventeen years later. By increasing incentives to work, produce and invest, real GDP growth increased in the years following the tax cuts, more people worked and the tax base expanded. Additionally, the expenditure side of the budget benefited as well because the unemployment rate was significantly reduced.

TABLE 4
A Look at the Kennedy Tax Cut

		Before and After: Total Income Tax Revenue (Personal and Corporate) (in $billions, calendar year BEA NIPA data)							
		Federal Government				Total Government (Federal, State and Local)			
	Year	Revenue	yr/yr % change	Inflation-Adjusted Revenue	yr/yr % change	Revenue	yr/yr % change	Inflation-Adjusted Revenue	yr/yr % change
4-Year Average Before Tax Cut	1960	$63.2		$63.2		$67.0		$67.0	
	1961	$64.2	1.6%	$63.5	0.5%	$68.3	1.9%	$67.6	0.9%
	1962	$69.0	7.5	$67.5	6.2	$73.7	7.9	$72.1	6.6
	1963	$73.7	6.8	$71.2	5.5	$78.7	6.8	$76.0	5.5
	1964	$72.1	-2.2	$68.8	-3.4	$78.0	-0.9	$74.4	-2.1
			3.3%		2.1%		3.9%		2.6%
4-Year Average After Tax Cut	1965	$80.0	11.0%	$75.1	9.2%	$86.4	10.8%	$81.1	9.0%
	1966	$90.0	12.5	$82.0	9.2	$97.7	13.1	$89.1	9.8
	1967	$94.4	4.9	$83.7	2.1	$103.2	5.6	$91.5	2.8
	1968	$112.5	19.2	$95.7	14.3	$123.6	19.8	$105.1	14.9
			11.8%		8.6%		12.2%		9.0%

Before and After: Revenue, Output, and Employment
annual average rate over four year period
before and four year period after the tax cut

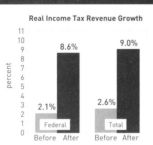

Real Income Tax Revenue Growth

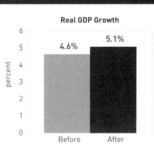

Real GDP Growth

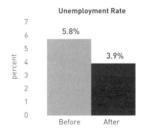

Unemployment Rate

TABLE 5

Actual vs. Forecasted Federal Budget Receipts
1964-1967 (in $billions)

Fiscal Year	Actual Budget Receipts	Forecasted Budget Receipts	Difference	Percentage Actual Revenue Exceeded Forecasts
1964	$112.7	$109.3	+$3.4	3.1%
1965	$116.8	$115.9	+$0.9	0.7%
1966	$130.9	$119.8	+$11.1	9.3%
1967	$149.6	$141.4	+$8.2	5.8%

Source: Congressional Budget Office, A Review of the Accuracy of Treasury Revenue Forecasts, 1963-1978 (February, 1981), p. 4.

Using the Congressional Budget Office's revenue forecasts made with the full knowledge of, yet prior to, the tax cuts, revenues came in much higher than had been anticipated, even after the "cost" of the tax cut had been taken into account (Table 5).

In addition, in 1965, one year following the tax cut, personal income tax revenue data exceeded expectations by the greatest amounts in the highest income classes (Table 6).

TABLE 6

Actual vs. Forecasted Personal Income Tax Revenue by Income Class, 1965

(calendar year, revenue in $millions)

Adjusted Gross Income Class	Actual Revenue Collected	Forecasted Revenue	Percentage Actual Revenue Exceeded Forecasts
$0 - $5,000	$4,337	$4,374	-0.8%
$5,000 - $10,000	$15,434	$13,213	16.8%
$10,000 - $15,000	$10,711	$6,845	56.5%
$15,000 - $20,000	$4,188	$2,474	69.3%
$20,000 - $50,000	$7,440	$5,104	45.8%
$50,000 - $100,000	$3,654	$2,311	58.1%
$100,000+	$3,764	$2,086	80.4%
Total	$49,530	$36,407	36.0%

Source: Estimated revenues calculated from Joseph A. Pechman, "Evaluation of Recent Tax Legislation: Individual Income Tax Provisions of the Revenue Act of 1964," Journal of Finance, *vol. 20 (May 1965), p. 268. Actual revenues are from* Internal Revenue Service, Statistics of Income—1965, *Individual Income Tax Returns, p. 8.*

Testifying before Congress in 1977, Walter Heller, President Kennedy's Chairman of the Council of Economic Advisors, summed it all up:

> What happened to the tax cut in 1965 is difficult to pin down, but insofar as we are able to isolate it, it did seem to have a tremendously stimulative effect, a multiplied effect on the economy. It was the major factor that led to our running a $3 billion surplus by the middle of 1965 before escalation in Vietnam struck us. It was a $12 billion tax cut, which would be

about $33 or $34 billion in today's terms, and within one year the revenues into the Federal Treasury were already above what they had been before the tax cut.

Did the tax cut pay for itself in increased revenues? I think the evidence is very strong that it did.[3]

THE REAGAN TAX CUTS

In August of 1981, Ronald Reagan signed into law the Economic Recovery Tax Act (ERTA, also known as Kemp-Roth). ERTA slashed marginal earned income tax rates by 25 percent across-the-board over a three-year period. The highest marginal tax rate on unearned income dropped to 50 percent from 70 percent immediately (the Brodhead Amendment) and the tax rate on capital gains also fell immediately from 28 percent to 20 percent. Five percentage points of the 25 percent cut went into effect on October 1, 1981. An additional 10 percentage points of the cut then went into effect on July 1, 1982, and the final 10 percentage points of the cut began on July 1, 1983.

Looking at the cumulative effects of ERTA in terms of tax (calendar) years, the tax cut provided a reduction in tax rates of 1.25 percent through the entirety of 1981, 10 percent through 1982, 20 percent through 1983, and the full 25 percent through 1984.

As a provision of ERTA, Reagan also saw to it that the tax brackets were indexed for inflation beginning in 1985.

To properly discern the effects of the tax-rate cuts on the economy, I use the starting date of January 1, 1983, given that the bulk of the cuts were in place on that date. However, a case could be made for a start date of January 1, 1984, the date the full cut was in effect.

These across-the-board marginal tax-rate cuts resulted in higher incentives to work, produce and invest, and the economy responded (Table 7). Between 1978 and 1982 the economy grew at a 0.9 percent rate in real terms, but from 1983 to 1986 this growth rate increased to 4.8 percent.

Prior to the tax cut the economy was choking on high inflation, high interest rates and high unemployment. All three of these economic bellwethers dropped sharply after the tax cuts. The unemployment rate, which had peaked at 9.7 percent in 1982, began a steady decline, reaching 7.0 percent by 1986 and 5.3 percent when Reagan left office in January 1989.

Inflation-adjusted revenue growth dramatically improved. Over the four years prior to 1983, federal income tax revenue declined at an average rate of 2.8 percent per year, and total government income tax revenue declined at an annual rate of 2.6 percent. Between 1983 and 1986 these figures were a positive 2.7 percent and 3.5 percent, respectively.

These across-the-board marginal tax-rate cuts resulted in higher incentives to work, produce and invest, and the economy responded.

The most controversial portion of Reagan's tax revolution was the big drop in the highest marginal income tax rate from 70 percent when he took office to 28 percent in 1988. However, Internal Revenue Service data reveal that tax collections from the wealthy, as measured by personal income taxes paid by top percentile earners, increased between 1980 and 1988 despite significantly lower tax rates (Table 8).

TABLE 7
A Look at the Reagan Tax Cut

		Before and After: Total Income Tax Revenue (Personal and Corporate) (in $billions, calendar year BEA NIPA data)							
		Federal Government				Total Government (Federal, State and Local)			
	Year	Revenue	yr/yr % change	Inflation-Adjusted Revenue	yr/yr % change	Revenue	yr/yr % change	Inflation-Adjusted Revenue	yr/yr % change
	1978	$260.3		$260.3		$307.4		$307.4	
4-Year Average Before Tax Cut	1979	$299.0	14.9%	$268.7	3.2%	$350.8	14.1%	$315.3	2.6%
	1980	$320.3	7.1	$253.5	-5.7	$377.4	7.6	$298.7	-5.3
	1981	$356.3	11.2	$255.6	0.8	$419.6	11.2	$301.0	0.8
	1982	$344.0	-3.5	$232.5	-9.0	$410.0	-2.3	$277.1	-7.9
			7.2%		-2.8%		7.5%		-2.6%
4-Year Average After Tax Cut	1983	$347.5	1.0%	$227.6	-2.1%	$421.7	2.9%	$276.2	-0.3%
	1984	$376.6	8.4	$236.5	3.9	$462.9	9.8	$290.7	5.2
	1985	$412.3	9.5	$250.0	5.7	$504.6	9.0	$306.0	5.3
	1986	$433.9	5.2	$258.2	3.3	$534.0	5.8	$317.8	3.9
			6.0%		2.7%		6.8%		3.5%

Before and After: Revenue, Output and Employment
annual average rate over four-year period before and four-year period after the tax cut

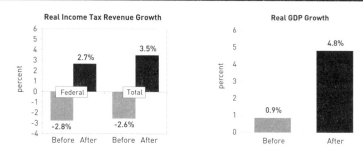

Real Income Tax Revenue Growth — Federal: Before -2.8%, After 2.7%; Total: Before -2.6%, After 3.5%

Real GDP Growth — Before 0.9%, After 4.8%

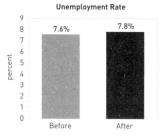

Unemployment Rate — Before 7.6%, After 7.8%

TABLE 8

Percentage of Total Personal Income Taxes Paid by Percentile of Adjusted Gross Income (AGI)

Calendar Year	Top 1% of AGI	Top 5% of AGI	Top 10% of AGI	Top 25% of AGI	Top 50% of AGI
1980	19.1%	36.8%	49.3%	73.0	93.0%
1981	17.6	35.1	48.0	72.3	92.6
1982	19.0	36.1	48.6	72.5	92.7
1983	20.3	37.3	49.7	73.1	92.8
1984	21.1	38.0	50.6	73.5	92.7
1985	21.8	38.8	51.5	74.1	92.8
1986	25.0	41.8	54.0	75.6	93.4
1987	24.6	43.1	55.5	76.8	93.9
1988	27.5	45.5	57.2	77.8	94.3

Source: Internal Revenue Service

THE LAFFER CURVE AND THE CAPITAL GAINS TAX

Changes in the capital gains maximum tax rate provide a unique opportunity to study the effects of taxation on taxpayer behavior. Taxation of capital gains is different from taxation of most other sources of income because people have more control over the timing of the realization of capital gains (i.e., when the gains are actually taxed).

The historical data on changes in the capital gains tax rate show an incredibly consistent pattern. Just after a capital gains tax-rate cut, there is a surge in revenues; just after a capital gains tax-rate increase, revenues take a dive. Also, as would be expected, just before a capital gains tax-rate cut there is a sharp decline in revenues, and just before a tax-rate increase there is an increase in revenues. Timing really does matter.

This all makes total sense. If you could choose when to realize capital gains for tax purposes you would clearly realize your gains before tax rates are raised (Figure 2). No one wants to pay higher taxes.

In the 1960s and 1970s capital gains tax receipts averaged around 0.4 percent of GDP, with a nice surge in the mid-1960s following

President Kennedy's tax cuts and another surge in 1978-79 after the Steiger-Hansen capital gains tax-cut legislation went into effect.

FIGURE 2
Inflation Adjusted Revenue

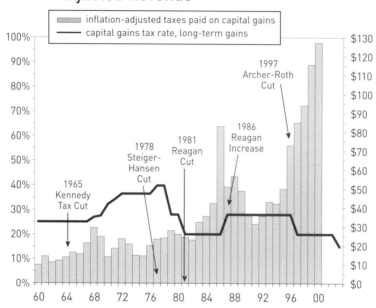

Following the 1981 capital gains cut from 28 percent to 20 percent, nominal capital gains tax revenues leapt from $12.5 billion in 1980 to $18.7 billion by 1983—a 50 percent increase. During this period capital gains revenues rose to approximately 0.6 percent of GDP. Reducing income and capital gains tax rates in 1981 helped launch what we now appreciate as the greatest and longest period of wealth creation in world history. In 1981 the stock market troughed at about 1,000, compared to nearly 10,000 today (Figure 3).

As expected, the increase in the capital gains tax rate from 20 percent to 28 percent in 1986 led to a surge in nominal tax revenues prior to the increase ($52.9 billion in 1986) and a collapse in revenues after the increase took effect ($24.9 billion in 1991). (Please note that Figure 2 displays inflation-adjusted revenue).

FIGURE 3

U.S. Stock Market: "Bull vs. Bear"
Nominal and Inflation-Adjusted Appreciation
(monthly, 12/31/59 –1/6/04)

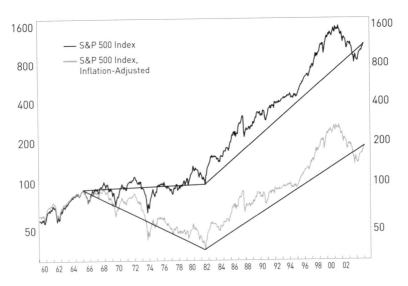

The return of the capital gains tax rate from 28 percent back to 20 percent in 1997 was an unqualified success and every claim made by the critics was wrong. The tax cut, which went into effect in May of 1997, increased asset values and contributed to the largest gain in productivity and private sector capital investment in a decade. Also, the capital gains tax cut was not a revenue loser for the federal Treasury.

In 1996, the year before the tax rate cut and the last year with the 28 percent rate, total taxes paid on assets sold was $66.4 billion (Table 9). A year later tax receipts jumped to $79.3 billion, and they jumped again one year later to $89.1 billion in 1998. The capital gains tax-rate reduction played a big part in the 91 percent increase in tax receipts collected from capital gains between 1996 and 2000—a percentage far greater than the most ardent supply-siders expected.

TABLE 9

1997 Capital Gains Tax Rate Cut: Actual Revenues vs. Government Forecast
(in $billions)

	1996	1997	1998	1999	2000
Long-Term Capital Gains Tax Rate	28%	20%	20%	20%	20%
Net Capital Gains:					
Pre-Tax Cut Estimate (Jan-97)	- -	$205	$215	$228	n/a
Actual	$261	$365	$455	$553	$644
Capital Gains Tax Revenue:					
Pre-Tax Cut Estimate (Jan-97)	- -	$55	$65	$75	n/a
Actual	$66	$79	$89	$112	$127

Seldom in economics does real life so conveniently conform to theory as this capital gains example does to the Laffer Curve. Lower tax rates change people's economic behavior and stimulate economic growth, which can create more, not less, tax revenues.

THE STORY IN THE STATES

California

In my home state of California, we have an extremely progressive tax structure which lends itself to Laffer Curve types of analyses. During periods of tax increases and economic slowdowns, the state's budget office almost always overestimates revenues because they fail to take into account the economic feedback effects incorporated in the Laffer Curve analysis (the economic effect). Likewise, the state's budget office also underestimates revenues by wide margins during periods of tax cuts and economic expansion. The consistency and size of the mis-estimates are quite striking. Figure 4 demonstrates this effect by showing current-year and budget-year revenue forecasts taken from each year's January budget proposal compared to actual revenues collected.[4]

FIGURE 4

California General Fund Revenue (Plus Transfers): Forecast vs. Actual

(in $billions)

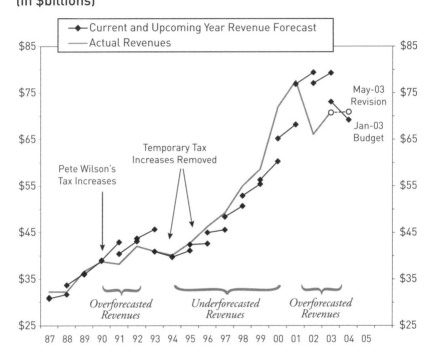

Year of January Forecast for Current and Upcoming Fiscal Year

	Revenue Estimates as of						Actual
	Jan-01	May-01	Jan-02	May-02	Jan-03	May-03	
00-01 Revenues	$76.9	$78.0					$77.6
01-02 Revenues	$79.4	$74.8	$77.1	$73.8			$66.1
02-03 Revenues			$79.3	$78.6	$73.1	$70.8	$70.9
03-04 Revenues					$69.2	$70.9	??

State Fiscal Crises of 2002/2003

The National Conference of State Legislatures (NCSL) conducts surveys of state fiscal conditions by contacting legislative fiscal directors from each state on a fairly regular basis. It is revealing to look at the NCSL survey from a little over one year ago (November 2002), just about the time when state fiscal conditions were hitting rock bottom. In the survey, each state's fiscal director reported its state's projected budget gap—the deficit between projected revenues and projected expenditures for the coming year—used when hashing out their state's FY2003 budget. As of November 2002, 40 states reported they faced a projected budget deficit, and eight states reported they did not. Two states (Indiana and Kentucky) did not respond to the survey.

Figure 5 plots each state's budget gap (as a share of the state's general fund budget) versus a measure of the degree of taxation faced by taxpayers in each state, or the "incentive rate." This incentive rate is the value of one dollar of income after passing through the major state and local taxes. This measure takes into account the state's highest tax rates on corporate income, on personal income, and on sales. (These three taxes account for 73 percent of total state tax collections).[5]

California, New Jersey and New York, three large states with relatively high tax rates, were among those states with the largest budget gaps.

These data have all sorts of limitations. Each state has a unique budgeting process, and who knows what assumptions were made when projecting revenues and expenditures. As California has repeatedly shown, budget projections change with the political tides and are often worth less than the paper they're printed on. In addition, some states may have taken significant budget steps (such as cutting spending) prior to FY2003 and eliminated problems for FY2003. Also, each state has a unique reliance on various taxes, and the incentive rate below doesn't factor in property taxes and the myriad of minor taxes out there.

That having been written, FY2003 was a unique period in state history given the degree that the states, almost without exception, all experienced budget difficulties, so it does provide a good opportunity for comparison. In this illustrative example, those states with high rates of taxation tended to have greater problems than those states with lower tax rates. California, New Jersey and New York, three large states with relatively high tax rates, were among those states with the largest budget gaps. In contrast, two "biggies" with no personal income tax at all—Florida and Texas—somehow found themselves with relatively few fiscal problems when preparing their budgets.

FIGURE 5

Incentive Rate vs. Initial FY2003 Projected Budget Gaps:The 50 States

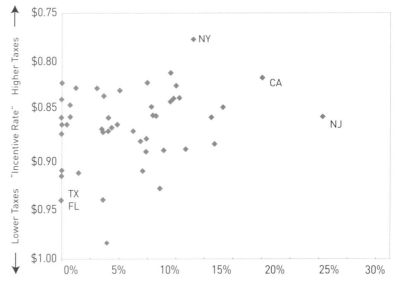

Impact of Taxes on State Performance Over Time

Over the years, Laffer Associates has chronicled the relationship between tax rates and economic performance at the state level. This relationship is more fully explored in our research covering the Laffer Associates State Competitive Environment model. Table 10 is a perfect example of this relationship and reflects the importance of taxation—both the level of tax rates and changes in relative competitiveness due to changes in tax rates—on economic performance.[6]

In contrast, two "biggies" with no personal income tax at all—Florida and Texas—somehow found themselves with relatively few fiscal problems when preparing their budgets.

Combining each state's current incentive rate (the value of a dollar after passing through a state's major taxes) with the sum of each state's net legislated tax changes over the past ten years (taken from our historical State Competitive Environment rankings) allows us to reach a composite ranking of which states have the best combination of low and/or falling taxes, and which have the worst combination of high and/or rising taxes. Those states with the best combination made the top ten of our rankings (1=best), while those with the worst combination made the bottom ten (fifty = worst). Table 10 shows how the "Ten Best States" and the "Ten Worst States" have fared over the past ten years in terms of income growth, employment growth, unemployment, and population growth. The ten best states have outperformed the bottom ten states in each category examined.

TABLE 10
Taxation (Level and Change) vs. Economic Performance:
A Look at 10-Year Performance of the Top 10 and Bottom 10 States

	Overall Rank[1]	Incentive Rate and Rank[2] 2003		Net Change in Taxes and Rank[3] 1994-03		10-Year Personal Income Growth[4]	10-Year Employment Growth[5]	Current Unemployment Rate[6]	10-Year Population Growth[7]
The 10 Best States									
Washington	1	$0.91	8	-$5.74	4	75.3%	17.5%	6.8%	16.8%
Connecticut	2	$0.88	14	-$4.91	7	56.9	7.4	5.0	6.4
Hawaii	3	$0.87	20	-$11.56	2	33.9	6.7	4.1	8.3
Colorado	4	$0.87	19	-$7.96	3	91.5	27.1	5.6	27.8
Florida	5	$0.91	5	-$0.13	17	72.3	30.4	4.7	24.1
Wisconsin	6	$0.87	22	-$5.73	5	61.6	13.8	5.0	8.2
Massachusetts	7	$0.88	13	-$0.78	14	65.2	11.3	5.4	7.0
Delaware	8	$0.91	7	$0.54	22	62.7	18.5	4.1	16.9
Georgia	9	$0.86	23	-$1.69	10	84.8	25.3	4.2	26.0
Virginia	10	$0.89	11	$0.79	25	67.8	19.7	3.6	14.3
10 Best Average						67.2%	17.8%	4.9%	15.6%
U.S. Average						**63.5%**	**16.3%**	**5.9%**	**12.8%**
10 Worst Average						60.0%	15.3%	5.5%	9.8%
Michigan	41	$0.87	18	$10.93	48	52.2	8.5	7.0	5.8%
California	42	$0.82	48	$0.30	20	66.2	20.2	6.4	13.9
Rhode Island	43	$0.82	45	$0.64	23	55.6	11.5	4.9	7.8
Maine	44	$0.85	32	$3.30	37	61.2	15.1	4.9	5.4
Louisiana	45	$0.84	38	$2.63	34	54.1	13.0	5.5	4.9
Oklahoma	46	$0.83	42	$4.22	40	54.4	17.0	5.3	8.8
Idaho	47	$0.83	43	$4.54	41	74.8	29.4	5.1	24.1
Alabama	48	$0.83	44	$6.86	45	55.3	8.3	5.8	7.3
Vermont	49	$0.83	41	$12.01	49	66.0	16.0	4.0	7.9
Arkansas	50	$0.82	47	$7.72	46	60.3	13.7	6.0	12.5
The 10 Worst States									

[1]Ranking based on equal-weighted average of each state's incentive rank and net change in taxes rank; [2]The incentive rate is the value of an after-tax dollar using the following weighting method: 80 percent, value of a dollar after passing through the personal tax channel (personal and sales taxes) and 20 percent, value of a dollar after passing through the corporate tax channel (corporate, personal and sales taxes); [3]Equals the sum of Laffer Associates' relative tax burden rankings (change in legislated tax burden per $1,000 of personal income relative to the U.S. change) over the 1994-2003 period, a negative indicates decreasing in taxes, a positive indicates increasing in taxes; [4]Nov-93 through Nov-03 (Bureau of Economic Analysis); [5]Nov-93 through Nov-03 (Bureau of Labor Statistics); [6]As of Nov-03 (Bureau of Labor Statistics); [7]7/1/93 though 7/1/03 (U.S. Census Bureau).

LOOKING GLOBALLY

For all the brouhaha surrounding high tax rates, Maastricht and the like, it is revealing, to say the least, that the highest tax rate G-12 countries have as many, if not more, fiscal problems (deficits) than do those countries with lower tax rates (Figure 6). While not shown here, cases such as Ireland, where tax rates were dramatically lowered and yet the budget moved into huge surplus, are pretty commonplace. Also not shown here, yet probably true, is the fact that the highest tax rate countries probably have the highest unemployment rates as well. High tax rates surely don't guarantee fiscal solvency, that's for sure.

FIGURE 6

Degree of Taxation vs. 5-Year Average Government Budget Surplus(+)/Deficit(-) as a % of GDP: The G-12[7,8]

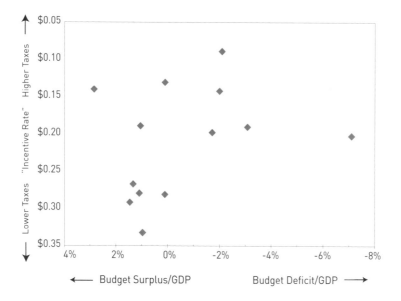

TAX TRENDS IN OTHER COUNTRIES: THE FLAT TAX FEVER

I have for many years lobbied for the implementation of a flat tax not only just here in California but also for the entire U.S. Hong Kong adopted their flat tax ages ago (and has performed like gangbusters ever since), and it is truly exciting that a flat-tax fever has seemingly infected Europe in recent years. In 1994 Estonia became the first country in Europe to adopt a flat tax, and their 26 percent flat tax dramatically energized what had been a faltering economy. Just prior to the adoption of the flat tax in 1994 Estonia had an impoverished economy which was literally shrinking—making the gains following the flat tax implementation all the more impressive. Over the eight-year period since 1994, Estonia has sustained real economic growth averaging 5.2 percent per year.

Latvia followed Estonia's lead one year later with a 25 percent flat tax. The five years before adopting the flat tax, Latvia's real GDP had fallen over 50 percent. The rest has been history (Figure 7). Lithuania has followed with a 33 percent flat tax, and has experienced similar positive results.

Russia has become one of the latest Eastern Bloc countries to give the flat tax an opportunity to take hold. In the years since the advent of the 13 percent flat personal tax (on January 1, 2001) and the 24 percent corporate tax (on January 1, 2002), the Russian economy has had amazing results. Tax revenue in Russia has gone way up (Figure 8). And the Russian system is simple, fair, and much more rational and effective. An individual whose income is only from a wage doesn't have to file an annual return—the employer deducts tax from the employee and transfers it to the Tax Authority every month.

Largely due to Russia and other Eastern European nations' successes with flat tax reform, Ukraine and Slovak Republic just implemented their 13 percent and 19 percent flat taxes, respectively, on January 1, 2004.

FIGURE 7
Average Annual Real GDP Growth
(%) in Selected Countries
5 Years Before and 5 Years After Flat Tax Implementation

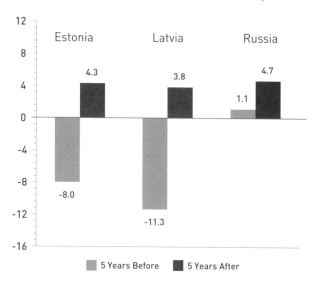

FIGURE 8
Annual Russian Tax Revenue
(in billions of Rubles)

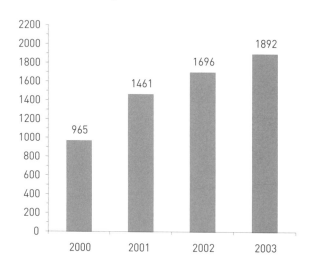

Endnotes

CHAPTER 1

1 Arthur B. Laffer and Charles W. Kadlec, "The Point of Linking the Dollar to Gold," *Wall Street Journal*, Oct. 13, 1981, and "Has the Fed Already Put Itself on a Price Rule?" Oct. 28, 1982.

2 This point explicitly addresses the reasonable criticisms as reflected in comments by a number of observers. Especially noteworthy are the *Wall Street Journal* columns by Lindley Clark.

3 "The U. S. Proposals for Using Reserves As An Indicator of the Need for Balance-Of-Payments Adjustment," Supplement to Chapter 5, *Economic Report of the President*, January 1973, pp. 160-174.

4 *Ibid.*, p. 171.

5 *Ibid.*, p. 160.

6 The specific values used in this paper are intended as illustrations. They are not definitive. Abstract description of such a system becomes almost incomprehensible.

7 *Ibid.*, p. 165; Herman E. Krooss and Paul A. Samuelson, *Documentary History of Banking and Currency in the United States*, McGraw-Hill, New York, 1969, p. 2457.

8 "The U.S. Proposals," pp. 173-174.

9 *Ibid.*, pp. 166-67.

10 *Ibid.*, p. 164.

11 *Ibid.*, p. 164.

12 *Ibid.*, p. 164.

13 Charles W. Kadlec and Arthur B. Laffer, "The Monetary Crisis: A Classical Perspective," Economic Study, A. B. Laffer Associates, November 12, 1979.

14 *Ibid.*

15 *Ibid.*

16 Arthur B. Laffer and R. David Ranson, "Inflation, Taxes and Equity Values," Economic Study, H.C. Wainwright & Co., Economics, September 20, 1979.

17 *Ibid.*

CHAPTER 2

1 Clayton Jones, *Christian Science Monitor,* March 10, 1981, p. 1.
2 Warren T. Brookes, "Welfare States Are Really No Friends to the Poor," *The Boston Herald American,* March 28, 1982, p. 44.
3 "An Analysis of Fiscal Policy and Economic Growth in Massachusetts," A.B. Laffer Associates, April 16, 1981, p. 70.
4 *1983 Massachusetts Budget,* Economy Section, p. 1.
5 "Hearing on the New Federalism," Governor Edward J. King's testimony before the Joint Economic Committee on February 24, 1982.
6 *1983 Massachusetts Budget,* Economy Section, p. 2.
7 "Hearing on the New Federalism," *op. cit.*
8 *Ibid.*
9 *Becker Institute Poll,* Survey No. 11, Report No. 2, p. 1.
10 "Supply-Side Roots of the Founding Fathers," *Wall Street Journal,* November 17, 1981, p. 26.

CHAPTER 3

1 Charles W. Kadlec and Arthur B. Laffer, "On the Road Again," A.B. Laffer Associates (October 26, 1982).
2 *Ibid.*
3 "Business This Week," *The Economist* (April 23-29), p. 69.

CHAPTER 4

1 Milton Friedman, "Why a Surge of Inflation Is Likely Next Year," *Wall Street Journal,* (September 1, 1983).
2 Nancy Brandon Tuma, Michael T. Hannan and Lyle T. Groeneveld, "Variation Over Time in the Impact of the Seattle and Denver Income Maintenance Experiments on the Making and Breaking of Marriages," *Research Memorandum* 43 (Menlo Park, CA: Center for the Study of Welfare Policy, Stanford Research Institute, 1977) p. 13, Table 1.
3 "Inside the Trojan Horse," *Research Reports of the American Institute for Economic Research* 50 No. 34 (August 22, 1983), pp. 133-34, and "A Review of the Budget," *Research Reports of the American Institute for Economic Research* 49 No. 52 (December 27, 1982), pp. 207-28.

CHAPTER 5

1   *1985 OASDI Trustees Report,* p. 28.
2   *Stocks, Bonds, Bills, and Inflation: 1984 Yearbook,* R.C. Ibbotson Associates, Inc., Chicago: 1984, p. 15; *1985 Economic Report of the President.*
3   *Ibid.*
4   This study was performed in response to an inquiry by Senator Steven Symms (R-Idaho).
5   Congressional Budget Office, Revised Estimates of the President's FY86 - Budget Request, (April 1985).
6   *1984 OASDI Trustees Report,* pp. 36, 130-1.
7   *1985 HI Trustees Report,* p. 42; *1985 OASDI Trustees Report,* p. 123.
8   Federation of American Hospitals, Washington, D.C.
9   *1985 HI Trustees Report,* p. 42.
10 Author's calculations based on data from p. 62 of the *1985 HI Trustees Report.*
11 *Report of the National Commission on Social Security Reform,* Appendix J, p. 23, (January 1983); SSA Alternative II-B Computer Run of March 18, 1982 by Orlo Nichols.
12 Public Law 98-21, section 111, April 20, 1983.
13 Public Law 92-21, section 121, April 20, 1983; acting Social Security Commissioner Martha McSteen, quoted in the *Washington Post,* December 11, 1984, p. A12.
14 Public Law 98-21, section 114, April 20, 1983.
15 Memorandum from the Executive Director of the National Commission on Social Security Reform, May 14, 1982; testimony before the Select Committee on Aging, U.S. House of Representatives, April 15, 1985.
16 March 20, 1985 Statement submitted to the *Los Angeles Times* by Congressman Edward Roybal.

CHAPTER 6

1   Paul R. Krugman, *Peddling Prosperity: Economic Sense and Nonsense in the Age of Diminished Expectations* (New York: W. W. Norton & Company, 1994).
2   Robert Eisner and Paul J. Pieper, "A New View of the Federal Debt and Budget Deficit," *American Economic Review* 74, no. 1 (March 1984), pp. 11-29.
3   Robert L. Bartley, *The Seven Fat Years: And How To Do It Again* (New York: The Free Press, 1992).

CHAPTER 7

1   Robert L. Bartley, *The Seven Fat Years: And How to Do It Again* (New York: The Free Press, 1994), 276.

CHAPTER 8

1   Robert Rector and Rea S. Hederman, Jr., "Two Americas: One Rich, One Poor? Understanding Income Inequality in the United States," Heritage Foundation Backgrounder No. 1791 (August 24, 2004), p. 9. It should also be noted that the size of the average household has fallen over time, from 2.78 people per household in 1978 to 2.57 people in 2003.

2   In recent years, a considerable amount of research has focused on the distribution of consumption, rather than income. The effect is to greatly reduce measures of poverty and inequality. See especially the work of economist Daniel Slesnick.

3   Macaulay made the same point regarding the impact of the Industrial Revolution. Writing in 1830, he said, "The advice and medicine which the poorest labourers can now obtain, in disease or after an accident, is far superior to what Henry the Eighth could have commanded." Thomas Babington Macaulay, "Southey's Colloquies on Society," in *Thomas Babington Macaulay: Selected Writings*, eds. John Clive and Thomas Pinney (Chicago: University of Chicago Press, 1972 [1830]), pp. 34-78; Census Bureau, *Supplemental Measures of Material Well-Being: Expenditures, Consumption, and Poverty, 1998 and 2001*, Current Population Report P23-201 (September 2003); Fredrik Bergström and Robert Gidehag, *EU versus USA* (Stockholm, Sweden: Timbro, 2004).

4   Angus Maddison, *The World Economy: Historical Statistics* (Paris: Organization for Economic Cooperation and Development, 2003), pp. 262-63. Robert MacCulloch points out that people will tolerate a high degree of income inequality if their standard of living is rising, but will turn to revolution when there is both inequality and slow growth. MacCulloch, "Income Inequality and the Taste for Revolution," *Journal of Law and Economics* 48, no. 1 (April 2005), pp. 93-123.

5   Alexis de Tocqueville, *Democracy in America*, trans. George Lawrence, ed. J.P. Mayer (New York: Harper & Row, 1966 [1850]), p. 54.

6   Karl Marx, *Value, Price and Profit* (New York: International Publishers, 1935 (1865]), p. 59.

7 Bob Herbert, "The Mobility Myth," *New York Times* (June 6, 2005).

8 I should note that I was randomly chosen by the Census Bureau to participate in the SIPP program for several years in the mid-1990s, so my finances during that period are included in the data.

9 "Rich Man, Poor Man," *Wall Street Journal*, November 28, 1984.

10 Census Bureau, *Transitions in Income and Poverty Status: 1985-86*, Current Population Report P70-18 (June 1990), and *Transitions in Income and Poverty Status: 1987-88*, Current Population Report P70-24 (August 1991).

11 Bruce Bartlett, "A Class Structure That Won't Stay Put," *Wall Street Journal*, November 20, 1991.

12 Sylvia Nasar, "Even Among the Well-Off, the Richest Get Richer," *New York Times*, March 5, 1992.

13 Contained in House Ways and Means Committee, *Background Material on Family Income and Benefit Changes*, Committee Print, 102nd Congress, 1st session (Washington: U.S. Government Printing Office [GPO], 1991).

14 See Joint Economic Committee Republican Staff, *Distorting the Data Base: CBO and the Politics of Income Redistribution*, April 1991; Paul Craig Roberts, "The Congressional Budget Office's Skewed Numbers," *Business Week*, March 23, 1992, pp. 18-19; "CBO Sues for Divorce," *Wall Street Journal*, May 11, 1992; John Greenlees, Memorandum to Bruce Bartlett and Robert Gillingham, U.S. Treasury Department, March 13, 1992; Congressional Budget Office, "Measuring the Distribution of Income Gains," CBO Staff Memorandum, March 1992.

15 For Krugman's efforts to try and explain himself, see Paul Krugman, "Disparity and Despair," *U.S. News & World Report*, March 23, 1992; "Like It or Not, the Income Gap Yawns," *Wall Street Journal*, May 21, 1992; "Ignorance and Inequality," *U.S. News & World Report*, June 1, 1992; "The Right, the Rich, and the Facts," *The American Prospect* (Fall 1992), pp. 19-31; on the CEA critique, see Michael Boskin, Letter to the Editor, *Wall Street Journal*, July 3, 1992; and "On Keeping the Record Straight," *Wall Street Journal*, May 21, 1992.

16 Sylvia Nasar, "However You Slice the Data, the Richest Did Get Richer," *New York Times*, May 11, 1992.

17 Sylvia Nasar, "The 1980s: A Very Good Time for the Very Rich," *New York Times*, March 5, 1992.

18 Suppose that aggregate income is $100 and the top 1 percent get 10 percent of it or $10. Now suppose that the income of the bottom 99 percent rises 10 percent and the top 1 percent sees its income rise 60 percent faster or 16 percent. The aggregate income has risen to

$110.60. Of the $10.60 increase in total income, the top 1 percent got $1.60 or 15 percent and the bottom 99 percent got $9 or 85 percent.

19 Daniel Okrent, "Setting the Record Straight (But Who Can Find the Record?)," *New York Times*, March 14, 2004.

20 I did not discover this discrepancy myself, but cannot give credit because I don't remember who did.

21 Michael M. Weinstein, "Why They Deserve It," *New York Times Magazine*, November 19, 1995.

22 Sylvia Nasar, "Is the U.S. Income Gap Really a Big Problem?" *New York Times*, April 4, 1999. Perhaps Miss Nasar's changed view was the result of having become rich herself as author of the best-selling book, *A Beautiful Mind*, which was made into an Academy Award-winning movie.

23 Easterlin, Schaeffer and Macunovich, and Sabelhaus and Manchester, show that Baby Boomers are indeed better off than their parents. Richard A. Easterlin, Christine M. Schaeffer, and Diane J. Macunovich, "Will Baby Boomers Be Less Well Off Than Their Parents? Income, Wealth, and Family Circumstances Over the Life Cycle in the United States," *Population and Development Review* 19, no. 3 (September 1993), pp. 497-522; John Sabelhaus and Joyce Manchester, "Baby Boomers and Their Parents: How Does Their Economic Well-Being Compare in Middle Age?" *Journal of Human Resources* 30, no. 4 (Fall 1995), pp. 791-806. It's worth mentioning that studies have long shown that lifetime income is much more equal than annual income. See Don Fullerton and Diane Lim Rogers, *Who Bears the Lifetime Tax Burden?* (Washington: Brookings, 1993), and John Sabelhaus, "What Is the Distributional Burden of Taxing Consumption?" *National Tax Journal* 46, no. 3 (September 1993), pp. 331-344.

24 See Chuck Collins, "Back From the Dead," *The American Prospect* (June 2005), pp. 60-61.

CHAPTER 9

1 The late Herb Stein coined the term "supply side fiscalists" in 1976. Herbert Stein, *Presidential Economics* (New York: Simon and Schuster, 1984).

2 Daniel Patrick Moynihan, "Reagan's Inflate-the-Deficit Game," *New York Times*, July 21, 1985; William Greider, "The Education of David Stockman," *The Atlantic Monthly*, December 1981, pp. 27-54.

3   Paul Craig Roberts, *The Supply-Side Revolution* (Cambridge: Harvard University Press, 1984), pp. 30-33. Roberts later was Assistant Secretary of the Treasury for Economic Policy in the Reagan Administration. Ture was named Under Secretary of the Treasury for Tax and Economic Policy.

4   William A. Niskanen, *Reaganomics: An Insider's Account of the Policies and the People* (New York: Oxford University Press, 1988). In 1981, the Congressional Budget Office (CBO) showed revenue loss estimates virtually identical to the Reagan Administration's. CBO, *Economic Policy and the Outlook for the Economy* (Washington: U.S. Government Printing Office [GPO], March 1981).

5   Ibn Khaldun, *The Muqaddimah* (3 vols.), trans. Franz Rosenthal (New York: Pantheon, 1958), vol. 2., p. 89.

6   "The President's News Conference, October 1, 1981," in *Public Papers of the Presidents of the United States: Ronald Reagan, 1981* (Washington: GPO).

7   Jonathan Swift, "An Answer to a Paper Called A Memorial of the Poor Inhabitants, Tradesmen, and Laborers of the Kingdom of Ireland" [1724], in *Jonathan Swift: Irish Tracts*, ed. Herbert Davis (Oxford: Basil Blackwell, 1964), pp. 17-25; Bruce Bartlett, "Jonathan Swift: Father of Supply-Side Economics?" *History of Political Economy* 24, no. 3 (Fall 1992), pp. 745-748.

8   Adam Smith, *An Inquiry into the Nature and Causes of the Wealth of Nations* (New York: Modern Library, 1937 [1776]), p. 835.

9   Baron de Montesquieu, *The Spirit of the Laws*, trans. Thomas Nugent (New York: Hafner, 1949 [1748]), p. 216.

10 Jean-Baptiste Say, *A Treatise on Political Economy*, 6th American ed., trans. C.R. Prinsep and Clement C. Biddle (Philadelphia: Grigg & Elliott, 1834), pp. 143, 453-54.

11 I am indebted to Kurt Schuler for calling this quote to my attention. John C. Calhoun, Statement, *Congressional Globe*, Appendix, 27th Congress, 2nd session, August 5, 1842.

12 Edwin Cannan, "Equity and Economy in Taxation," *Economic Journal* 11, no. 44 (December 1901), pp. 469-479; John Maynard Keynes, "The Means to Prosperity," in *The Collected Writings of John Maynard Keynes* (London: Macmillan, 1972 [1933]), vol. 9, p. 338.

13 Colin Clark, "The Scope for, and Limits of, Taxation," in *The State of Taxation* (London: Institute of Economic Affairs, 1977), pp. 19-28. Clark quotes Keynes (p. 23) that "25 percent taxation is about the limit of what is easily borne."

14 Ludwig von Mises, *Human Action: A Treatise on Economics* (New Haven: Yale University Press, 1949), p. 734.

15 C. Northcote Parkinson, *The Law and the Profits* (Boston: Houghton Mifflin, 1960), p. 95.

16 Richard B. McKenzie, "The Micro and Macro Economic Effects of Changes in the Statutory Tax Rates," *Review of Social Economy* 31, no. 1 (April 1973), pp. 20-30.

17 Woodrow Wilson, "Annual Message of the President," *Congressional Record*, December 2, 1919. See also Lawrence L. Murray, "Bureaucracy and Bi-partisanship in Taxation: The Mellon Plan Revisited," *Business History Review* 52, no. 2 (Summer 1978), pp. 200-225.

18 Andrew W. Mellon, *Taxation: The People's Business* (New York: Macmillan, 1924). The Treasury Secretary's annual reports throughout this period strongly stressed supply-side arguments for tax reduction.

19 Benjamin G. Rader, "Federal Taxation in the 1920s: A Re-examination," *The Historian* 33, no. 3 (May 1971), pp. 415-435; Gene Smiley and Richard H. Keehn, "Federal Personal Income Tax Policy in the 1920s," *Journal of Economic History* 55, no. 2 (June 1995), pp. 285-303.

20 Ture worked on the Joint Economic Committee, of which Mills was also a member, and functioned as Mills' staff economist.

21 The memo is reprinted in Bruce Bartlett, *Reaganomics: Supply-Side Economics in Action*, 2nd ed. (New York: Morrow/Quill, 1982), pp. 226-227.

22 Walter W. Heller, *The 1977 Economic Report of the President*, Joint Economic Committee, U.S. Congress, 95th Congress, 1st session (Washington: GPO), p. 161.

23 Walter W. Heller, "'Supply-Side' Tax Reductions" *New York Times*, December 17, 1980.

24 Some liberal supporters of the Kennedy tax cut even used Mellon's arguments to tease Republican opponents. See Donald F. Swanson, "Andrew Mellon on Tax Cuts," *The New Republic*, March 23, 1963, p. 22. On the other hand, some liberals, like John Kenneth Galbraith, opposed the Kennedy tax cut precisely because it was too Republican for their taste. John F. Kennedy, "Address and Question and Answer Period at the Economic Club of New York, December 14, 1962," in *Public Papers of the Presidents of the United States: John F. Kennedy, 1962* (Washington: GPO).

25 Wilbur Mills, Statement, *Congressional Record*, September 24, 1963; Council of Economic Advisers, *Economic Report of the President, 1965* (Washington: GPO); Lawrence B. Klein, "Econometric Analysis of the Tax Cut of 1964," in *The Brookings Model: Some Further Results*, eds. James Duesenberry et al. (Chicago: Rand McNally, 1969), pp. 459-472; Arthur M. Okun, "Measuring the Impact of the 1964 Tax Reduction," in *Perspectives on Economic Growth*, ed. Walter W. Heller

(New York: Random House, 1968), pp. 25-49. It should be noted that Kennedy's official revenue estimates, like Reagan's, all showed significant revenue losses. Henry Fowler, Statement, in *Meetings With Department and Agency Officials*, Committee on Banking and Currency, U.S. House of Representatives, 90th Congress, 1st session (Washington: GPO, 1967).

26 CBO, *Understanding Fiscal Policy* (Washington: GPO, April 1978).

27 Ronald Reagan, "The President's News Conference, October 1, 1981," in *Public Papers of the Presidents of the United States: Ronald Reagan, 1981*. Canto, Joines & Webb come closest to proving that the Kennedy tax cut paid for itself by including higher revenues that accrued to state and local governments with those obtained by the federal government. Victor A Canto, Douglas H. Joines, and Robert I. Webb, "The Revenue Effects of the Kennedy Tax Cuts," in *Foundations of Supply-Side Economics: Theory and Evidence*, eds. Victor A. Canto, Douglas H. Joines, and Arthur B. Laffer (New York: Academic Press, 1983), pp. 72-103.

28 Michael K. Evans, "The Source of Personal Saving in the U.S.," *Wall Street Journal*, March 23, 1981; Paul Craig Roberts, "The Tax Cut Will Help Savings," *Fortune*, August 24, 1981, pp. 44-45

29 Ronald E. Grieson, "Theoretical Analysis and Empirical Measurements of the Effects of the Philadelphia Income Tax," *Journal of Urban Economics* 8, no. 1 (July 1980), pp. 123-137.

30 The literature on these matters is extensive.

31 "Mr. Callaghan Talks Business," *New York Times*, October 10, 1976. Shortly thereafter, German Chancellor Helmut Schmidt of the liberal Social Democratic Party, also rejected Keynes, saying, "The time for Keynesian ideas is past, because the problem of the world today is inflation." Leonard Silk, "Major Change in Theory Seen," *New York Times*, March 5, 1980.

32 Paul Craig Roberts, "Idealism in Public Choice Theory," *Journal of Monetary Economics* 4, no. 3 (August 1978), pp. 603-615. Roberts posited a version of the Laffer Curve on page 611 of this review, showing that an increase of government rules, by which he meant the size of government, lowered GNP and, presumably, government revenue. A similar figure in a book by the same author appeared in Roberts, *Alienation and the Soviet Economy* (Albuquerque: University of New Mexico Press, 1971), p. 54. In a personal note to me about the latter, Roberts explicitly drew a parallel to the Laffer Curve.

33 CBO, *Temporary Measures to Stimulate Employment: An Evaluation of Some Alternatives* (Washington: GPO, September 1985). The Tax Reduction Act of 1975 gave taxpayers up to a $200 rebate to stimulate

demand. Subsequent research, however, found that almost all of it was saved in the short run, and thus provided no stimulus to demand, exactly as Milton Friedman had predicted.

34 Paul Craig Roberts, "The Breakdown of the Keynesian Model," *The Public Interest*, Summer 1978, pp. 20-33.

35 Russell Long, Statement, in *Incentives for Economic Growth*, Committee on Finance, U.S. Senate, 95th Congress, 1st session (Washington: GPO, 1977).

36 Harley H. Hinrichs, "An Empirical Measure of Investors' Responsiveness to Differentials in Capital Gains Tax Rates Among Income Groups," *National Tax Journal* 16, no. 3 (September 1963), pp. 228.

37 Martin Feldstein, Statement, in *The President's 1978 Tax Reduction and Reform Proposals*, Committee on Ways and Means, U.S. House of Representatives, 95th Congress, 2nd session, Serial 95-78; Feldstein, Statement, in *Revenue Act of 1978*, Committee on Finance, U.S. Senate, 95th Congress, 2nd session (Washington: GPO, 1978). See also Martin Feldstein, Joel Slemrod, and Shlomo Yitzhaki, "The Effects of Taxation on the Selling of Corporate Stock and the Realization of Capital Gains." *Quarterly Journal of Economics* 94, no. 4 (June 1980), pp. 777-791.

38 See among other entries by these authors, Geoffrey Brennan and James M. Buchanan, "Towards a Tax Constitution for Leviathan," *Journal of Public Economics* 8, no. 3 (December 1977), pp. 255-273.

39 Perry Shapiro and Jon Sonstelie, "Did Proposition 13 Slay Leviathan?" *American Economic Review* 72, no. 2 (May 1982), pp. 184-190.

40 Herbert Stein, "The Real Reasons for a Tax Cut," *Wall Street Journal*, July 18, 1978; George Will, "Reining In the Federal Spending Urge," *Washington Post*, July 27, 1978; Irving Kristol, "Populist Remedy for Populist Abuses," *Wall Street Journal*, August 10, 1978.

41 Milton Friedman, "The Kemp-Roth Free Lunch," *Newsweek*, August 7, 1978.

42 Ronald Reagan, "Address to the Nation on the Economy, February 5, 1981," in *Public Papers of the Presidents of the United States: Ronald Reagan, 1981*.

43 Alberto Alesina, Roberto Perotti, Francesco Giavazzi, and Tryphon Kollintzas, "Fiscal Expansions and Adjustments in OECD Countries," *Economic Policy* 10, no. 21 (October 1995), pp. 205-248; Gary S. Becker, Edward P. Lazear, and Kevin Murphy, "The Double Benefit of Tax Cuts," *Wall Street Journal*, October 7, 2003.

44 Robert A. Mundell, "The Dollar and the Policy Mix: 1971," International Finance Section, Department of Economics, Princeton University.

45 *The Phenomenon of Worldwide Inflation*, eds. David Meiselman and Arthur B. Laffer (Washington: American Enterprise Institute, 1975). Laffer discusses his work with Mundell in Arthur B. Laffer, "Economist of the Century," *Wall Street Journal*, October 15, 1999.

46 *The Phenomenon of Worldwide Inflation*, p. 145. See statements by Alan Blinder, John Brittain, Edward Denison, Otto Eckstein, Martin Feldstein, John Kenneth Galbraith, Edward Gramlich, and Joseph A. Pechman in Committee on Ways and Means, *Tax Reductions: Economists' Comments on H.R. 8333 and S. 1860 (The Kemp-Roth Bills)*, U.S. House of Representatives, Committee Print, 95th Congress, 2nd session (Washington: GPO, 1978).

47 Jude Wanniski, "It's Time to Cut Taxes," *Wall Street Journal*, December 11, 1974; Wanniski, "The Mundell-Laffer Hypothesis—A New View of the World Economy," *The Public Interest*, Spring 1975, pp. 31-52.

48 Douglas was a Democratic senator from Illinois from 1948 to 1966. He chaired the JEC during the 84th, 86th and 88th Congresses.

49 Joint Economic Committee, *1980 Joint Economic Report*, U.S. Congress, 96th Congress, 1st session, Senate Report 96-618 (Washington: GPO).

50 Leonard Silk, "Major Change in Theory Seen," *New York Times*, March 5, 1980.

51 Steven Rattner, "Economic Panel Splits on Policy," *New York Times*, February 27, 1981.

52 Bert Lance, Statement, *The 1977 Economic Report of the President*, Joint Economic Committee, U.S. Congress, 95th Congress, 1st session (Washington: GPO), p. 478.

53 CBO, *An Analysis of the Roth-Kemp Tax Cut Proposal* (Washington: GPO, October 1978).

54 Peter M. Gutmann, "The Subterranean Economy," *Financial Analysts Journal* 33, no. 6 (November-December 1977), pp. 26-27, 34. Gutmann's work was well known on Capitol Hill (it was the subject of three congressional hearings) and spawned a vast literature.

55 A first entry in a long list of literature is Henry S. Farber, "Individual Preferences and Union Wage Determination: The Case of the United Mine Workers," *Journal of Political Economy* 86, no. 5 (October 1978), pp. 923-942.

56 *Tax Reductions: Economists' Comments on H.R. 8333 and S. 1860 (The Kemp-Roth Bills)*, 64.

57 Arthur B. Laffer, Statement, in *The 1978 Midyear Review of the Economy* (Joint Economic Committee), U.S. Congress, 95th Congress, 2nd session (Washington: GPO).

58 Arthur B. Laffer, "An Equilibrium Rational Macroeconomic Frame-work," in *Economic Issues of the Eighties*, eds. Nake M. Kamrany and Richard H. Day (Baltimore: Johns Hopkins University Press, 1979), pp. 44-57. The original text is in error. It says "increased poverty," but Laffer meant it to read, "reduced poverty." In addition, "exchanged rates" in the original text should have read "unchanged rates." These quotations have been corrected.

59 Arthur B. Laffer, "Government Exactions and Revenue Deficiencies," *Cato Journal* 1, no. 1 (Spring 1981), pp. 1-21. Martin Feldstein cited this quotation in refutation of the statement by Martin Anderson that the Reagan Administration never predicted higher revenues from its tax cut. Of course, Laffer was not an administration official, although he was a member of President Reagan's Economic Policy Advisory Board, a group of private economists who met with him occasionally to give informal advice. As noted above, all the official revenue estimates of the Reagan Administration showed no feedback effects at all and were consistent with those of the CBO. Feldstein, "American Economic Policy in the 1980s: A Personal View," in *American Economic Policy in the 1980s*, ed. Martin Feldstein (Chicago: University of Chicago Press, 1994), p. 25; Anderson, *Revolution* (New York: Harcourt Brace Jovanovich, 1988).

60 *Tax Reductions: Economists' Comments on H.R. 8333 and S. 1860 (The Kemp-Roth Bills)*, 96; Michael K. Evans, Statement, in *Leading Economists' Views of Kemp-Roth*, U.S. House of Representatives, and Committee on the Budget, U.S. Senate, Joint Committee Print, 95th Congress, 2nd session (Washington: GPO, 1978).

61 David A. Stockman, Statement, *Congressional Record*. March 1, 1978.

62 David A. Stockman, Statement, in *Individual and Business Tax Reduction Proposals*, Committee on Finance, U.S. Senate, 95th Congress, 2nd session (Washington: GPO, 1978).

63 *A Program for Economic Recovery* (Washington: GPO, 1981), p. 16.

64 Richard A. Musgrave, Statement, in *The 1981 Economic Report of the President*, Joint Economic Committee, U.S. Congress, 97th Congress, 1st session (Washington: GPO).

65 Gardner Ackley, Statement, in *Tax Aspects of the President's Economic Program*, Committee on Ways and Means, U.S. House of Representatives, 97th Congress, 1st session, Serial 97-10 (Washington: GPO, 1981).

66 *Tax Aspects of the President's Economic Program*, pp. 430, 469.

67 David A. Stockman, Statement, in *Nomination of David A. Stockman*, Committee on Finance, U.S. Senate, 97th Congress, 1st session (Washington: GPO, 1981).

68 David A. Stockman, *The Triumph of Politics: Why the Reagan Revolution Failed* (New York: Harper & Row, 1986), pp. 67, 94-95; see Richard B. McKenzie, "Supply-Side Economics and the Vanishing Tax Cut," *Economic Review*, Federal Reserve Bank of Atlanta, May 1982, pp. 20-24; "Why Only a Popgun Tax Cut?" February 26, and "Kemp-Roth: Too Large and Too Small," April 27, 1981, *New York Times*; and Dimitri Andrianacos and Ali T. Akarca, "Long-Run Impact of Tax Rate Changes on Government Receipts," *Public Finance Quarterly* 26, no. 1 (January 1998), pp. 80-94.

69 Lawrence B. Lindsey, *The Growth Experiment: How the New Tax Policy Is Transforming the U.S. Economy* (New York: Basic Books, 1990), p. 76. See also Rosemarie M. Neilsen, Frank J. Sammartino, and Eric Toder, "CBO Replies to Lindsey," *Tax Notes* 35, no. 5 (May 4, 1987), pp. 496-501.

70 Martin Feldstein, "Supply-Side Economics: Old Truths and New Claims," *American Economic Review* 76, no. 2 (May 1986), pp. 26-30.

71 Paul Craig Roberts, "How the Defeat of Inflation Wrecked the U.S. Budget," *Los Angeles Times*, January 27, 1987; "What Really Happened in 1981," *Independent Review* 5, no. 2 (Fall 2000), pp. 279-281.

72 Arthur M. Okun said that to bring the basic inflation rate down by one percent would cost 10 percent of a year's GNP. Okun, "Efficient Disinflationary Policies," *American Economic Review* 68, no. 2 (May 1978), pp. 348-352.

73 The White House anticipated an increase in the GNP deflator of 36 percent between 1981 and 1986. It actually came in at 21 percent. *A Program for Economic Recovery*, p. 25.

74 Office of Management and Budget, *Budget of the United States Government: Fiscal Year 1982* (Washington: GPO, 1981), pp. 3, 59.

75 M.A. Akhtar and Ethan S. Harris, "The Supply-Side Consequences of U.S. Fiscal Policy in the 1980s," *Quarterly Review*, Federal Reserve Bank of New York, Spring 1992, pp. 1-20.

76 Paul A. Samuelson, "The '80s Are an Economic Success Story," *Christian Science Monitor*, Oct. 4, 1989; *1994 Economic Report of the President* (Washington: GPO), p. 88.

77 Representative examples from the literature on these points is as follows: Robert J. Barro, "Economic Growth in a Cross Section of Countries," *Quarterly Journal of Economics* 106, no. 2 (May 1991), pp. 407-443; Charles L. Ballard, John B. Shoven, and John Whalley, "The Total Welfare Cost of the United States Tax System: A General Equilibrium Approach," *National Tax Journal* 38, no. 2 (June 1985), pp. 125-140; Jon Gruber and Emmanuel Saez, "The Elasticity of Taxable Income: Evidence and Implications," *Journal of Public Econom-*

ics 84, no. 1 (April 2002), pp. 1-32; Austan Goolsbee, "Evidence on the High-Income Laffer Curve from Six Decades of Tax Reform," *Brookings Papers on Economic Activity* 1999, no. 2, pp. 1-64; Edward C. Prescott, "Why Do Americans Work So Much More Than Europeans?" *Staff Report* 321, Federal Reserve Bank of Minneapolis, September 2003; "IMF Seminar Discusses Revenue Implications of Trade Liberalization," IMF News Brief No. 99/8, February 25, 1999; and Austan Goolsbee, "What Happens When You Tax the Rich? Evidence from Executive Compensation," *Journal of Political Economy* 108, no. 2 (April, 2000), pp. 352-378.

78 Robert Lucas, "Supply-Side Economics: An Analytical Review," *Oxford Economic Papers* 42, no. 2 (April 1990), 293-316.

79 Joseph A. Pechman, "The Future of the Income Tax," *American Economic Review* 80, no. 1 (March 1990), p. 1.

80 Gerard Baker, "The White House Fights the Last Economic War," *Financial Times*, December 13, 2001; Floyd Norris, "Japan's Budget Deficit Has Soared. It's Time for a Tax Cut," *New York Times*, August 17, 2001.

81 Downloaded at www.msnbc.com.

CHAPTER 10

1 Martin Anderson, *Revolution: The Reagan Legacy* (Stanford: Hoover Institution Press, 1990), 148.

2 John Maynard Keynes, The Collected Writings of John Maynard Keynes (London: Macmillan Cambridge University Press, 1972).

3 Walter Heller, in testimony before the Joint Economic Committee of Congress, 1977, quoted by Bruce Bartlett in *National Review,* October 27, 1978.

4 Our most recent research paper covering this topic: Arthur B. Laffer and Jeffrey Thomson, "The Only Answer: A California Flat Tax," Laffer Associates, October 2, 2003.

5 For our purposes here we have arrived at the value of an after-tax dollar using the following weighting method: 80 percent, value of a dollar after passing through the personal tax channel (personal and sales taxes); 20 percent, value of a dollar after passing through the corporate tax channel (corporate, personal and sales taxes). Alaska is excluded from consideration due to the state's unique tax system and heavy reliance on severance taxes. U.S. Census Bureau, "State Government Tax Collections Report," 2002.

6   See Arthur B. Laffer and Jeffrey Thomson, "The 2003 Laffer State Competitive Environment," Laffer Associates, January 31, 2003; and previous editions.

7   The G-12 includes 13 countries: Australia, Belgium, Canada, France, Germany, Italy, Japan, Netherlands, Spain, Sweden, Switzerland, the U.K. and the U.S.

8   The "Incentive Rate" here is the value of $1.00 once it has passed through a country's highest tax rates (national and sub-national combined) on corporate income, on personal income, on payrolls, and on value added/sales. For the U.S., Chicago, Illinois is used for the sub-national location.

ACKNOWLEDGEMENTS

In the course of preparing two books on the history of supply-side economics, first *Econoclasts* (2009) and now *The Pillars of Reaganomics*, I have come to benefit from the recollections, and the friendships, of the people who were there, in the arena, as the supply-side revolution developed and took hold in the 1970s and 1980s. First among these is the central figure of this volume, Arthur B. Laffer, who along with his wife Traci, and very able protégés at his firm including Ford Scudder, drew me in to the voluminous sphere of the supply-side source base and spurred me on to point out its salience in our current circumstances.

Beyond Nashville and Laffer Associates, Lewis E. Lehrman and John Mueller have been boon companions, as have Alan Reynolds, Charles Kadlec, and Larry Kudlow. Bruce Bartlett has assisted me in many ways. Rich Lowrie, Louis Woodhill, Wayne Stoltenberg (along with the whole of the Herman Cain for President economic team), Sean Rushton, Ralph Benko, and John Tamny, not to mention our generation's greatest monetary sage, Nathan K. Lewis, all deserve recognition for advancing the best of economic traditions in an enlightened and practical fashion. Sam Houston State University has, as always, showed me every assistance.

Rowena Itchon of the Pacific Research Institute perfected this volume, and Dana Beigel made it handsome. Many thanks to them. My wife Jessica assisted me in this project very much once again, not least as my webmaster, as the children have indeed, and in a native fashion, developed interests in money and taxes. It was a pleasure to prepare another volume in their company.

—Brian Domitrovic

ABOUT THE EDITOR
BRIAN DOMITROVIC

Brian Domitrovic is Senior Associate of the Laffer Center for Supply-Side Economics and author of the standard history of supply-side economics, *Econoclasts: The Rebels Who Sparked the Supply-Side Revolution and Restored American Prosperity* (2009). His essays have appeared in *The Wall Street Journal* and *Investor's Business Daily* and on Forbes.com, where he writes a biweekly column. He chairs the Department of History at Sam Houston State University in Huntsville, Texas, and holds a Ph.D. in history from Harvard University.

ABOUT THE LAFFER CENTER AT THE PACIFIC RESEARCH INSTITUTE

Founded in 2012, The Laffer Center at the Pacific Research Institute is dedicated to preserving and promoting the core tenets of supply-side economics. The Laffer Center is named after Arthur B. Laffer, one of the nation's leading economic minds and considered by many to be the "Father of Supply-Side Economics." The Laffer Center houses Dr. Laffer's life's work and seeks to be the leading source for supply-side research and thought, including the research and published works of other economists and thought leaders whose ideas have played an instrumental role in the supply-side movement in the United States and abroad. Most important, The Laffer Center is focused on educating people on economic ideas and ensuring that the lessons of supply-side economics are as relevant and applicable today as they were in the 1980s when the supply-side revolution swept the country.